Praise for Karen Elliott House's

On Saudi Arabia

"Fascinating. . . . An important book that offers insights into the kingdom's fault lines, as well as gentle suggestions for a positive diplomacy." —*The Washington Post*

"The vignettes [House] assembles are not only entertaining and lucidly drawn, but also offer a rare glimpse into a world that is normally closed to Western reporters. . . . Eloquent and timely. . . . Presenting these issues in a readable yet serious book is a rare feat indeed, and she should be commended for it." —*The New Republic*

"Vivid. . . . House tells us that the goal of her book is 'to peel back the bindings of tradition and religion that wrap the Saudi mummy.' In this she succeeds brilliantly." —*The Wall Street Journal*

"A gem of reporting on one of the hardest stories to crack. . . . [House] is one of the wiliest and most determined newspaperwomen of her generation. . . . Illuminating. . . . Masterful." —*The New York Sun*

"An incisive analysis of divisive dynamics inside the world's most important supplier of oil." —Graham Allison, Director of the Belfer Center for Science and International Affairs, Harvard University

"A valuable assessment of where the kingdom is and where it might go. A stimulating and worthwhile read."
—George P. Shultz

"A book that future Saudi leaders should read carefully. It exposes incisively and dispassionately the social contradictions and the potential political vulnerabilities of contemporary Saudi Arabia. . . . Timely and truly important."
—Zbigniew Brzezinski,
former United States National Security Advisor

Karen Elliott House

On Saudi Arabia

Karen Elliott House is a graduate of the University of Texas at Austin. She studied and taught at Harvard University's Institute of Politics and was a senior fellow at the John F. Kennedy School of Government at Harvard University. House lives in Princeton, New Jersey, with her husband, Peter R. Kann, and their children.

www.karenelliotthouse.com

On Saudi Arabia

Its People, Past, Religion,
Fault Lines—and Future

Karen Elliott House

Vintage Books
A Division of Random House, Inc.
New York

FIRST VINTAGE BOOKS EDITION, JUNE 2013

The Library of Congress has cataloged the Knopf edition as follows:
House, Karen Elliott.
On Saudi Arabia : its people, past, religion, fault lines, and future /
by Karen Elliott House.—1st ed.
p. cm.
Includes bibliographical references.
1. Saudi Arabia—Civilization.
2. Saudi Arabia—Politics and government.
3. Saudi Arabia—Social life and customs. 4. Saudi Arabia—Religion.
5. Al Saud, House of. I. Title.
DS215.H68 2012
953.8—dc23 2012018977

Vintage ISBN: 978-0-307-47328-8

www.vintagebooks.com
www.karenelliotthouse.com

Author photograph © Pryde Brown
Map by David Lindroth

Printed in the United States of America
10 9 8 7 6

CONTENTS

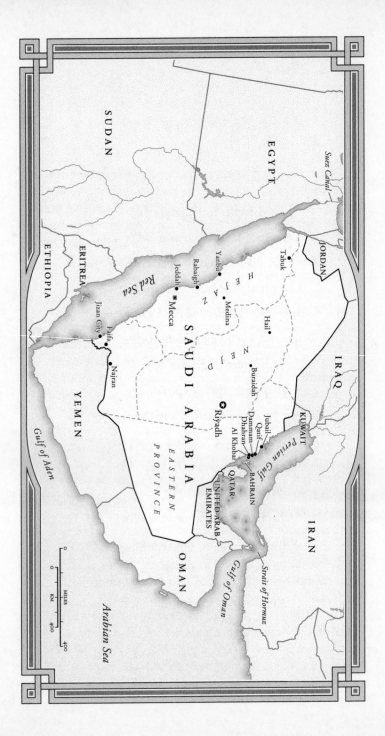

When I first began visiting Saudi Arabia nearly thirty-five years ago as diplomatic correspondent for *The Wall Street Journal,* my focus was on the kingdom's role in the Middle East issues that affected the security of the United States—Arab-Israeli peace, Iran-Iraq War, Gulf War, and oil production and pricing. Saudi Arabia clearly mattered; yet the Saudi people did not matter much to me.

Over the decades, as I encountered more ordinary Saudis, I became fascinated by their passivity, their unquestioning acceptance of rules laid down by elders, teachers, religious scholars, and their Al Saud rulers, who have governed the kingdom on and off for nearly three centuries. How, I kept asking myself, could people be so docile, so unquestioningly obedient? These were not, after all, enslaved people living under tyranny's lash. Nor were they primitives on some uncharted island.

I understood from personal experience the impact of rigid religion, authoritarian parents, and isolation from the wider world. I grew up on the hot, barren plains of the Texas panhandle, so similar to Saudi terrain, in a small town where, as in Saudi Arabia, religion defined daily life and where the only available social events were attending one of the town's four churches several times a week. Those churches were all Protestant, of course, ranging from our Church of Christ, which forbade any musical instruments, to the relatively more liberal—and we were told sinful—Methodists who were rumored to dance in their church basement.

In my family, strictly ruled by a loving but authoritarian father, we were forbidden to play games with cards or dice; we had no telephone or television; and shorts were banned as immodest dress. Alcohol was not allowed in our home or, indeed, anywhere in our county. Ours was a family in which on any important issue the wife was seen but not heard, and that expectation was the same for a daughter. Matador, Texas, with its population of nine hundred, was isolated enough that very few of my neighbors had ever been to a big city, flown on an airplane, or encountered a Roman Catholic—much less a Jew or a Muslim.

It was a way of life that held little resemblance to that of most Americans, but was remarkably similar to what I found in Saudi Arabia. The pervasive Muslim religion was different, of course, as were the language, the dress, and many of the Arab customs like the endless cups of bitter coffee and sweet tea served to a visitor. Yet, I also discovered on my early Saudi travels that a stranger could be as welcome and well treated in a remote Saudi desert town as were the strangers my father brought home for Sunday lunch after church. Saudi society, strict in virtually every sense, was also welcoming to a young woman journalist. Over time I grew less interested in Saudi Arabia as an oil-rich and influential country, and more and more determined to understand the Saudi people and the lives they led—and what that portends for the future stability of a country feared by many for the terrorists it has spawned but so essential to the West for the oil it provides.

Paradoxically, Saudi Arabia achieves a remarkable degree of anonymity. Its fate is so important to the rest of the world and the world is so vested in maintenance of its status quo that it's almost as if talking about Saudi Arabia might jinx that stability. Thus, as unrest in the Middle East and the toppling of lesser regimes consumed global attention in 2011, Saudi Arabia was largely ignored. Indeed, when President Barack Obama delivered a major speech on the Middle East in late spring, the words *Saudi Arabia* were never mentioned.

Saudi Arabia is a difficult country to visit, much less to understand. Driven by curiosity, I have visited the country repeatedly since I retired from active journalism in 2006 to explore and explain this shrouded society that is the antithesis of open, individualistic Western societies. This book is the result of those five years of deep diving. In the course of them I have traveled throughout the kingdom, a country nearly three times the size of my native Texas, spent time in villages as well as cities, interviewed paupers as well as princes, conservative Muslim imams as well as modern reformers, young as well as elderly, and women as well as men.

The last are important because contrary to what many might think about a foreign woman reporting in a male-dominated and gender-segregated society, my gender proved to be a genuine advantage. By and large, as a Western woman I had access to men, even some of the most religiously conservative ones, who met with me so long as I was appropriately shrouded in my floor-length *abaya* and head scarf. As a woman I also had a degree of access to traditional Saudi women that would have been impossible for any man. Often, I would visit a Saudi home to sip coffee and converse with my male host and his friends in one room and then move to another room to chat over dates and tea with the women of the household. As the intrepid early English Middle East explorer Gertrude Bell discovered more than a century ago, for all practical purposes of access in that society, the Western woman in Saudi Arabia is treated as a "third sex."

This book focuses on the lives of individual Saudis and how they are shaped and suppressed by traditions and authorities, whether religious figures, tribal elders, or princely rulers. This web of traditions and rules means that women are not free but neither are men. Both sexes are trapped by societal expectations. As a result, individual initiative and enterprise are virtually nonexistent. Society is a maze in which Saudis endlessly maneuver through winding paths between high walls of religious rules, government restrictions, and cultural traditions. Men must obey Allah and women must obey men. As a result, all too few Saudis have the energy, enterprise, curiosity, or confidence even to try to leave this labyrinth. However, in recent years, information via the Internet and youthful demands are penetrating the labyrinth and threatening the very foundations of these walls.

Outside Saudi Arabia, the 2011 Arab Spring has left many once seemingly stable Arab regimes in varying states of turmoil. While much of the world focused its attention on the fall of Arab dictators, the turmoil that transfixed the Al Saud was the assault on the monarchy in Bahrain. To the Al Saud,

Arab dictators come and go but dynastic monarchies are sacrosanct. Royals are beloved by their people and, of course, by Allah, both of whom they serve. Bahrain was a mirror in which this Al Saud myth was being shattered. Frightened that the fall of one small royal domino could expose Saudi Arabia, the Al Saud dispatched Saudi troops to shore up their fragile fellow royals. For the moment, at least, the monarchies have survived.

When I first began traveling in the kingdom in the late 1970s, the West could view Saudi Arabia with a mix of curiosity and mild concern, but today its future is critical to the West. The industrial world's insatiable appetite for energy has made us ever more dependent on the kingdom, which provides one of every four barrels of oil exported around the globe. Despite talk of U.S. energy self-sufficiency due to oil from shale, the reality is the rest of the world relies more than ever on Saudi oil. Meanwhile, Saudi Arabia no longer is the tame American ally of a generation ago. The once monogamous Saudi-U.S. marriage has become a polygamous Muslim one as the Saudis build bonds with multiple powers. The royal family may still depend upon the United States for its ultimate survival, but widespread anti-Americanism among conservative Saudis means even princes cannot appear to be in America's pocket. Saudi Arabia, then as now, is the heart of Islam with its two holy cities of Mecca and Medina, but today extremist Muslims see Islam in a clash of civilizations with the West. Among these extremists are the modern-day terrorists, very much including the largely Saudi suicide killers of September 11, 2001. These days they are underground, but they are still there.

The kingdom I first visited has become more important and much more threatening to our livelihoods and lives. The goal of the following chapters is to peel back the bindings of tradition and religion that wrap the Saudi mummy to explain how the society works, how Saudis think and live, and how events in the desert kingdom may unfold. It is the interplay of multiple issues—religion, royalty, economics, culture, tradition, and modernity—in a society still largely shrouded in its robes and *abayas* that is the subject of this book.

On Saudi Arabia

CHAPTER I

Fragile

Observing Saudi Arabia is like watching a gymnast dismount the balance beam in slow motion. As the body twists frame by frame through the air, we instinctively hold our breath to see if the hurtling gymnast will nail the landing or crash to the mat. So it is with the Al Saud monarchy of Saudi Arabia.

As revolutionary fervor sweeps the Middle East, the world watches with trepidation the aged princes at the head of the House of Saud struggle to maintain a precarious balance. Because Saudi Arabia produces fully one of every four barrels of oil sold on the world market, what happens in this most veiled of Arab societies will affect not only the future of 19 million Saudis but also the stability and prosperity of the global economy, and it will touch the lives of every citizen in the world. The stakes for all Americans are far higher here than anywhere else in the volatile Middle East. After all, the United States, which imports two-thirds of its oil, has gone to war twice in a period of thirteen years in no small part to ensure access to Persian Gulf oil.

For nearly eighty years, a succession of Al Saud princes have traversed the balance beam, skillfully maintaining control of a deeply divided, distrustful, and increasingly dispirited populace, by cunningly exploiting those divisions, dispensing dollops of oil money, and above all, bending religion to serve Al Saud political needs. This ruling family never promised democracy—and still doesn't. Nor does it bother with sham elections to present the appearance of legitimacy, as do so many other Arab regimes. The Al Saud believe they have an asset more powerful than the ballot box: they have Allah.

Nearly three hundred years ago, when Arabia was nothing but harsh desert inhabited by wild and warring tribes, Muhammad al Saud, leader of one such tribe, discovered a magic lamp in the person of Muhammad ibn Abd al Wahhab, a fundamentalist Islamic scholar bent on imposing on Arabia his version of the pure Islam of the Prophet Muhammad a millennium earlier. So fanatical was this preacher that by the time the two men met, Abd al Wahhab was fleeing for his life, having destroyed the tomb of one of the Prophet's companions and stoned to death a woman accused of adultery in a public display of his Islamic fervor. None of this bothered Muhammad al Saud. He saw in the preacher's call for Islamic jihad the opportunity to use religion to trump his tribal enemies and conquer Arabia. Sure enough, the Al Saud sword, wielded in the name of religion rather than mere tribal conquest, proved triumphant. The first Saudi state was declared in 1745. Arabia has been under the sway of the Al Saud—and their religious partners—off and on ever since, with the most recent Saudi state established in 1932 by the current king's father, Abdul Aziz bin Al Saud.

Over all those years, religion has been a pillar of strength, steadying the Al Saud atop the kingdom that bears their name. To this day, the monarchy justifies its rule by claiming to personify, protect, and propagate the one true religion. The Saudi monarch styles himself as "Custodian of the Two Holy Mosques," a unique title intended to convey his spiritual leadership of all Islam. *King*, after all, is a temporal and rather common title.

These days, however, the old magic of divide and conquer, the majesty of appropriated religion, and even the soothing balm of money, lots of money, are not enough to blind a new generation of Saudis to the decay rotting the very foundations of their society and threatening their future and that of their children. Islam as preached is not practiced. Jobs are promised but not delivered. Corruption is rampant, entrapping almost every Saudi in a web of favors and bribes large and small, leaving even the recipients feeling soiled and resentful. Powerful and powerless alike are seeking to grab whatever they can get, turning a society governed by supposedly strict Sharia law into an increasingly lawless one, where law is whatever the king or one of his judges says it is—or people feel they can get away with.

All of this is widely known to Saudis. For the first time, the Internet allows the young generation—70 percent of Saudis are under thirty years of age, with more than 60 percent age twenty or younger—to know what is taking place at home and abroad. These young people are aware of government inefficiency and princely corruption, and of the fact that 40 percent of Saudis live in poverty and at least 60 percent cannot afford a home. They know that nearly 40 percent of Saudi youth between twenty and twenty-four are unemployed, at the very age when most men would like to marry if only they could afford the bride price. They know that 90 percent of all employees in the private sector of their economy are imported foreign workers, whom business owners, often including Al Saud princes, exploit for low wages. Saudis, undereducated and often indolent, sit idly by rather than work for what they regard as slave wages doing menial jobs. If all too many Saudi men who could work do not, even educated Saudi women who want to work often cannot. The female half of the Saudi population remains sheltered, subjugated, and frustrated.

Saudis hear their minister of labor say the kingdom must create two hundred thousand well-paying jobs every year until 2030 to sop up the currently unemployed Saudi men (leave aside women) and provide work for wave after wave of young men who will enter the labor market over the next two decades. Yet it is no secret to Saudis that in each of the past five years, the government has created only about fifty thousand new jobs, and that the 2.5 million jobs created by private industry over that period have gone overwhelmingly to foreigners.

All this they know, and now share with each other through social media. These young Internet-savvy Saudis are breaching the walls that have been so carefully constructed and maintained over decades by the regime to keep Saudis separated and distrustful of those outside their family or tribe, to ensure their near total dependence on Al Saud protection and largesse. Stability (more recently coupled with the promise of prosperity) in exchange for loyalty was for most of the last three hundred years the social contract binding the people to their Al Saud rulers. But no longer. These days young Saudis compare their lives with those of contemporaries in neighboring Gulf states and elsewhere, and that comparison leaves many of them humiliated and embittered. All too many of these young Saudis know they are living third-world lives in a country that has more than $400 billion in foreign reserves and, in recent years, annual oil revenue in excess of $200 billion. Yet the government fails to provide basic services like quality education, health care, or even proper sewage and drainage to protect from floods.

And things just keep happening to stoke anger and forge bonds among the young. In January 2011, as Cairo was erupting in revolution, the kingdom's second largest city, Jeddah, flooded for the second time in little more than a year in a deluge of rainwater and sewage. For decades corrupt businessmen and bureaucrats had stolen billions of dollars allocated for construction of a proper sewage and drainage system, leaving the city vulnerable to floods of sewage-polluted rainwater. The first flood, in 2009, killed more than 120 people, displaced another 22,000, and destroyed 8,000 homes. King Abdullah promised "never again," yet in less than fourteen months, once again Jeddah was drowning. Young Saudis using Facebook and Twitter helped stranded citizens find safety and shelter when authorities were scarcely seen. "Hang your head, you are a Saudi," one angry youth posted on the Internet, a cynical reversal of a favorite royal admonition to the young to "Hold your head high. You are a Saudi." Another depicted the Saudi national emblem—two swords crossed over a palm tree—as two mops crossed atop a stack of buckets. Even the generally respected monarch, King Abdullah, was the target of unprecedented criticism for such

Senior Al Saud royals: King Abdullah, 89, above right, is on his third crown prince in eight months. Crown Prince Sultan, 84, upper left, died in October 2011 and was succeeded by Crown Prince Nayef, 77, below left, who died in June 2012. Crown Prince Salman, 76, below right, served forty-nine years as governor of Riyadh. (GETTY IMAGES)

a visible failure to deliver on his previous promise. His photo was posted on the Internet with a giant red X and the words, "Why do you give them all this power when they all are thieves?"

The Internet, and the power of knowledge that it provides to Saudis, may be the biggest threat to the Al Saud, but it is not the only one. If Saudi citizens increasingly are in touch, their rulers are increasingly out of touch. King Abdullah, eighty-nine, generally popular for his effort to make at least modest reforms, is seen as isolated by his retainers and, at any rate, was slowed by age and serious back surgery in 2010 and again in 2011. Despite his age and infirmities, the king has largely governed without a crown prince since taking the monarchy's mantle in 2005 because Sultan, eighty-four, was suffering from cancer and Alzheimer's and finally died in October 2011. The new crown prince, Nayef, seventy-seven and ailing from diabetes and poor circulation, died after less than eight months, to be followed by yet another brother.

After them? No one knows. What scares many royals and most ordinary Saudis is that the succession, which historically has passed from brother to brother, soon will have to jump to a new generation of princes. That could mean that only one branch of this family of some seven thousand princes will have power, a prescription for potential conflict as thirty-four of the thirty-five surviving lines of the founder's family could find themselves disenfranchised. Saudis know from history that the second Saudi state was destroyed by fighting among princes. Older Saudis vividly recall how this third and latest Saudi state was shaken by a prolonged power struggle between the founder's two eldest sons after his death in 1953.

Today's Saudi Arabia is reminiscent of the dying decade of the Soviet Union, when one aged and infirm Politburo chief briefly succeeded another—from Brezhnev to Andropov to Chernenko—before Gorbachev took power with reform policies that proved too little too late. "They keep dying on me," Ronald Reagan famously said of the four Soviet leaders he dealt with in less than three years. The next U.S. president almost surely will have the same experience with ailing Saudi rulers.

Beyond all this, religion, once a pillar of stability, has become a source of division among Saudis. Many Saudis, both modernists and religious conservatives, are offended by the Al Saud's exploitation of religion to support purely political prerogatives. The accommodating flexibility of religious scholars is eroding the legitimacy of both the Al Saud and their religious partners in power. Saudis hear religious scholars condemning infidels in the sacred land of the Prophet, yet they recall that the religious hierarchy obediently approved the presence of U.S. troops when the king needed them to confront Saddam Hussein in 1990. The scholars similarly condemn any mixing of men and women and deploy their religious police to enforce this ban on ordinary Saudis, but they acquiesced in 2009, when the king opened a richly endowed university where Saudi men and women mix with each other and with foreign infidels. And of course, they have long accepted all sorts of heresies, including movie theaters and women driving at the large compound of Saudi ARAMCO, the national oil company, which almost alone produces the funds that fill the kingdom's treasury. Sin in the company that funds the kingdom—including privileges for the religious establishment—apparently is permissible.

The modernizers see this and whisper to each other that if the Al Saud can manipulate the religious when it suits their interests, why not press religious authorities to permit more change more rapidly? For their part, religious fundamentalists feel betrayed by both the religious establishment and the Al Saud putting their mutual interest in power and money ahead of the word of Allah. "We are hypocrites tricking each other, lying to each other as the government has taught us," laments one devout imam. "We are not Islamic."

For all their frustrations, most Saudis do not crave democracy. To conservative Saudis, especially the many devoutly religious, the idea of men making laws rather than following those laid down by Allah in the Koran is antithetical and unthinkable. More modern and moderate Saudis, aware the Al Saud have banned any political and most all social organizations even down to something as apolitical as photography clubs, fear that without Al Saud rule, the country would face tribal, regional, and class conflict—or rule by religious zealots. With seventy thousand mosques spread across the kingdom, only the religious are an organized force; moderates fear that power inevitably would be seized by the most radical. Whatever lies in Saudi Arabia's future, it is not democracy.

What unites conservatives and modernizers, and young and old, is a hunger not for freedom but for justice; for genuine rule of law, not rule by royal whim. They want a government that is transparent and accountable, one that provides standard services such as are available in far less wealthy societies: good education, jobs, affordable housing, and decent health care. Saudis of all sorts resent having to beg princes for favors to secure services that should be a public right. They also want to be allowed to speak honestly about the political and economic issues that affect their lives. Yet when a conservative professor of religion at Imam University, the cornerstone of religious education in the kingdom, dared to suggest on the Internet that Saudis be permitted to take public their pervasive private discussions on royal succession, he was jailed.

The country fundamentally is a family corporation. Call it Islam Inc. The board of directors, some twenty senior religious scholars who theoretically set rules for corporate behavior, are handpicked by the Al Saud owners, can be fired at royal whim, and have nothing to say about who runs the company. Al Saud family members hold all the key jobs, not just at the top but right down through middle management, even to regional managers. (The governors of twelve of the kingdom's thirteen provinces are princes.) At the bottom of the company, ordinary employees are poorly paid and even more poorly trained because management doesn't want initiative that might threaten its control. Imagine working for a company where you can't aspire even to a regional management position, let alone influence those who control the company that determines your livelihood and your children's future. Not surprisingly, the Saudi employees of such a stultifying company are sullen, resentful, and unmotivated. Most feel no pride in their country but focus on getting even with their overlords by chiseling on their expense accounts and showing up late for work—in effect, by grabbing what they can get from their corporate masters. And given the widespread Saudi cynicism over the unholy alliance of profligate princes and pliable religious leaders, it is not surprising that many Saudis see the kingdom not as Islam Inc. but rather as Un-Islam Inc.

All this raises the question: Can the Al Saud regime reform in time to save itself? Are the royal princes capable of curbing corruption, improving government efficiency, and permitting people honestly to express themselves on taboo topics like religion, the role of women, and the royal family? Can they abandon a history of divide and conquer—of exploiting deep religious, tribal, regional, and gender divisions—and recognize that those divisions now threaten rather than enhance Al Saud survival? If so, can they begin to help Saudis bridge divides and reach a consensus that allows the kingdom to move forward, rather than flounder in perpetual checkmate? Or will the House of Saud prove to be a house of cards?

"If we do not share responsibility and create action, we will face stagnation or catastrophe," says Prince Saud bin Abdul Mohsin, a grandson of the founder and one of a dozen royal provincial governors. "This family has delivered for people in the past. But if we can't do it now, they will not see the need for the family."

CHAPTER 2

Al Saud Survival Skills

Allah has revealed to me that you must be humble. No one
should boast over one another, and no one should oppress
another.

—PROPHET MUHAMMAD

Over the generations, the Al Saud princes have displayed
remarkable skill at survival. In the eighty years since
Abdul Aziz bin Al Saud used a combination of religion
and ruthlessness to reunite Arabia under the Al Saud, his
extended family has evolved as perhaps the most successful family enterprise in modern history—and certainly the
wealthiest.

Saudi Arabia remains an absolute monarchy, the last significant one on earth. Its power centers all are controlled
by princes. The king appoints the country's senior religious
leaders, all judges, and all 150 members of its toothless parliament. His relatives own the news media. No social or civic
organizations that might be a breeding ground for citizen
organization are allowed. Slavery was abolished only in 1962!
Royals also control the kingdom's oil wealth, which has
subsidized—and subdued—Saudi citizens while enriching
and entrenching the royal rulers. The wealth of the family,
like its internal politics, is veiled from public view, a growing
source of public anger. Yet as the royal family has expanded
exponentially, as times have changed and outside information and infidel influences have seeped into the kingdom,
and as a succession of aged and infirm kings have occupied

the throne, the Al Saud sovereign skills appear less and less adequate to the challenges at home and abroad.

How has an absolute monarchy and a royal family by now consisting of some seven thousand princes—sons, grandsons, even great-great-grandsons of the founder—continued to maintain near-absolute power amid the winds of change sweeping in from the outside world and the pressures boiling up from a young population?

One answer is the skill of the family at adapting the founding father's strategy of divide and conquer from an age of manipulating desert tribes to a modern era of manipulating social groupings and foreign allies. Second, there is the family's clever use of money—whether the limited gold coins in the founder's portable money chest or today's billions from oil revenue—to buy loyalty, or at least submission. Third, there is the pervasive and so often oppressive role of religion that preaches obedience to Allah, and inextricably to the Al Saud, who, unlike ruling dynasties in Western societies, are not simply a temporal power but also Allah's instruments on earth. Finally, there is the somnolence of Saudi society itself. Notwithstanding the occasional terrorist who blasts onto the world stage, the society has been overwhelmingly passive, imbued from birth with a sense of obedience to God and ruler and with customs of conformity such that only the rarest of Saudis steps outside the strict social norms to leave his place in the labyrinth that divides Saudis one from another. Saudis vividly demonstrate Karl Marx's axiom that religion is the "opium" of the people.

The divide-and-conquer pattern was set early by Abdul Aziz. A strapping man in his twenties, Abdul Aziz rode out of Al Saud exile in Kuwait in 1902 to reconquer Arabia, which had been lost after family squabbles had cost the family its rule in 1891. For thirty years, Abdul Aziz used a combination of brutality and guile to subdue the Arabian Peninsula, an area nearly four times the size of France, and declare the modern Kingdom of Saudi Arabia in 1932. Civil war in Saudi Arabia is not a dim and distant memory for Saudis but something elderly Saudis survived. While the

British supported Abdul Aziz with money and weapons, his dynasty is strengthened by the fact that it springs from Arabia rather than being imported and imposed by an outside power. Indeed, Arabia, unlike much of the Middle East, was never colonized by any Western power.

Abdul Aziz's challenge was to establish his rule over an impoverished and backward Arabian Peninsula that had been fragmented for centuries by region and tribe, by urban and desert lifeways. He began by launching a predawn raid that left him wounded and the ruler of Riyadh dead at Masmak, a mud fort still standing in Riyadh, and went on to win the loyalty of townspeople who traditionally had been forced to buy their safety by paying off one or another warrior tribe to protect them. With the city dwellers fighting for him on the promise of security for loyalty, Abdul Aziz began to harness

Saudi Arabia preserves little history but is proud of its modern malls and skyscrapers. *Above,* the ruins of Fort Masmak, captured in 1902 by Abdul Aziz al Saud. (ROGER HARRISON) *Opposite,* the skyline of Riyadh, a city of 5 million, dominated by Faisaliah Tower, owned by one of Abdul Aziz's grandsons. (GETTY IMAGES)

the loyalties of Bedouin tribes, which historically had survived by raiding towns, caravans, and other tribes. Realizing that these nomadic people could switch loyalties almost instantly, Abdul Aziz knew he had to find a way to control them.

He used religion—just as his ancestors had. And he chained them to the land. He convinced the *bedu* to congregate in agriculturally oriented settlements called *hijra* and

adopt a more sedentary life focused on the puritanical form of Islam promoted by Muhammad ibn Abd al Wahhab, an imam who had teamed with the Al Saud to found the first Saudi state some 150 years earlier. The imam had taught that belonging to the *umma,* or community of believers, took precedence over all other social bonds. Anyone who made a judgment based on anything other than the Koran was a *kafir,* or nonbeliever, Sheikh Abd al Wahhab had preached. This meant that tribal law must be subjugated to God's law. Working with the imam's descendents, Abdul Aziz harnessed his political ambition to their religious conviction.

All men who joined *al-wahhabiya* were called Ikhwan, or brethren, and were promised equal treatment regardless of their tribal origins or race, something new in Arabia. This latter-day *hijra,* or migration, was akin to the Prophet's move from Mecca to Medina some thirteen hundred years earlier to escape his opponents and signified a renunciation of tribal bonds in favor of loyalty to the larger brotherhood of Islam. Abd al Wahhab wanted to purify Arabia for the one true God. Abdul Aziz, taking a page from his ancestors, wanted to subdue Arabia again for the Al Saud. It was, as the famous *Casablanca* line has it, "the start of a beautiful friendship." Subjugating tribal loyalty to devotion to Allah—and of course to his temporal ruler—was the beginning of Abdul Aziz's successful strategy to divide and conquer, co-opt and coerce, persuade and punish.

As a founding father, Abdul Aziz looms far larger in the creation of modern Saudi Arabia than does even George Washington in U.S. history. George Washington's ragtag army of colonists fought the British to free America, founded in part on the idea of religious freedom, to grow into first a confederation and then a federation of states. By contrast, Abdul Aziz fought not foreigners but his fellow Arabs with the help of his religious Ikhwan to conquer Arabia exclusively for only one religion (fanatical Islamic Wahhabism) and, of course, one family (the Al Saud).

Like Washington, Abdul Aziz was a giant of a man, towering above most of his fellow countrymen. Like Washington, he exuded a courage and dignity that set him apart from and above his people. But unlike Washington, who refused to be king and retired to his private estate after two terms as president, leaving no sons, Abdul Aziz ruled the Kingdom of Saudi Arabia until his death in 1953 and fathered forty-four sons by twenty-two wives, thirty-six of whom lived to adulthood. (He limited himself to no more than the four wives at a time allowed by Islam. But he is estimated to have had brief marriages for political purposes to nearly three hundred women over his lifetime.) His elderly sons continue to rule the kingdom to the present.

To this day, the Al Saud princes insist they are the glue that holds Saudi Arabia together. As Cairo was engulfed in one of its many "days of rage," one middle-aged prince assured me: "Without our family, this country would dissolve into chaos. Our people revere the family as you revere George Washington." There is, of course, a big difference between citizens revering one remarkable man, whether he is Abdul

King Abdul Aziz bin Saud, founder of the current
Kingdom of Saudi Arabia, with five of his forty-four sons
plus household servants. Five sons have succeeded him
on the throne since his death in 1953. (GETTY IMAGES)

Aziz or George Washington, and their extending that sentiment many decades later to some thousands of progeny who just happened to be born with the same last name.

If George Washington is famous for never telling a lie, Abdul Aziz is equally famous for cunning and duplicity, traits still much admired in Saudi Arabia. For instance, Abdul Aziz's admirers tell the story of a clash between a religious sheikh and the king over the length of Abdul Aziz's *thobe,* the floor-length garb resembling a long shirt that is the Saudi national dress. The religious man told his monarch his *thobe* was too long, a sign of extravagance and vanity that displeases Allah. Abdul Aziz asked that the critical cleric be given a pair of scissors to cut the *thobe* to the proper length. Once that was done and the satisfied cleric departed, Abdul Aziz ordered his guards never to let the man into his presence again. The gesture of submission to religious dictate had been only for appearance.

Knowing when to yield and when to fight is a survival instinct the founding ruler perfected—and passed to his sons. When his Ikhwan urged him to declare a holy war on the British infidels, who after World War I had replaced the Ottoman Turks as the dominant foreign power in the Middle East, Abdul Aziz demurred because he needed British money and cooperation to drive his rival, Sharif Hussein, the great-great-grandfather of Jordan's King Abdullah, from Mecca and complete his conquest of Arabia. Once the Ikhwan helped conquer Mecca and the surrounding Hejaz region, Abdul Aziz fought a brutal war with these same religious extremists because they wanted to continue to wage jihad beyond Arabia into Iraq, a British protectorate. He was not about to risk his precariously constructed kingdom to expand into Iraq and turn the powerful British against him. Instead, he turned on the Ikhwan, precisely the people whom he had used to help him secure power, and destroyed them. Abdul Aziz's devotion to religion took a backseat to his determination to retain his rule of Arabia. (And the same is true today of his sons who, when it suits them, confront religious leaders and even fire some of them, while professing total devotion and obedience to Allah.)

"Draw the sword in their face and they will obey; sheathe the sword and they will ask for more pay," Abdul Aziz once told a British official, to explain his modus operandi. To the Ikhwan leaders, he warned before destroying them, "Are there not a number of you upon whose fathers' and grandfathers' necks my sword and that of my fathers and grandfathers made play?"

To demonstrate his willingness to use power where persuasion failed, Abdul Aziz razed the villages of some of his own cousins who had massed an army to threaten his hold on Riyadh. He forced the surrender of one village, Laila, and condemned to death nineteen of its leaders. Demonstrating an unerring flair for dramatic brutality, Abdul Aziz granted the leaders a twenty-four-hour stay of execution while a platform was built outside the main gate of town. At dawn, he took his seat before an assembly of men summoned from the countryside around Laila. In pairs the condemned men were led before him, and each was put to death on his command by a black slave wielding a sword. With eighteen men dead, he abruptly pardoned the nineteenth and told him to go tell all he met what he had seen of the just vengeance of Abdul Aziz. It was classic Al Saud—offering people a choice between brutality and submission. The lessons learned and taught by Abdul Aziz are deeply imprinted in the minds of his elder sons, who helped him subdue Arabia in their youth and who have followed him on the throne.

Like his father, the current king, Abdullah, has practiced the art of balance. Much as his father subdued the Ikhwan, Abdullah has faced the challenge of subduing its modern variant, the Islamic jihadists. In a striking parallel to the Ikhwan, whom Abdul Aziz used and then destroyed, the modern-day Islamic extremists were indulged in the 1980s by a royal family eager to burnish its religious credentials, as Islamic fundamentalism swept the region in the wake of the religious revolution in Iran. The regime supported the jihadists as they fought the Soviets in Afghanistan and imposed rigid religiosity in the kingdom. The Saudi regime then ruthlessly suppressed religious extremists some thirty years later when they began terrorist attacks inside Saudi

Arabia in 2003 and thus were seen to pose a threat to Al Saud rule.

This embrace of extreme religiosity began in 1979 after a Bedouin preacher and several hundred followers did the unthinkable: they used firearms, forbidden in any mosque, to seize control of Islam's holiest site, the Grand Mosque in Mecca. Just as the imam was concluding the dawn prayer on November 20, gunshots rang out, freezing worshippers who stood in concentric circles emanating from the Kaaba, a large cube covered in black silk in the center of the mosque. Juhayman al Uteybi, age forty-three, with intense black eyes and unruly black hair, seized the microphone from the imam and barked orders to his followers to secure the mosque. Juhayman and his cohorts were determined to end what they saw as the Al Saud's excessive tolerance of infidel innovations—women newscasters on television, cinemas, and even tolerance of Shias, who in their fanatical minds, are members of a heretical sect of Islam not worthy to be called Muslim. Panicked worshipers tried to flee, only to find all fifty-one gates of the mosque chained shut. Thus began the first jihadist attack in modern Saudi history, one whose repercussions continue to this day.

The shocked Al Saud first tried to black out any news of the dramatic event. But when days passed with no progress in dislodging Juhayman and his followers, the government laid bloody siege to the holiest site in Islam for nearly two weeks, severely damaging the mosque and finally destroying Juhayman and his compatriots with help from the Western infidels he decried: French commandos deployed CB, a deadly chemical that blocks breathing and inhibits aggressiveness, immobilizing the religious rebels, who were rounded up by Saudi troops. But the siege claimed at least one thousand lives. Juhayman and his compatriots were quickly executed. The traumatized royal family soon curbed the societal liberties Juhayman had condemned. Women announcers were ordered off television, women were forced to wear the veil, and cinemas were closed (except at Saudi ARAMCO). In short, the Al Saud killed Juhayman and his cohorts but adopted their agenda of intolerance, spawning yet more radical Islamists and eventually their deadly attacks on the United States on September 11, 2001, and on Saudis in 2003.

This incident marked the beginning of a now widespread sense among Saudis that their government was incompetent. That sense only grew in 1990, when the kingdom's rulers, despite hundreds of billions of dollars in defense purchases over the decades, nonetheless concluded they needed U.S. troops to protect the country from Saddam Hussein, who had invaded Kuwait and had his eye on Saudi oil fields as well. That cynicism continues to compound to this day, with incidents like the repeated floods in Jeddah in 2009 and 2011 and with the government's inability to diversify the Saudi economy to create jobs for the growing number of unemployed youth.

In the wake of the attack on New York's Twin Towers by Saudi nationals, both political reformers and religious fundamentalists began to call for reforms inside the kingdom. Fundamentalists sought reforms that essentially would make religious leaders full partners of the Al Saud. Seeing the regime on the defensive, Saudi intellectuals and other moderates too began to press for political pluralism, including a constitution limiting the government's powers and even direct elections to the country's Potemkin parliament, the Majlis Ash Shura, or Consultative Council.

Faced with these mounting and seemingly irreconcilable demands, Crown Prince Abdullah, the de facto ruler (as King Fahd lay dying), deftly sought to defuse both threats. The regime imprisoned some of its critics and co-opted others. In 2003 Abdullah launched what he called "National Dialogues" that moved the debate from substantive political reform of the monarchy to superficial reform of the society. The articulate activists from the religious and the reformer ranks soon were subsumed and diluted by a broader and far less threatening group of public representatives selected by the government to participate in the nationally televised "dialogue." In short, the government picked the topics for discussion, such as the role of women, youth, tolerance, and unemployment, and selected those who would discuss them. These National Dialogues soon sucked the energy out of the incipient reform movement and within a year had become just another somnolent event under royal sponsorship, ignored by most of society and viewed with cynicism by more politically aware Saudis. The recommendations of the National Dialogues were bound in expensive volumes at the conclusion of each session but most were never acted upon. As so often happens in Saudi Arabia, a large new building called the Center for National Dialogue is the only remaining monument to that latest reform movement.

As delicately as the regime co-opted demands for power sharing, it met the violent attacks of extremists on Saudi citizens with matching brutality. For two years after the attack on the World Trade Center, as the United States pressured Riyadh to cut Saudi citizens' financing of terrorists, the Saudi government largely denied that extremism was a problem. But when frustrated extremists turned to violent attacks on Saudi civilians in 2003, the government met the challenge with massive force, killing hundreds and arresting thousands, many of whom remain incarcerated without trials nearly a decade later.

Like Abdul Aziz, his sons strongly prefer to co-opt rather than to confront, to buy rather than to bully, to deflect rather than to directly deny. But in extremis, they are willing to employ pretty much the same harsh practices as neighboring Arab rulers or Abdul Aziz himself. Saudi Arabia is replete with secret police, surreptitious surveillance, grim prisons, and torture chambers, even if this is an aspect of the regime that most Saudis manage to avoid.

Since becoming king in 2005, Abdullah, more than any modern Saudi king, has sought to introduce modest reforms to please modernizers and to blunt the kingdom's image at home and abroad as a breeding ground for fanaticism. Among other things, he has advocated that women be allowed greater opportunities—a handful of prominent females for the first time even joined a monarch's official entourage for foreign visits. In 2011 he announced that women would be appointed (by him) to the Majlis Ash Shura and would actually be allowed to vote in 2015, albeit only in elections for municipal councils, powerless bodies first elected in 2005 to help defuse Western criticism of the kingdom in the wake of 9/11. Still, women are expected to be segregated from men in the Consultative Council and participate only by closed-circuit television. Being members of the council may be one thing; mixing with male members is another.

King Abdullah also began sending a flood of Saudi youth abroad for education—more than one hundred thousand attend foreign universities now, roughly half in the United States. In 2009, to reinforce his call for improvements in the kingdom's notoriously poor education system, he established King Abdullah University of Science and Technology (KAUST), the new gender-mixed research university, a first in Saudi Arabia, with an endowment reported to be second only to Harvard's.

When one of the senior religious *ulama* had the temerity to criticize this unprecedented mixing as an infidel innovation forbidden by Islam, the mild-mannered king promptly fired him, a modern form of his father's beheadings. The sacking of this sheikh had the desired effect of prompting supportive statements on KAUST from other tame religious leaders, but it angered religious conservatives who see the approval of gender mixing as yet further prostitution by a religious establishment that puts pleasing the king and retaining its privileges ahead of pleasing Allah. Always careful to balance, the king, who had secured *ulama* approval for gender mixing at his elite university, did nothing to curb the country's religious police from roaming the kingdom's streets and harassing ordinary Saudis mixing with anyone of the opposite gender.

As is clear by now, the regime perpetually performs a delicate minuet, dancing closer at times to the religious establishment and at other times to modernizers, but always focused on retaining Al Saud control. None of King Abdullah's reforms, of course, provides any real sharing of power by the Al Saud who, even as revolutions have toppled regimes all around them, still appear determined to salve Saudis' frustrations with money alone rather than with meaningful political freedoms.

Indeed, the second source of Al Saud survival is money. Abdul Aziz understood this well even in the pre-oil era, when he had little of it. Until the discovery of oil in 1938, his only sources of modest revenue were a tax on pilgrims making the hajj to Mecca; the *zakat,* an annual tax on wealth and assets of Muslims required by the Koran; and a small subsidy from the British. All this he freely dispersed at his daily *majlis* to a succession of tribal chiefs and other supplicants. He regularly fed thousands at his palace from huge communal trays of rice and mutton and passed out clothes to the needy from his basement storerooms. He literally kept his gold and silver coins in a metal chest that was carried about the kingdom wherever he went, as omnipresent as the black doomsday box that accompanies modern American presidents wherever they go.

"Neither I nor my ancestors have kept a chest in which to hoard money," he told one of his ministers. "Hoarded money does no good. In peace I give all, even this cloak, to anyone who may need it. In war I ask and my people give all they have to me."

By the 1930s, the cost of government salaries, an army, payments to tribal leaders to maintain loyalty, and efforts at nation building such as installing radio and telegraph stations and creating a water supply for townspeople left Abdul Aziz almost always broke. So desperate was he that in 1933 for only 50,000 pounds (about $250,000) he granted Standard Oil of California, which a year earlier had struck oil in neighboring Bahrain, a concession in Saudi Arabia. "Put your trust in God and sign," the king instructed his finance minister. In 1938 Standard Oil struck oil—gushers of it— in the kingdom's Eastern Province.

Abdul Aziz's first royalty check exceeded $1.5 million. He was so delighted, he led a group of two thousand people in a caravan of five hundred cars to the oil fields to turn the tap to allow the first Saudi oil to flow into tankers for export. Having heard a radio report that man would one day reach Mars, a planet deemed as desolate as the deserts in Eastern Arabia, Abdul Aziz asked one of the American oil men, "Do you know what they will find when they reach Mars?" Answering his own question, he said, "They will find Americans out there in the desert hunting for oil."

The succeeding Al Saud monarchs have lived more or less luxurious lifestyles, but the family as a whole has become infamous around the world for the profligacy of its numerous playboy princes. While Abdul Aziz would have disapproved of such profligacy, his strategy of using at least some of the kingdom's wealth to buy the loyalty of its subjects continues to this day. Buying loyalty in Saudi Arabia is not, as in so many countries, a matter of greasing the palms of purchased politicians, since there are no independent Saudi politicians to purchase. Purchasing loyalty is far more pervasive than that.

Indeed, Saudi Arabia is a wealthy welfare state, in which the public pays no taxes yet receives widespread, if often poor-quality, services, from free education and health care to water and electricity and, of course, cheap energy. At least 80 percent of the revenues in the Saudi treasury accrue from petroleum. All revenue, whether from oil, earnings on the country's $400 billion in foreign reserves, or even traffic fines, flows into the central government in Riyadh—that is, to the royal family. No accounting is given to the public of either total revenues to the Al Saud coffers or total spending by the Al Saud—on behalf of the people and on behalf of the ever-expanding royal family. The public has no say in the formation of the annual government budget, which represents that portion of government spending that is disclosed publicly. The Majlis Ash Shura, appointed by the king to "represent" the people has no role in budget formation. Fully 40 percent of the budget that is disclosed publically is labeled "Other Sectors" (including defense, security, intelligence, and direct investment of the kingdom's revenues outside the country) and is opaque to the public. In sum, what the royal family takes in from national oil revenue and spends on itself is secret. Not surprisingly, Saudis increasingly are demanding not only that more of the wealth be spent on better government services, but also a transparent accounting of the nation's oil revenue, which they believe belongs to the people, not to the royal family.

More important than these entitlements, which, as in all welfare states, the public largely takes for granted, is the largesse that the Al Saud directly distribute. From multibillion-dollar contracts passed out to powerful families like the Bin Ladens to the many royal charities sponsored by princes and princesses, from the King Abdullah Housing Development Fund to the Prince Sultan Humanitarian City, royal benevolence pervades the society in such big ways but also in myriad minor ones. A seriously sick Saudi waits outside a princely office for a letter that will admit him to one of the premier military hospitals. A reformed terrorist is the beneficiary of a new Toyota, an Apple iPhone, and a job arranged under the sponsorship of Muhammad bin Nayef, the prince in charge of fighting terrorism in the kingdom. A father wants a scholarship for his son to study abroad—he petitions a prince for the favor. A hungry mother wants to procure food for her family—she stands outside any royal household. The list of petitions and royal favors is as long as the line of supplicants who once gathered outside the desert tent of King Abdul Aziz seeking free meals and clothes. In those early days, the king would dip into his money chest and hand out gold coins when he had them, though there were never enough to go around. Nevertheless, the old king's subjects undoubtedly were more appreciative of what little he had to give than modern Saudis are of the oil-funded welfare benefits now widely—but far from equitably—dispersed. "We have been made a nation of beggars," laments one government official privately critical of the regime.

A third source of Al Saud survival is the pervasive and often oppressive role of religion. Indeed, if finely honed political skills and oil riches are essential components of the Al Saud survival kit, Islam is the monarchy's survival manual. To many Saudis, the Al Saud royals are not merely a ruling family of a secular state like any Western royal dynasty but the religious exemplars of an Islamic community of believers. To find a Western analogy, one has to think back a thousand years to an age of Holy Roman emperors blessed by the pope—except in Saudi Arabia, the monarch is both emperor

Saudi grand mufti Sheikh Abdul Aziz al Ashaikh, left,
holding hands with King Abdullah. The legitimacy of this
marriage made in heaven between the Al Saud and Islam is
increasingly being challenged by Saudis. (GETTY IMAGES)

and, in effect, pope, or head of Islam styling himself as Custodian of the Two Holy Mosques.

Not only is the Saudi monarch effectively the religious pri-
mate, but the religious leaders of the puritanical Wahhabi sect
of Islam that he represents instruct Muslims to be obedient
and submissive to their rulers, however imperfect, in pursuit of
a perfect life in paradise. In their view only if a ruler directly
countermands the commandments of Allah should devout
Muslims even consider disobeying. "O you who have believed,
obey Allah and obey the Messenger and those in authority
among you," enjoins the Koran in Sura 4:59. A popular hadith
quotes the Prophet Muhammad urging believers to "stick to
obedience even if it is to an Abyssinian slave, since the believer
is like a submissive camel, wherever he is led, he follows."

In Sunni Islam, the sect that dominates Saudi Arabia and most of the Arab world, there is no single spiritual leader on earth. Rather, since the death of the Prophet Muhammad, God's messenger and spiritual leader on earth, the community of believers was first guided by a Commander of the Believers, or caliph, selected from among the faithful, and in more modern times by consortia of religious scholars or sheikhs in each Islamic country.

Sadly for Islam, those who led the believers after the Prophet quickly abandoned his commitment to austere living and humble service to Allah in favor of using religion to procure power and personal profit, not unlike the Al Saud today. Only the first caliph, Abu Bakr, truly patterned himself on the Prophet's life of sacrifice and service to believers. "Obey me for so long as I obey God and His Messenger," Abu Bakr said. "But if I disobey God and His Messenger, you owe me no obedience." All three caliphs who followed Abu Bakr died violently, although they are, along with Abu Bakr, regarded by most Muslims as the four "rightly guided" caliphs. Within fifty years of the Prophet's death, Muslims murdered a succession of leaders; shot, trampled, and beheaded the Prophet's grandson; and sacked the holy cities of Medina and Mecca, even burning the Kaaba and breaking the embedded black stone into several pieces. The saintly rule of the Prophet was supplanted by the temporal empire ruled by the fifth caliph, Mu'awiyah, son of a nobleman of Mecca who commanded the pagan opposition to the Prophet Muhammad when he was driven from Mecca. At Mu'awiyah's death, he was succeeded by his son, setting up the same sort of dynastic pattern that persists today in Saudi Arabia. Mu'awiyah's Umayyad dynasty lasted nearly one hundred years before being conquered by the Abbasids, who accused his heirs of abandoning the true Islam. The conquerors invited the surviving Umayyad rulers to dinner, and after pleasantries, by prearrangement, the waiters locked the doors and clubbed to death their ruler's guests. The debauchery and cruelty of these early caliphs is reminiscent of some of Roman Catholicism's medieval popes.

Not surprisingly, this depressing history has bred a political fatalism down through the centuries among many Muslims who believe that if just rule couldn't be established even when the Prophet's example was so fresh, there's no possibility that it could happen now. This resignation to living under corrupt temporal leaders and focusing not on improving life on earth but rather on securing a better life in the hereafter helps explain why oppressive and greedy rulers reign for so long in so many Arab countries.

In today's Saudi Arabia, the senior religious scholars, or *ulama,* are supposed to be the interpreters and arbiters of the teachings of the Koran and the Sunna, Muhammad's life example. They are not regarded as holy men but simply men well versed in the holy book and in Muhammad's life and teachings. While these men rise in the faith as a result of their scholarship and righteous living, the select group that form the Council of Senior Ulama, the body of some twenty scholars who advise the monarch on major religious issues, are appointed by the king. This council is the group to whom the Saudi king turned, for example, for the fatwa approving his request to invite U.S. troops into the kingdom in 1990 after Saddam Hussein invaded Kuwait. Similarly, it was senior members of this group who approved using violence inside the Grand Mosque of Mecca to evict the homegrown terrorists who occupied it for some weeks in November 1979. These appointed *ulama,* not surprisingly, often remind Saudis of their obligation to submit to their rulers—in this case, the Al Saud, who appointed them religious scholars—not exactly conflict-free advice.

Over recent decades, the Al Saud and their religious partners have engaged in a delicate tug-of-war. In the wake of the attack on the Grand Mosque in 1979, a shaken King Fahd, as we have seen, gave them near carte blanche over Saudi society. Beyond subjugating women, young Saudis were pressured to attend after-school training in religious fundamentalism, and over the next decade, the government gave billions of dollars to aid jihadists fighting in Afghanistan, Chechnya, and Bosnia, spawning the global jihadists who two decades later brought down the World Trade Center and then, more seriously to the Al Saud, carried their attacks into Saudi Arabia itself.

Only after the Al Saud felt themselves targeted in 2003 did the regime begin to crack down on these indigenous jihadists and on the religious fundamentalists in whose waters jihadists swim. The voices that preach a more radical and puritanical brand of Islam have been largely silenced in recent years in the name of antiterrorism. For instance, nearly two thousand mosque leaders were fired in the aftermath of terrorist bombings inside Saudi Arabia in 2003, for what the government regarded as supporting extremism. Furthermore, messages can no longer be posted inside mosques, a common recruiting place for extremists, without government permission. Friday midday sermons that touch on any controversial topic, such as jihad or politics, must be cleared in advance by the Ministry of Islamic Affairs. The security directorate also monitors mosques, religious lecturers, and camps as well as schools. In short, the religious are scrutinized carefully by the regime's security apparatus to ensure that their devotion to Allah also includes loyalty to the regime.

Like an earthquake-proof building, the Al Saud have long had the wisdom to bend ever so slightly at the moment of greatest pressure and then later reclaim, over time, most of what they yielded. And so the delicate dance between the royals and the religious, sometimes smooth and sometimes awkward, continues, but always with the Al Saud as the leading partner. The Al Saud have taken a lesson from Mu'awiyah, the seventh-century caliph who, when asked to explain his long twenty-year rule given that three of his four predecessors had been murdered, said, "I place a hair strand between myself and the people. If they pull it from their end, I would loosen it from mine so that the strand would not break. If they loosened it from their end, I would pull on it from mine." This explains why government decisions, such as allowing Saudis to vote, can be altered. As noted, the government allowed elections for toothless municipal councils in 2005 in part to please Western critics but postponed the same elections in 2009, agreeing to schedule them only in 2011, after the Arab Spring brought sweeping demands for more participation by publics all across the Middle East, including Saudi Arabia. So there is no guarantee that women will actually be allowed to participate in the municipal elections due again in 2015. What the king promises, the king can postpone.

The combined effect of Al Saud survival skills, vast oil riches, and the religious requirement of obedience all add up to a largely somnolent and passive Saudi populace. The willingness, at least so far, of Saudi citizens to live with their lot is the ultimate gift to the Al Saud. However many resentments, however much the society may seethe beneath the surface, however divided segments of the society may be, the Al Saud have retained control. Indeed, Saudis have a joke that summarizes their society's passivity.

The king decides to check the will of his people. So he sets up a checkpoint on a busy road. No one complains. So he asks his security officers to further test people's patience by also doing an identity check at the checkpoint. Still no one complains. Determined to find the public's limit of tolerance, the king asks the officer not only to stop the people and check their identities but also to ticket them. The line of cars grows ever longer on the busy Riyadh road, but still no public complaint emerges from a Saudi. So the king asks the officer to go one step further and slap those he stops, identifies, and tickets. Finally one Saudi man goes ballistic. The ruler asks that his angry countryman be brought before him to explain the outburst. "I have waited for hours in the queue," the man tells the king. "If you are going to do this to us, at least get two officers to slap us so the line moves faster."

Saudis' overwhelming desire to conform, to pass unnoticed among the rest of society, is surely a boon to Al Saud control. If Westerners love individualism, most Saudis are literally frightened at the mere thought of being different. To be different is to attract attention. To attract attention is to invite envy from peers and anger from family. It is one of the many paradoxes of Saudi Arabia that a society determined to see its collective self as unique from other Islamic countries, and surely from the West, is made up of individuals each so fearful of being unique. "Saudis do not control their own behavior," explains a U.S.-educated Saudi. "Society does. Now that we have moved to cities, it is the family rather than the tribe who controls our behavior with unwritten rules. So we do not have freedom or we will lose the support and protection of our family."

Imagine a life spent anticipating the unspoken desires of an extended family and acquiescing to the unwritten rules of society. This need for conformity forces Saudis to wear multiple faces and change them multiple times each day. The need to adapt and fit in is stressful, so most Saudis tend to reduce the stress by keeping primarily to those they know, thereby reinforcing their isolation from others who aren't members of their extended family or tribe. "Americans have one face," says the Saudi who studied in the United States. "We have multiple faces—two, three, four, five, six faces. Our views depend on which face we are wearing, and which face we are wearing depends on who we are with. Saudis don't have the same views here that we have in Paris."

Young Saudis, however, are increasingly frustrated with this consuming focus on appearance and pervasive social conformity, and they are much more willing than their parents to try to discover who they are rather than just follow the dictates of parents, teachers, imams, and royal rulers. "Our minds are in a box," says a middle-aged Saudi businessman. "But the young are being set free by the Internet and knowledge. They will not tolerate what we have. No one knows how the spark will come, but things will change because they have to."

Paradoxically, it is the Al Saud's deft duplicity, their paternal dispersal of favors, their arrogant exploitation of religion for their own purposes, and their rendering of Saudis to powerless passivity that now threaten the family's survival, because more and more Saudis—especially women and youth—now share a growing awareness of the rather non-Islamic tactics so artfully employed to cage them and they are determined to press for change that allows more freedom and more dignity for individual Saudis.

CHAPTER 3

Islam: Dominant and Divided

Religion is very easy and whoever overburdens himself in
his religion will not be able to continue in that way. So you
should not be extremists, but try to be near to perfection
and receive the good tidings that you will be rewarded.

—PROPHET MUHAMMAD, SAHIH BUKHARI HADITH,
VOL. I, BK. 2I, NO. 38

Lulu, invisible in her black *abaya,* tugs open the heavy
steel door of the high wall that surrounds her Riyadh
home in the poor district of Suwaidi. The dusty street is
empty, but she is careful to avoid exposing even a glimpse of
herself to any passerby, as she ushers me onto a tiny concrete
courtyard leading to the modest two-story home she shares
with her seven children and her husband—every other day.
On alternate days he is downstairs with his first wife of nearly
forty years, with whom he shares another eight children, all
older than Lulu's brood, who range from ages five to twenty.

As we climb the bare tile stairs to her home, Lulu nods
toward the ground-floor door as we pass and says simply,
"That is her home, and up here is mine."

Lulu is a gentle woman in her early forties who speaks
halting but passable English, learned as a student at King
Saud University. Deeply devout and eager to win a convert
to Islam, she has agreed to let me live with her to experience traditional, rigorously religious Saudi life. Converting
an infidel to Islam, which means "submission," entitles one
to paradise, she believes, so religion is the centerpiece of her

conversation. While Saudis these days can access hundreds of satellite television channels, the Internet, modern shopping malls, and even illicit drugs and alcohol, her home is free of any worldly modernity. The family has one television and viewing is limited to Al Majd, a religious network that bans any appearance by women in its programming. Similarly, the family's sole computer is used only under Lulu's supervision and then only for homework, most of it studies of the Koran, or for accessing religious sites. The walls of her home, like those of any devout Wahhabi Muslim, are devoid of photos or any human representations because they are forbidden by this strict interpretation of Islam. She is the primary caregiver to her seven children and has no household help, as the salary of her professor husband can't cover maids for both wives, and Islam requires that a husband treat his wives equally. Her life is that of a lower-middle-class Saudi: no frills.

Like all Wahhabis, Lulu follows the Hanbali school of law, the most conservative of Islam's four schools of Islamic jurisprudence. The Hanbali school relies not only on the Koran but more than other schools relies on hadith, traditions of the Prophet Muhammad and sayings of his companions. While Wahhabi religious practice is considered austere by most Muslims, the Islam practiced by Lulu and her family is strict even by Wahhabi standards.

By choice, Lulu rarely leaves home. She has no interest in the world outside her home, where her focus is on serving her husband and ensuring that her children follow a strictly religious path. As the days go by, it becomes clear Lulu not only accepts but welcomes the confines of her life. She has no aspiration beyond living life in a way that pleases Allah and ensures her entry to paradise. An essential element of achieving this goal is serving every need of her husband, a professor of hadith, the thousands of stories about the words and deeds of the Prophet Muhammad, collected and passed down by his contemporaries as a guide for devout Muslims' daily lives. If her husband should be dissatisfied with her or, even worse, be somehow led astray, the fault would be hers. "Men are in charge of women," says the Koran. "So righteous women are devoutly obedient, guarding in [the husband's] absence what Allah would have them guard." Serving Allah means serving her husband.

Lulu's children, including teenage girls, admire and obey her. I ask Lulu if she wants her daughters to have opportunities she did not have. "No, I pray they have a life like mine," she says instantly. Her eldest daughter, a student at King Saud University, says, "She is dedicating herself to helping us have a life just like hers." The daughter, dressed in a modest floor-length skirt and long-sleeved sweater even at home, speaks with deep reverence, not the sarcasm that a Western teenager might use.

Lulu and her household illustrate the deep and genuine commitment of a majority of Saudis to their religion. Most Westerners, who live in an aggressively secular environment, would find it impossible to imagine the pervasive presence of religion, which hangs over Saudi Arabia like a heavy fog and has been a source of stability, along with the Al Saud, for nearly three centuries. But the growing gap between Islam as revealed in the Koran and Islam as practiced in the kingdom is undermining the credibility of the religious establishment and creating divisions among religious conservatives and between them and modernizers. As a result, the religious pillar is cracking, with serious implications for the kingdom's future stability. But for devout Muslims like Lulu, these troubling divisions simply mean redoubling their effort to follow the true Islam by adhering strictly to the example set by the Prophet Muhammad fourteen hundred years ago.

Even small children in Saudi Arabia can be preoccupied with religion. An hour outside Riyadh in rocky desert terrain, a Saudi family concludes a daylong outing. A bright full moon illuminates the black line of silhouettes in prayer. Ahmad, six, and his father, brother, and sister bend, straighten, and prostrate themselves in unison in the direction of Mecca. I sit alone nearby on a blanket beside the dying embers of the fire, where we cooked chicken kebab for dinner. Observing my failure to pray, a concerned little Ahmad comes over and says, "I need to teach you something." Sure, what is it? I say. "Do you know what to say when the angel of death comes?"

he asks earnestly. Assuming my ignorance, this sweet child immediately provides the dialogue that the dying can expect to have if they want to transit successfully from death to the hereafter:

"The angel asks you 'Who is your God?' and you say 'Allah,'" prompts Ahmad. "Then he asks 'Who is your Prophet?' You say 'Muhammad.' What is your faith? You say 'Islam.' Then he asks 'What is your work?' and you say 'I heard and believed in Allah.'" It is impossible to imagine a child of that age in any other society on earth being similarly concerned about the hereafter—for himself, let alone a stranger. And Ahmad is the child of open-minded parents educated in the United States.

As both Lulu's and Ahmad's stories demonstrate, the emerging divisions and debates have not diminished the omnipresent ritual of religion. Every airport, shopping mall, and government or private office building includes a large area spread with prayer rugs indicating the direction of Mecca, so worshipers know where to kneel and pray. Every hotel room has a sticker on the wall or bed or desk with an arrow pointing toward Mecca. Even new cars often include complimentary prayer rugs so travelers can stop alongside a road and pray. The sound of the muezzin calling the faithful to prayer begins in the predawn hours and is heard four more times throughout the day and evening from mosques so numerous that the effect in cities is a chorus of prayer calls in surround sound. All retail businesses close several times a day, supposedly for thirty minutes but sometimes longer, while men go to pray in designated public locations or at mosques. (Women usually pray at home, as the strict segregation of sexes in Wahhabi Islam discourages most from going to mosques though women prayed with men during the Prophet's time.)

Lying on my pallet on the floor of Lulu's home, I awake at four A.M. when the muezzin in the nearby mosque begins to call *"Allahu akbar,"* or "God is most great." He repeats twice, "I testify that there is no god but God." Then he adds, "Hurry to prayer. Hurry to salvation. Prayer is better than sleep." Soon I hear the sound of men's sandals clickety-clacking down the stairs outside my door, as Lulu's husband and two teenage sons rush to the mosque. The big steel door clanks shut behind them. Then silence.

A few hours later Lulu's husband, sole driver of the family's SUV, drops the children at a special school that focuses on teaching students to memorize the entire Koran by ninth grade. Along with study of more conventional subjects. Even when her husband and children are out, Lulu almost never leaves home. All her interests are there. Asked if she would like to drive, she seems genuinely puzzled. "Why would I want to drive? In Islam it is a man's responsibility to drive his wife and children. Some women just want to drive to have fun. But this is wrong."

When her husband is home, I am banished to my room, where I read the Koran to pass the time. A religious man like her bearded husband would never mix unnecessarily with a woman who is not a relative, even if she covers her body and face. Indeed, during the week I spend with Lulu, I see her husband only once—when he picks us up from a rare outing to her sister's home. Fully veiled, I silently slip into the seat behind him, but we are not introduced and the conversation continues as if I were as invisible as Casper the friendly ghost.

Doing Allah's will is Lulu's consuming focus. At age nineteen, when her husband offered himself to her family, Lulu willingly chose to be a second wife. "Some men need another wife for many reasons, perhaps to keep from doing something bad," she explains, clearly meaning adultery, though she doesn't speak the word. "I prayed to Allah, 'Let me do this if it is good.'" She is separated from the first wife only by a set of stairs, yet they rarely visit. "It is natural that sometimes there is jealousy," she says, "if he gives her a gift or spends more time there. But I just say '*humdililah*' [praise be to God]." She beats her breast with her fist for emphasis.

For someone accustomed to an overactive American life, the ennui in Lulu's home is frustrating at first. After a few days, however, it begins to feel eerily similar to my youth in Matador, a tiny windswept West Texas town, in a home with strict religious parents—a father who read the Bible every night and a mother who, like Lulu, served him and was subservient to him. We had no television or telephone and few escapes other than attending church every Sunday morning and evening. So boring was that existence that as a teenager I set myself the goal of emulating the town's newspaper editor, who had ventured as far as California— a wider ambition wasn't imaginable in my limited life, so I surely didn't ever dream then of any place as distant or exotic as Saudi Arabia. My later fascination, over a thirty-year career as an international reporter and editor, was with the myriad places to which I traveled and the diverse people I met. Now here I was far from Matador but once again confined to a home focused only on religious asceticism similar to that of my family.

Clearly Lulu is a genuinely devout woman who sincerely wants to save me. Just as my father forbade shorts and pants, Lulu tells me that my pants and sweater are not pleasing to God. Lulu would no sooner wear a pantsuit even at home than run down the street naked, because anything that reveals the human form is forbidden. My floor-length black *abaya* similarly is gently criticized because it fits across the shoulders and features modest decoration on its long sleeves. Fingering the blue and orange stitching, she says, "This is wrong. Your *abaya* shows the body, and this decoration attracts men to look at you." Outside the home, Lulu and her daughters shroud head to toe in shapeless black *abayas* that are akin to wrapping oneself in a black bedsheet. Before exiting, they also cover their faces with a separate black *niqab,* securing it firmly in a knot behind their head. The *niqab* features a slit for the eyes, but these devout ladies cover even that slit with another black cloth, which can be flipped up or lowered over the slit depending on whether one needs to see clearly.

From the first day until the last—and on subsequent visits to her home—Lulu is persistent in seeking to convert me to Islam. On my first day, she seats me before the family computer to watch an hourlong video of a fundamentalist Christian preacher from Texas explaining his conversion to Islam. When this example didn't induce my conversion, she next issues a stern warning: "It is very bad to die believing Allah had a son," she says, debunking Christians' view that Jesus is the son of God. *"Allah* has no sons." When I observe that

Christians, like Muslims, believe in one God and that a righteous life on earth is required to gain admission to heaven, she politely rejects any equation between the two religions. "It is bad for you to believe Christians have their religion and Muslims have theirs. No," she says emphatically, "you must believe in Islam. Allah says this."

Finally, when this conversion effort fails, a disappointed Lulu assumes it can only be fear, not any failing of Islam. "Why are you not a Muslim, Miss Karen? What stops you? Are you afraid of some people in your country when you go home?"

Lulu represents the cloistered and benign Islamic conservatism that the Al Saud and their religious partners, the Council of Senior Ulama, profess to believe dominates the kingdom. Lulu wishes she were in such a majority but says fewer than 50 percent of women any longer share her views and lifestyle. Lulu is not interested in the world beyond her walls—or even in the here and now—but only in the hereafter. She is far more concerned about whether God had a son than about which elderly son of Abdul Aziz will next rule Saudi Arabia. She is content to criticize those outside her walls who adopt modern ways she considers non-Islamic while focusing on preserving her family's religious piety inside her walls. A greater openness in recent years has allowed some Saudis to choose a more liberal lifestyle—where men and women sometimes mix, where women can check into a hotel without a male relative, where there is even talk of women being allowed to drive; but if it were to become the new norm, Lulu would undoubtedly resist adapting with all her might. This is the challenge for the kingdom: how to accommodate those citizens who want more freedom to change and those, like Lulu and her family, who truly see change as a road to hell.

As old divisions among tribes, regions, genders, and classes grow ever more visible, religion's ability to serve as a unifying force is becoming weaker. Indeed, rather than unifying Saudi believers, Islam is now becoming another source of division. This is true for at least four reasons.

First, the Al Saud have politicized Saudi Islam. For two

decades they used their religious establishment to support jihadists in Afghanistan and religious extremists at home. Then they abruptly switched course in 2003 to insist that the same religious leaders promote the regime's campaign for a kinder, gentler interpretation of Islam, to undermine Islamic extremists, whom the Al Saud belatedly recognized as threatening their rule. This shift, which followed the terrorist attacks by Islamic extremists inside the kingdom in 2003, has led many Saudis, moderates as well as conservatives, to view the religious establishment, or Council of Senior Ulama, as apologists for the Al Saud and, worse, as indirect puppets of America. The Al Saud regime always has been the dominant partner in the relationship with religious leaders, but in recent years the religious partner has come to be seen as so openly compliant with Al Saud political needs rather than Allah's commands that it has lost much of its credibility—and as a consequence, the Al Saud also are losing theirs.

Secondly, while Islam often is seen as a very literal faith, whose adherents follow the injunctions of the Koran to the letter, in fact, in the Muslim world, many interpretations of Islam exist. For most of Saudi history, religious scholars of the Wahhabi sect provided the only valid interpretations. But that is changing dramatically with the advent of the Internet and education. More Saudis are reading and interpreting the Koran for themselves. Thus, for example, women seeking more social equality are plucking verses from the Koran to justify an expanded role for women, even as fundamentalists cite other verses to justify keeping them sequestered and subordinated. In sum, the Al Saud and their Wahhabi *ulama* no longer have a lock on interpreting Islam.

Third, while the many muezzins call to the faithful in scripted words in perfect harmony, the religious voices reaching Saudi citizens these days through the Internet and satellite television are anything but harmonious. Saudi Islam has become discordant. On any given day, at any hour, Saudis are logging on to the Internet or tuning in to a satellite television channel, where they hear a wide range of Islamic voices preaching everything from modern and moderate Islam to extreme fundamentalist and even violent Islam. While the regime tries hard to prop up and promote the authority of its official Council of Senior Ulama by, among other things, creating an official Web site for fatwas by this group only (www.alifta.com), the regime has largely lost control of an increasingly diffuse and divided Islam. Thanks to the Internet, fatwa "shopping" is common among young Saudis.

Fourth, modern society presents a whole range of challenges that the Prophet Muhammad did not have to deal with and could not foresee. A youthful population with Internet access to the rest of the world has raised a profusion of issues that are taxing the theology and ingenuity of Islamic scholars. Sheikh Mutlag, a member of the senior *ulama* and an adviser to King Abdullah, surely didn't expect, when he was pursuing his religious studies, that he would be called upon to issue a fatwa on the appropriateness of carrying into a toilet a cell phone that included downloaded selections from the Koran. He settled the issue by permitting cell phones in a toilet on the clever justification that the Koran is (or should be) completely "downloaded" into every Muslim's mind at all times.

Senior *ulama* are usually stern and inaccessible where foreign females are concerned. But Sheikh Mutlag agrees to meet me to discuss the role of a religious scholar in the lives of Saudis. The sheikh is something of a homespun humorist— a latter-day Will Rogers, the Oklahoma cowboy commentator famous for quips such as "Be thankful we're not getting all the government we pay for." In a similar vein, when a devout Saudi asked the sheikh if it was religiously permissible to eat a penguin, a remote possibility in Saudi Arabia, the amused Sheikh Mutlag responded, "If you find one, eat it."

His common touch and practical advice have made him popular with young Saudis, even though some of their elders consider him a buffoon. Those same traits apparently appealed to King Abdullah when he named Sheikh Mutlag an adviser on issues such as whether the kingdom should have a minimum marriage age for girls. Public anger forced this issue on King Abdullah after a Saudi father married his twelve-year-old daughter to his eighty-year-old cousin, who paid the father a dowry of 85,000 Saudi riyals (about $20,000).

While the sheikh declines to disclose his advice to the king, he does volunteer, "If there is harm to the girl, it is forbidden. This is what the Prophet Muhammad said." When I point out that the Prophet Muhammad was betrothed to the six-year-old daughter of one of his righteous companions and consummated the marriage when she was only nine, an annoyed Sheikh Mutlag waves off any comparison. "Her mother and father and she all agreed," he says. "And Aisha was not like a nine-year-old today. The Prophet consulted her on all issues." The sheikh then promptly excuses himself to pray. When he returns, he terminates the meeting, promising to reschedule in a few days. Of course, he never does. But what's one little broken promise to an infidel?

Or perhaps he was just seeking to chalk up one credit with God. Muslims believe that each human is flanked by two angels who record good and bad deeds. If a believer even thinks of doing something good, the angel records the thought as a single good deed. If the believer actually does what he or she says, God gives credit for ten good deeds. So perhaps this is why Saudis so often make promises even if they have no intention of keeping them. Partial credit is better than none at all.

There are myriad modern issues to which scripture offers no specific guidance. The religious scholars must find justification for any ruling they issue in the Koran, the hadith, or fatwas issued down through the ages, much as late medieval monks pored through scripture to debate how many angels could stand on the head of a pin, even as the Renaissance swept across Western Europe.

To understand where Saudi Islam is going these days, it is necessary to step back and understand its outlines and origins. As Muslims see it today, and have always seen it, Islamic law recognizes five categories of acts: those God requires of man, those recommended but not required (like visiting Medina after the required pilgrimage to Mecca), those God prohibits (theft, alcohol, fornication), those discouraged but not forbidden, and last, those to which God is indifferent and neither rewards nor punishes. Only in this last category is man free to make laws governing conduct. Otherwise, these broad categories govern all legal and ethical conduct of devout Muslims—and of a truly Islamic nation.

There is considerable disagreement among Muslim scholars as to distinctions within and between categories. Religious scholars to this day study and debate fatwas, but all such rulings should find foundation in the Koran, or in the traditions and sayings of the Prophet and his companions, or in the scholarship of Muslim jurists in the first few centuries after Muhammad—in short, in events and judgments made more than a millennium ago.

What is authentic, of course, is sometimes a matter of dispute. The Sunna, the example set by the Prophet's words, deeds, and practices, is considered the ideal and thus this pattern of behavior is practiced and passed on by pious Muslims. While Christians seek to emulate the sinless life of service that Jesus Christ, their spiritual leader, led on earth, they make no attempt to copy Jesus, the man, in his earthly personal habits, dress, or lifestyle. It is Jesus, holy figure of faith, who matters to Christians. Muslims, on the other hand, see Muhammad as only a man but one worthy of emulating in minute detail as a role model for daily life.

"For nearly 1,400 years Muslims have tried to awaken in the morning as the Prophet awakened, to eat as he ate, to wash as he washed himself, even to cut their nails as he did," writes Seyyed Hossein Nasr, a Muslim scholar, in *Ideas and Realities of Islam.* "There has been no greater force for unification of the Muslim peoples than the presence of this common model for the minutest acts of daily life."

The actual religious requirements of Islam are quite simple—in contrast to the requirements of religion in daily life. To be a Muslim, one has only to fulfill five requirements. The first is the *shahada,* or statement of belief: "There is no god but God, and Muhammad is the Messenger of God." Say those words, and you are a Muslim. The second requirement is that a believer pray five times daily, an act of worship that reminds man that he must submit to God's will rather than his own. The third is the requirement that every Muslim pay *zakat,* an annual tax of 2.5 percent on all his various forms of wealth, not simply his cash or income. The fourth is fasting during the holy month of Ramadan from sunrise to sunset. And finally, good Muslims must make a pilgrimage to Mecca at least once in their lifetime if at all possible.

The obligatory Muslim prayers, or *salat,* are not requests for intercession or offers of thanks, as common Christian prayers are. While Muslims also offer this sort of prayer, or *du'a,* the *salat* is something very different. It is a precisely regulated, formal ritual that features bodily bending while repeating specific verses from the Koran and that climaxes in prostration to God in the direction of Mecca to demonstrate submission to God's will.

The entire procedure requires nearly ten minutes and can be performed only after the worshiper has properly purified himself—and his heart—for the act of worship. This washing, or ablution, is a critical part of preparing for prayer; it requires the worshiper to wash his hands up to the wrist, rinse the mouth, clean the nose, and scrub the face, forearms up to the elbows, head (by rubbing a wet finger from the forehead to the nape of the neck and back), ears, and finally feet. The Prophet is quoted as saying, "The key to paradise is prayer [*salat*] and the key to prayer is purification."

When Muslims pray, they begin in a standing position and repeat the opening sura of the Koran:

In the name of God, the Compassionate, the Merciful
Praise be to God, Lord of the Worlds,
The Compassionate, the Merciful
Owner of the Day of Judgment.
Thee only do we worship; and unto Thee alone do we turn for
help.
Guide us to the straight path,
The path of those whom thou has favored; not the path of those
who have
earned thine anger nor of those who go astray. Be it so.

It is routine for a Saudi—male or female—to interrupt a conversation to pray. Men go to a nearby mosque, while women cover themselves and pray wherever they are indoors. Other times, in public places, a man will simply roll out a prayer rug in the lobby of a hotel and fall to his knees as others continue to traipse past, scarcely taking notice of the prostrate worshiper. Occasionally, a host will simply prostrate himself across the room, leaving his guest to watch as he subjugates himself to Allah.

Against the backdrop of all this religious tradition and ritual, every decision taken in Saudi Arabia by anyone from the king on down involves religion. But religion cannot serve to direct society down a common path when the religious guides themselves are divided. So beyond the cacophony of Islamic voices now bombarding Saudis from television and the Internet is the even more serious spectacle of a religious establishment at war within itself.

In recent years, the senior religious scholars have publicly criticized first the king and then each other over the issue of the religious rectitude of men and women mixing. The king's firing in 2009 of Sheikh Shetri, a member of the senior *ulama* who criticized the mixing of men and women at the king's new namesake university, unleashed the unholy spectacle of other compliant *ulama* suddenly discovering and disclosing that, lo and behold, the Prophet himself had mixed with women, even to the extent of allowing unrelated women to wash his hair. Then the head of the Hai'a, or Commission for the Promotion of Virtue and Prevention of Vice, in the holy city of Mecca, Sheikh Ahmad Qasim al Ghamdi, not only supported men and women mixing in public places but also said he instructed his *mutawa'a,* or religious police, not to interfere with such mixing. The grand mufti, the kingdom's senior religious scholar, then got involved and (according to Saudi newspaper reports) told Sheikh Al Ghamdi to stop making statements about religious issues that aren't his concern.

This display of discord played out in the media and became fodder for conversation and comment across the country. Under pressure from religious conservatives, the head of the Hai'a in Riyadh fired his chief in Mecca late one Sunday night. So the public was treated to the added spectacle of the king's appointee firing the king's defender. This paradox was not lost on King Abdullah, so things got worse. Within hours of the firing of Sheikh Al Ghamdi, the Hai'a issued an embarrassing retraction: "The information sent out today concerning administrative changes at some Hai'a offices, particularly those concerning Mecca and Hail, was inaccurate, and the administration has requested editors not to publish it."

It was too late. Both the firing and the retraction had become major news, not only on the Internet and television but even in the controlled print press. Outraged conservatives went to Sheikh Al Ghamdi's home, demanding to "mix" with his females. The sheikh also reported receiving angry text messages, and still other outraged opponents scrawled graffiti on his home. In another unprecedented move, the unrepentant Sheikh Al Ghamdi went on television after Friday prayer, when most Saudis are home relaxing, to defend himself and say of his fellow Saudis: "Most people want to be more religious than the Prophet. I don't expect to change them. They are fanatics. I just want to tell the truth because the relationship between men and women is not war."

While this kind of open, divisive debate is taking place within the official religious establishment, that establishment also is coming under external attack from respected fundamentalist and also moderate religious scholars. At the moderate end of the spectrum is Sheikh Salman al Awdah, once such a fierce fundamentalist that in the 1990s he was jailed for his virulent criticism of the regime. Since then he has moderated his views, helped the regime try to dissuade young Saudis from turning to terrorism, and been granted a weekly television show that became hugely popular with young Saudis, most of whom want to live a genuinely devout life, not one focused simply on the minutiae of religious ritual so popular in the fatwas of the elderly Council of Senior Ulama.

About fifty years of age, Sheikh Salman's intense face is

Islam in Saudi Arabia has many faces. *Above,*
the late blind grand mufti Sheikh Abdul Aziz
bin Abdullah bin Baz believed the world was
flat and was the unchallenged voice of Wahhabi
Islam until his death in 1999. (REUTERS)
Below, Sheikh Salman al Awdah, among
the most prominent of today's proliferating
religious voices, is popular among
Saudi youth for challenging Wahhabi
orthodoxy. (ABDULLAH AL SHAMMARI)

framed by a heavy black beard, and his penetrating eyes look straight through his rimless glasses at an interlocutor who asks what led to his change in religious views. "There is only one change," he says. "I am getting older and more logical in my thinking." This former religious extremist has become a multimedia phenomenon with a Web site (IslamToday.net), a newspaper column, videos, books, and lectures in addition to his television show. The sheikh dispenses advice on contemporary issues and temptations—and along with it, criticism of the society and by extension the Al Saud and their religious establishment. On just one Friday television show, the sheikh criticized the kingdom's education system as a failure, accused the government of insincerity and inadequacy in its latest plan to create a high-tech revolution in the kingdom, and charged the religious leaders with being more interested in building mosques than in building clinics to serve the poor. "Saudi society is slow to change and has no plan," he tells a visitor to his home. "So what is coming is a spontaneous change. My project is to teach the young to be honest and deal with each other in a good way. If we can change the young, they might change the country."

At the other end of the spectrum from this charismatic moderate is a deeply conservative imam who leads a much more private life but whose critiques of the regime, while less public, are thus free to be even more acerbic. The imam, who asks to remain anonymous, seeks to block out evil and live an austere, ascetic life focused on serving others. He drives a beat-up old car and wears a plain brown *thobe* cut above his ankles to indicate avoidance of extravagance. When meeting with guests in his home, he himself serves the coffee and tea that are obligatory expressions of hospitality. The imam is surrounded in his study from floor to ceiling by books, which he pores over to perfect his knowledge of authentic Islam. Sporting a frizzy, uncut black beard, a hallmark of conservative religious Muslims, he refuses to shake hands but is willing to converse on Islam and even seeks to convert me. He sums up his approach—and that which he clearly proposes for others—this way: "One who believes in God sees this life is short and he must live for the next life. Some others think this is the only life so they are corrupt and greedy."

The imam clearly puts the Al Saud in the camp of the corrupt and greedy. He seethes with anger at a regime that he sees as kowtowing to American infidels, encouraging the mixing of men and women, and leading corrupt lives focused on materialism rather than on the hereafter. "We are very weak," he says. "If the royal family can't renew itself, the regime will collapse. The young are attacking the government because it is loyal to the United States, not to Islam."

One year after the spirited religious debate on gender mixing and shortly after the Arab Spring, Sheikh Al Ghamdi was fired and Sheikh Salman left the kingdom for what he said would be temporary self-imposed exile in South Africa. Only the imam, who never went public with his thoughts, remained unaffected by a new crackdown on religious debate imposed by King Abdullah in the wake of Arab Spring rebellions across the Middle East. Eager to ensure the support of religious conservatives inside the kingdom, the monarch imposed a ban on public criticism of the religious establishment, the very kind of open dialogue that he had encouraged for half a dozen years in his efforts to curb religious extremism in Saudi Arabia. But with Al Saud survival possibly at risk from an unhappy, frustrated populace, the Al Saud compass pointed once again in the direction of the religious.

Not surprisingly, Saudi youth have a difficult time navigating all these conflicting currents of Islam. Whether motivated by moderates or by fundamentalists, young Saudis are far more likely to question religious authority than were their parents a generation ago. Meanwhile the religious authorities are faced with the problem of trying to issue fatwas that are relevant to modern life yet more often end up merely pointing up the inadequacy of religious rulings to current issues confronting young people.

So minute and myriad are the issues where religion impacts daily life that the government has established an official Web site for approved fatwas to guide the faithful. The site (www .alifta.com) is intended to discourage young Saudis from following fatwas they find posted on the Internet from some unapproved sheikh at home or abroad who doesn't represent Islam as propounded by Saudi Arabia's religious scholars. For instance, one Saudi sheikh issued a fatwa condemning soccer because the Koran, he insisted, forbids Muslims to imitate Christians or Jews. Therefore, using words like *foul* or *penalty kick* is forbidden. The country's grand mufti, Sheikh Abdul Aziz bin Abdullah al Ashaikh, rejected that fatwa and called on the religious police to track down and prosecute its author. Using a few non-Arabic words, said the grand mufti, is not forbidden, as even Allah used some non-Arabic words in the Koran. (Not incidentally perhaps, the grand mufti understood that soccer is a national passion.)

The official Web site even allows believers to query the *ulama,* much as Americans of earlier decades used to write Ann Landers for advice on life. For example, one young man asked religious authorities whether, having masturbated during the daytime in Ramadan when he was a teenager (and didn't know it was forbidden) and then having performed ablutions afterward, he had violated proper fasting and prayer.

The short answer: yes. "First, practicing masturbation is *haram* [prohibited] and it is even more sinful during the day in Ramadan," wrote the religious officials in fatwa number 10551. Furthermore, they noted, the young man would indeed need to make up with fasting and prayer for every day he masturbated during Ramadan, because masturbation invalidates his fasting and his prayer, making them void because he failed to cleanse himself with a bath prior to praying.

Not only is masturbation forbidden—so is shaking hands with women. The *ulama* insist the Prophet Muhammad said, "I do not shake hands with women." Therefore, modern-day Muslims should follow that example. Ironically, those same *ulama* have ruled in another fatwa that touching a woman after washing for prayer doesn't make one unclean and thus does not require repeating ablutions. Similarly, it is acceptable to wave one's hand to others while saying the Islamic greeting "Peace be upon you," but it is forbidden to wave one's hand as a substitute for the words of the peace greeting since waving is a Western practice.

More consequential life issues also are prescribed by the religion. For instance, Saudi religious scholars insist that a Muslim woman must cover her entire body in the presence of a man who is not a relative. While the Saudi religious authorities acknowledge, in a fatwa on veiling, that there is historic evidence of the permissibility of uncovering the face and hands, this, they say, was in practice before the revelation of Sura 33:59 requiring veiling ("O Prophet! Tell your wives and your daughters and the women of the believers to draw their cloaks all over their bodies") and before the Prophet commanded women to observe it. Therefore the former is abrogated by the latter.

Some rules apply to all Muslims, regardless of gender. Any sexual deviancy is forbidden. So is any public display of affection between opposite sexes, whether related or married. The only acceptable display of affection in Saudi Arabia (in contrast to the West) is between two men, whose hand holding is seen as a display of trust. Eating only with the right hand is required of all Saudis, because the left is reserved for toilet functions or touching other unclean objects.

Despite its great rigidity, Islam also is pragmatic enough for believers to meet its requirements without excessive hardship. For instance, those who are ill or traveling may forgo fasting during Ramadan and make up for it by fasting another time. Similarly, if a worshiper has no access to water to cleanse for prayer, there is what amounts to a dry cleaning procedure. The process is called *tayammum* and involves rubbing a bit of sand on one's hands and face or, if indoors, patting a cushion to make dust rise, a symbolic cleaning.

Educated, modern Saudis, especially the young, often chafe at the restrictive nature of Wahhabi Islam and even more so at the growing gulf between what is enunciated in mosques and fatwas and what is practiced by many of the ruling political and religious elite. Increasingly, traditional, conservative Saudis see the ruling authorities as corrupted, while more liberal Saudis see the same authorities as hypocrites who say one thing and do another.

"Things that used to be *haram* [forbidden] like music are now everywhere," says a professor at Imam University, one of the kingdom's premier religious schools. "We memorize the Koran but we don't live it." This man is offended to see the government erect a huge new mosque across from a run-down hospital, and to see a popular Saudi blogger imprisoned for exposing government corruption in an arms deal with Britain. "During the whole of Islamic history, these [the Council of Senior Ulama] are the most corrupt religious authorities."

A colleague, who confesses to fighting his brother to prevent him from committing the offense of listening to music, says, "We have replaced religion with ritual. Imam University teaches people to memorize, not question." The insistence that Muslims never ask "how" or "why" dates from at least the tenth century. During the first two centuries after the Prophet Muhammad's death, Islamic scholars debated a range of religious issues, but that pretty much ended in the tenth century. "The efforts to explore the content of faith by reason had led to a confusing mass of theories and views that threatened the community's harmony," wrote German scholar Tilman Nagel. So questioning "how" or "why" became forbidden and remains so in Wahhabi Islam.

Glaring contradictions abound. For instance, fatwas from religious *ulama* forbid the use of gold- or silver-plated dinnerware or utensils. "If anyone drinks from vessels of gold or silver, it is as if the fire of Hell is rumbling in their stomach," one fatwa quotes the Prophet as having said. The Prophet further said, "Do not drink from vessels of gold or silver and do not eat in plates made from them. They are for them [unbelievers] in this world and for you in the Hereafter." Yet it is common for members of the royal family to dine at home with silver utensils on food served on gold-rimmed china and to drink from gilded goblets and teacups. Such ostentatious display of wealth, and the contradiction with the Islam practiced by the Prophet, who ate with his right hand from a communal plate of food, disturbs religious purists. "We have become just consumers," laments the Imam University professor. "This leads to corruption and destruction."

This growing lack of respect for senior religious authorities, coupled with the increasing availability of other Islamic views to Saudis, is prompting more independent thinking and action in the daily lives of young Saudis. The globalization of the workplace also is altering religious habits. One young Saudi in his twenties who works as a salesman for an international company describes his soul searching over whether to shake hands with a female on whom he was paying a business call for his company. He consulted his imam not once but twice; each time he was told that shaking hands is *haram,* or forbidden. In the end, he decided to shake the woman's hand anyway as he felt it was simply good manners. "I shook her hand, and I don't feel unclean," he said.

Islam is a religion of doing, not hearing or preaching; of active faith, not passive belief. Like fundamentalist Christians, pious Muslims believe they will be accountable to God at a final judgment day for everything they do on earth, so they want to know precisely what God commands and to please him in all things. The stakes are high.

The Koran speaks repeatedly and graphically of the rewards in store for righteous believers and of the torments awaiting wrongdoers. Those who live by Allah's commandments "will be honored in gardens of pleasure on thrones facing one another. There will be circulated among them a cup [of wine] from a flowing spring. White and delicious to the drinkers; No bad effect is there in it, nor from it will they be intoxicated. And with them will be women limiting [their] glances, with large beautiful eyes."

By contrast, those who have not led humble, obedient lives will find themselves in hell. "We have made it a torment for the wrongdoers. Verily it is a tree that springs from the bottom of the Hellfire. Its emerging fruit is like the heads of devils. And indeed, they will eat from it and fill with it their bellies. Then indeed, they will have after it a mixture of scalding water. Then indeed, their return will be to the Hellfire."

Even before this final judgment day, Muslims believe, every human being—believer and nonbeliever—must undergo a so-called "grave trial" immediately after death. Once in the grave, the believer's soul is borne up by angels through seven heavens, whereupon God records the person's good deeds, and the Angel of Death conducts the grave trial asking, "Who is your God? What is your religion? Who is your prophet?" If the believer successfully answers, a window on paradise is opened for the individual with the words, "Rest in tranquillity."

But there is no tranquillity for the nonbeliever. His soul is ripped from his body and borne aloft by angels, although he is not permitted to view heaven. Instead, he is returned to his grave for trial. Two angels squeeze his body relentlessly as he fails to answer their questions. He is shown his place in hell, and then the angels hit him so hard his body turns to dust, only to be immediately restored and again hit so hard he crumbles into dust, and so on forever until Judgment Day. Only martyrs are spared the grave trial and allowed to go directly to paradise. Small wonder, then, that jihad appeals to devout young men.

Still, while many Saudis are focused on the afterlife, it is entirely possible to lead a largely Western lifestyle in this birthplace of the Prophet Muhammad—and a very small minority does. While restaurants are limited to serving non-alcoholic beer and wine and "Saudi Champagne" (a mixture of apple juice and Perrier), some private homes of the wealthy feature full liquor cabinets and, in more limited cases, large, well-stocked wine cellars. Children in these households often attend modern schools with international curricula, where girls' sports teams are acceptable, and teenage boys and girls are allowed to mix in their family homes. The children study voice and dance, listen to music, and watch television. The mothers watch Oprah Winfrey, visit spas, and contribute time to charity work. The fathers gather to drink and talk and watch soccer in each other's homes. These are, in effect, the Saudi version of the "millionaires and billionaires" in the United States who so trouble President Obama.

Many Saudis can't afford, or won't risk, indulgences like alcohol or prostitution while inside the kingdom but are eager to partake of them during travels abroad. Millions of Saudis cross the King Fahd Causeway that connects the kingdom to Bahrain, a sheikdom where they can enjoy cinema, alcohol, and prostitutes or just the pleasure of dinner in a relaxed environment with friends both male and female. Indeed, Saudis give proof to the old saying that opposites attract. The United States—which prides itself on individualism, not conformity, on openness, not secrecy, on rule by institutions, not by a royal family—seems to hold a special attraction for many Saudis, even those who condemn its morals. In this as in so many other things, Saudis see none of what Americans would call hypocrisy in saying one thing and doing another.

By "promoting good and forbidding evil"—even if occasionally indulging in some forbidden conduct—the majority of Saudi society continues to be committed to a righteous way of life and to exhibit a rectitude in public that these Saudis see missing in most Western nations, especially the United States. Isn't it better, such Saudis ask, to condemn extramarital sex, even while indulging in it occasionally, than to have more than 50 percent of all infants born to unwed mothers, as in the United States? Isn't it better to drink in private than to have open bars, alcoholics, and drunk drivers menacing the roads?

Saudi society of today is reminiscent of a simpler time in the United States when husbands and wives may have cheated on each other but didn't divorce; when a majority of Americans went to church even if the sermons didn't guide their conduct during the week; when unwed mothers were embarrassed about their condition; and when Americans didn't spill their most intimate secrets on Facebook or on reality TV shows. A healthy level of hypocrisy helped keep guardrails on society so that young people were presented— if only in public—with an ideal model for life.

Saudi Arabia, assaulted by technology and globalization, tipsy from a population explosion that has left more than 60 percent of its citizens age twenty or younger, and clinging to religion as an anchor in this sea of change, is trying to preserve a way of life exhibited by the Prophet fourteen hundred years ago.

For the Al Saud, navigating between those Wahhabi clerics

who insist that true religious orthodoxy is one of austere rules (not coincidentally interpreted by them) that must govern every aspect of social life, and those more liberal Saudis who insist that the true Islam of the Prophet is a kinder, gentler religion that loves learning and life, is a pressing challenge. It is compounded by a generational change in Al Saud leadership that can't be far off, given that all the remaining brothers who could be king are nearly seventy years old or older. So far, the royal family has chosen to let various voices compete in the marketplace of Islamic ideas rather than try to reconcile competing versions of orthodox Islam. But the longer these contending strains of Islam continue, and the more divided Saudi society becomes, the harder it will be for the Al Saud to reclaim the religious legitimacy that has largely cloaked them since the founding of their dynasty.

Ironically, this breakdown in social cohesion brought about by modern development was foreseen nearly seven centuries ago by Ibn Khaldun, an Islamic social thinker (A.D. 1332–1406). An historian, he sought to understand the basic causes of historical evolution that he believed were embedded in the economic and social structure of societies. Often described as the founder of sociology and demography, Ibn Khaldun, a Tunisian, in his *Muqaddimah* (An Introduction to History) outlines two main types of society: primitive and elementary society (*jawam al-bedoun*) and civilized and complex society (*jawam al-hazari*). He found *asabiya,* or social cohesion, greatest in primitive tribal societies. He saw the increasing power of the ruler and of government institutions that characterizes more complex societies, as well as unnecessary consumption and indulgence in luxury by the population, as features that inevitably would lead to a decline in social cohesion and a sense of individual alienation from society. This fourteenth-century analysis pretty accurately sums up the divisiveness and alienation in today's Saudi Arabia.

CHAPTER 4

The Social Labyrinth

Hold firmly to the rope of Allah all together and do not become divided.

—KORAN, SURA 3:103

A child born in Saudi Arabia enters a harsh and divided society. For millennia, Saudis struggled to survive in a vast desert under searing sun and shearing winds that quickly devour a man's energy, as he searches for a wadi of shade trees and water, which are few and far between, living on only a few dates and camel's milk. These conditions bred a people suspicious of each other and especially of strangers, a culture largely devoid of art or enjoyment of beauty. Even today Saudis are a people locked in their own cocoons, focused on their own survival—and that of family—and largely uncaring of others. While survival in the desert also imposed a code of hospitality even toward strangers, life in Saudi cities shuts out strangers and thus eliminates any opportunity and thus obligation for hospitality toward them.

Walk down the dusty and often garbage-strewn streets of any Saudi residential neighborhood, and all you will see are walls. To your right and to your left are walls of steel and walls of concrete. Walls ten or twelve feet high. Western neighborhoods offer grassy lawns, flower beds, front steps, and doorways that seem to invite you in, but Saudi Arabia's walls are there to shut out strangers—and to shut in those who live inside. The higher and more ornate the walls, the more prosperous or princely are the occupants. But rich or poor, royal or common, Saudis are shut-ins.

If America is a messy melting pot of nationalities, races, genders, and sexual orientations all mingling with perhaps too few guardrails, Saudi Arabia is the precise opposite: a society of deep divisions and high walls. Imagine an entire society living within a maze of myriad walls that block people from outside view but, more important, separate them from one another. The walls of this metaphorical Saudi maze are those of religion, tradition, convention, and culture. As with any maze, there are narrow pathways meandering through, but most Saudis have neither the curiosity nor the courage to explore, much less seek to escape, their prescribed warren.

Inside this labyrinth, the people present a picture of uniformity. From the king to the lowest pauper, men wear identical flowing white robes. Their heads most often are draped in red-and-white cotton scarves, usually held in place by a double black circle of woven woolen cord. Similarly, women—when in public—are invisible beneath flowing black *abayas,* head scarves, and generally full-face veils, or *niqab.* The society presents a somber cast as men move about their daily business, because laughter and visible emotion are discouraged by Islam as practiced in Saudi Arabia. Encouraged—and everywhere visible—is prayer. When the call to prayer sounds, as it does five times daily, men leave their beds or their work to kneel in rows and prostrate themselves in unison toward the holy city of Mecca, birthplace of the Prophet Muhammad.

Like the labyrinth constructed by Daedalus for King Minos to imprison his wife's son, the walls of the Saudi maze have been constructed by the Saudi ruling family, the Al Saud, and its partner, the religious establishment of Wahhabi Islam, to maintain their joint control over Saudis—and to keep them isolated enough that they cannot coalesce around common frustrations.

Beneath the surface, however, cracks in the facades of control and conformity were beginning to show well before revolutionary winds swept from Tunis to Cairo to Tripoli and across much of the Middle East. The regime faces growing

challenges from still largely docile reformers and, more seriously, from religious fundamentalists who view the Al Saud
as princely puppets of the infidel West and the religious establishment as hirelings of those princes. Meanwhile, the placid
surface of traditional society no longer can constrain or conceal its many internal divisions based on tribe, class, region,
and Islamic sect. These traditional divisions have been compounded by more recent ones including the growing gaps
between rich and poor and between conservatives (who cling
to religious and cultural traditions) and modernizers (who
believe Islam and greater individualism can coexist). While
Saudis still may be publicly passive, they are neither happy
nor harmonious.

From birth, they are raised in a religion that encourages
submission to Allah and his chosen leaders on earth. Oppression by a bad ruler is preferable to chaos among believers,
according to one of the most prominent eleventh-century
Sunni Islamic scholars, Muhammad al Ghazali. So Saudis
are instructed by religious leaders to obey their ruler even if
he is bad. "The religious leaders protect the government from
people instead of representing people to the government,"
says a male student at Imam University, the kingdom's premier institution for training religious scholars, reflecting the

A hapless Saudi woman escapes her car during
the Jeddah floods. (ARAB NEWS)

Cynical Saudis distort their national emblem with mops
and buckets to express anger at the government's failure to
deal with severe flooding in Jeddah in 2009 and 2011.

skepticism, common even among devout youth, of the ruling
partnership of the Al Saud and the religious establishment.

As this young man indicates, these days life in the labyrinth is under assault. Outside information and influences are
penetrating its walls through the Internet, satellite television,
ubiquitous cell phones, and social media. Saudi society no
longer is shrouded from the outside world and its influences.

Much as Ronald Reagan once challenged Mikhail Gorbachev to "tear down this wall," a growing number of Saudi
youth are tearing at the walls of their national labyrinth.
Saudi Arabia boasts 9.8 million Internet users, or 38 percent
penetration, according to the International Telecommunications Union, an agency of the United Nations. And with 5.1
million Saudis on Facebook in January 2012, a 25 percent
increase in six months, Saudi Arabia is second only to more
populous Egypt (with 10 million users) among Middle East
nations in use of this social networking site. (Saudi Arabia
ranks 30th in the world, right behind Russia, which has five
times the population.) Tellingly, Saudi users are overwhelmingly young (69 percent are under thirty-four), male (69 percent), and single (91 percent). While much of the Facebook
chatter is personal, not political, Saudis have learned to connect, and they did so spontaneously—and furiously—when
floods swept Jeddah in late 2009 and again in early 2011. The

government's failure to provide proper sewage and drainage systems in this wealthy kingdom encouraged conspiracy theories among angry citizens, who claimed the actual death toll in these floods was ten times the official number of 150 dead. "Add a zero to anything he says about casualties," a cynical young Saudi professor advises as we watch the prince in charge of Jeddah promising yet again on the evening news to aid victims, punish the guilty, and fix the problem. Unhappy Saudis these days routinely e-mail each other photos of flood damage, destitute children, dilapidated school buildings, and displays of lavish living by princes.

The regime is not blind to these cracks in its walls of control. Historically, when the Al Saud rulers are anxious, they slather on a new layer of religious restriction to hold Saudis inert in the labyrinth. When the regime is more confident, it chips off a small piece of this religious rigidity here and there to give citizens a sense of relative freedom. So, as noted earlier, when the Grand Mosque in Mecca was overrun in 1979 by homegrown jihadists seeking to remove the Al Saud and restore the kingdom to Islamic purity, the royal family tried to appease religious fanatics by forcing an already restrictive religious society to conform to an even more puritanical way of life.

After the shocking terrorist attack on New York's Twin Towers on September 11, 2001, carried out mostly by Saudi-bred terrorists, the royal family began belatedly to discern that it had made a pact with the devil. Just how deadly a pact was brought home two years later, when extremists started attacking Saudi targets, not merely foreign infidels. So once again the regime swung into action to combat extremism. With one hand, it got tough on homegrown terrorists, arresting jihadists and trying to root radical imams from the kingdom's seventy thousand mosques.

With the other hand, the regime relaxed some of the oppressive social restrictions it had imposed two decades earlier. Press controls were partially eased so that newspapers could criticize extremists, suddenly a popular whipping boy of the regime, and even once again publish photos of women. The regime convened national dialogues and, more important, curbed some of the worst excesses of the religious police—at least temporarily. Previously, any fanatic could proclaim himself a *mutawa*, or religious policeman, and bully his fellow citizens in the name of religious purity. Now the would-be bullies had to be appointed and trained by higher authorities. But as soon as uprisings began sweeping the Middle East, the nervous Al Saud once again began to cement the small nicks in the walls of Saudi society that the king had created less than a decade earlier. The religious establishment was given new money and new authority to expand its reach deeper into the kingdom by establishing fatwa offices in every province. More ominously, King Abdullah issued a royal decree making it a crime for print or online media to publish any material that harms "the good reputation and honor" of the kingdom's grand mufti, members of the Council of Senior Ulama, or government officials. So much for reform.

Beyond religious rules, tradition also binds Saudis within their walls. Most remain deeply averse to conduct that might be seen to violate social norms and invite shame upon themselves and their families. So myriad unspoken rules bind most Saudis in place as tightly as Lilliputians tied down Gulliver.

The tight-knit tribal unit tracing its lineage to a single ancestor is the key social grouping in Saudi Arabia and remains a powerful force for conformity. Over millennia, to survive the challenges of the desert and of competing tribes, these groups developed a set of core values such as generosity, hospitality, courage, and honor that bound the entire group and preserved its unity. These values, writes David Pryce-Jones in *The Closed Circle: An Interpretation of the Arabs,* can be summed up as self-respect, but not in the Western sense of conscience or relationship with God. For Arabs, a man's self-respect is determined by how others see him. So appearance is everything.

Honor, for Arabs who seek leadership in any sphere, is akin to favorable public opinion polls in a democracy. Loss of respect equates to loss of honor. "Honor is what makes life worthwhile: shame is a living death, not to be endured, requiring that it be avenged," Pryce-Jones writes. A man who kills his wife or daughter for unfaithfulness simply is preserving the honor of his family and his tribe. "Between the poles of honor and shame stretches an uncharted field where everyone walks perilously all the time, trying as best he can to interpret the actions and words of others, on the watch for any incipient power-challenging response that might throw up winners and losers, honor and shame." The determination of all Saudis to retain honor and avoid shame cannot be overstated. Understanding this begins to help Westerners like me, accustomed to spontaneity, grasp why Saudis are so passive and conformist.

Something as simple as a wife accompanying her husband on a brief trip abroad is laden with rules and norms that trap her into largely self-induced inaction. A young Saudi mother, the very picture of Western fashion in tight jeans and a Ralph Lauren polo shirt, describes with dismay how tradition prevented her mother from accompanying her father on a short trip to neighboring Dubai. If a Saudi woman is traveling, Rana explains, she is expected to visit senior relatives and even close neighbors to bid them good-bye. Upon her return, she is obliged to make another round of visits to the same individuals to pay her respects and dispense small gifts. To simply pack her bag and fly off for a few days with her husband would break society's conventions and thus disrupt social harmony, exposing her to negative gossip and bringing shame upon her family. So confronted with that heavy load of tradition, the wife simply stayed home. This little convention, multiplied and magnified throughout the Saudi maze, is what consumes so much of the time and saps so much of the initiative of Saudi citizens, confines them to their walled compounds, and restricts them largely to contact among family members.

Rana, the mother of two young boys, insists she is not bound by such cultural conventions: "I advised my mother to just go. But she worries that other people will judge her. I don't care what people think." As evidence of her independence, she recounts flying to neighboring Dubai with her two children for a four-day holiday after "only" two weeks of planning with her extended family. "It was as satisfying as if I had gone to the moon, to travel with so little planning," she says, explaining that normally Saudis require four to six months to check their plans with extended family before finalizing them. Imagine a mother in Paris or New York needing two weeks to clear plans for a long weekend with her children in London or Miami, trips on a par with Riyadh to Dubai! Rana's "rebellion" clearly indicates that change in Saudi Arabia still consists of very small steps.

For most Saudis, appearances remain far more important than actual behavior, a curious contradiction since Islam teaches that it is precisely individual behavior that Allah will reward or punish on the Day of Judgment. With urbanization, Saudis know little about the true piety of those they encounter in daily life, so appearances have become even more important. To be accepted as pious, a man simply has to sport a beard and short *thobe*. Covering herself completely in public similarly conveys a woman's devotion to Allah. This is precisely why many educated Saudi women say they veil: not to do so risks conveying antisocial behavior and being ostracized as liberal.

That this preoccupation with appearance of the flesh, not purity of the heart, can be misleading is illustrated by a little incident that occurred during Ramadan, a month when Muslims fast between sunrise and sunset to draw closer to Allah. Abdullah, a devout Muslim, driving to a predawn breakfast, recounts how his car was struck at an intersection by an SUV, whose driver sped away. Abdullah gave chase while calling the police. Nearly half an hour later, the offending driver finally stopped as he approached his own neighborhood. "Please don't confront me in front of my neighbors," the culprit begged. A disgusted Abdullah recalls, "He was only concerned about being humiliated in front of men, not that Allah had already seen his bad behavior—and in Ramadan, when we are supposed to be focused especially on Allah." As always, appearance is all important.

All this focus on appearances leads to timidity among Saudis. A reform-minded government official who spent decades working for a powerful prince with whom he remains friends is willing to confide to me his scathing criticism of the royal regime and his deep pessimism about the future of Saudi society, a view he didn't express a quarter-century ago, when I first met him. What, I ask, does his princely friend think of his analysis? Nothing. The official never dared mention his critique to the prince, and it clearly has never dawned on him that he might do so. Whatever truths are told furtively in the private sitting rooms of Saudi society, they rarely are told to power. And this clearly leaves a gaping hole in the rulers' knowledge of their people's genuine points of view.

Why, we might ask, are most Saudis so docile? After all, this is a culture that prides itself on the courage of ancestral tribal warriors raiding visiting caravans to ancient Arabia—and battling each other. Why are modern-day descendants of this fierce culture so willing to play the role of powerless pawns, resigned to the frustration of their everyday lives and to the uncertain future of a society over which they have so little influence? After all, they are increasingly well educated and well informed. Why don't they simply take more initiative, more freedom of action, for themselves?

The answer is that both tradition and religion have made most Saudis accustomed to dependence, to being reactive, not proactive; to accepting, not questioning; to being obedient, not challenging; to being provided for rather than being responsible for their own futures. During the centuries when Arabia was dominated by warring tribes, the tribal head was responsible for the needs of his tribe and expected to receive loyalty and obedience from others if he met those needs.

In more recent times, when the late King Abdul Aziz conquered Arabia and declared the modern Kingdom of Saudi Arabia, he sought to establish a stable state with himself in charge. To do so, he needed to remove the tribal leaders' freedom to switch loyalties—and warriors—to whoever promised the most booty. The king pledged that if the tribes fought only when he ordered and against whomever he ordered, he would provide for all their needs. To ultimately render tribes incapable of marauding, he persuaded them to settle down to raise crops rather than to pursue the dangerous and often desperately poor life of raiding. Most important, his regime took possession of traditional tribal lands and territory, making them state property, which then was redistributed, often to the very same tribal chiefs. But the state retained the right to repossess the land if a tribe didn't obey. Thus, tribal raiding was no longer a livelihood but a crime. The king and his family had become the arbiters of power and prosperity.

To this day, the pull of tribe and tradition can lock even the most educated and seemingly sophisticated Saudis in corners of the labyrinth. Such is the case with Abdul Rahman bin Humaid, who graduated from Harvard in the spring of 2003 and went on to earn a Ph.D. in international legal studies from American University. His goal was to serve Saudi Arabia as a diplomat wherever in the world he was needed. Instead, the spring of 2010 found a still youthful Abdul Rahman working in a dusty Saudi National Guard outpost in his birthplace, the small industrial city of Yanbu. There he heads the same tribal National Guard unit that once was commanded by his father and, before that, his grandfather.

What happened? With his Harvard degree and Ph.D. in hand, he had launched his diplomatic career in 2004 handling congressional affairs for the Saudi embassy in Washington, D.C. He and his young wife were enjoying walks along the Potomac and movies and dinners out with friends. Suddenly in 2007, his father was killed in a car accident. The young diplomat went home for the funeral. As tradition requires, he paid his respects to King Abdullah, then supreme commander of the National Guard, who had sent his condolences to the family. At their meeting, King Abdullah summarily appointed Abdul Rahman commander of his tribal *fouj*, or group of warriors on government retainer. It was not an offer—it was a royal request that tradition required him to accept. In that instant, Abdul Rahman's career in international diplomacy was replaced by one of adjudicating internal tribal disputes. His tribe, the Utaiba, is the kingdom's largest, with 3 million members; as one of Arabia's so-called *asil,* or noble tribes, it can trace its origins back to one of the original tribes of Arabia.

"Be patient," Abdul Rahman recalls King Abdullah telling him. "You will face a lot of problems."

Asked what kind of problems he has faced, Abdul Rahman says they range from internal tribal disputes to more mundane requests. "Sometimes someone wants me to translate a letter from American Express," he says. "Whatever it is, I try to help."

Abdul Rahman is sitting in the air-conditioned meeting room where he receives guests and tribal supplicants. A handsome man who resembles a young Omar Sharif, he is surrounded by photos of his father and grandfather and supported by a gaggle of uncles and sons. As *fouj* commander, he is, of course, wearing the traditional red-and-white scarf and white *thobe,* not the Western suits he donned in Washington. "I enjoyed going to Congress," he says, "but duty calls. My grandfather did this job. My father did too. So why not me?"

Later, over coffee with his wife, mother, and eight sisters, I ask him if his role as commander is for life. He says, "Who knows?" But here is a clue that the idea of being a diplomat hasn't yet died. In a country where most men wander to work late and spend most nights chatting with male friends, Abdul Rahman is an exception. "I try to keep everything like in America," he says. "I rise early and get to the office by eight and come home for lunch at twelve thirty or eat with my men; then home to visit my wife and children by three so I can have dinner at seven thirty and be in bed by nine thirty." It is a Potomac River schedule on the shores of the Red Sea. Yet Abdul Rahman is in Yanbu, not Washington; duty has prevailed over dreams; he has been relegated to a comfortable corner of the Saudi labyrinth.

Saudis, from poor supplicants at royal offices to impressive servants of the regime like Abdul Rahman, are accustomed to receiving their livelihood from the ruler. The unspoken but implicit social contract still is that rulers provide stability and prosperity, and the ruled obey. So far prosperity has been sufficient to secure most people's acquiescence, even as many grumble these days about too much religion, too much dependence on the United States, too much corruption among the princes, too great a gap between rich and poor, too much unemployment among the young. Perceptive Saudis also mutter about the reemergence of tribal loyalties because the regime, rather than create a spirit of nationalism, has sought to ensure control by keeping citizens divided and distrustful of one another, and by encouraging tribal leaders who still meet weekly with senior princes to compete for Al Saud loyalty and largesse.

Today's Saudi Arabia thus is less a unified nation-state than a collection of tribes, regions, and Islamic factions that coexist in mutual suspicion and fear. A resident of the Hejaz, the relatively cosmopolitan region encompassing the port of Jeddah and the holy city of Mecca, the kingdom's two international melting pots, resents the fact that men from the Nejd in central Arabia, and the original home of the Al Saud, occupy all key judicial and financial jobs in the kingdom and are allowed to force their conservative customs and religious views on all Saudis. Shia Muslims from the oil-rich Eastern Province, even more than the Sufi Muslims from Jeddah or the Ismaili Muslims from the impoverished south of Saudi Arabia, resent the total domination of the Wahhabi philosophy over every aspect of life and the pervasive discrimination against them. Tribal loyalties also divide the population, as few individuals ever marry outside their tribe. The preferred marriage partner is one's first cousin. A Saudi instantly can tell, from an individual's accent and name, the tribal origins of another Saudi. Social life consists almost entirely of family, and family connections are almost always within one tribe. Thus even the most modern and relatively liberal of Saudis who may mix at work with coworkers of various tribal backgrounds most likely is married to a cousin and socializes almost exclusively with other relatives.

In sum, division is a daily feature of Saudi life. While the cosmopolitan people of Hejaz resent those of Nejd for their power and provincialism, Nejdis see people of the Hejaz as a

polyglot people lacking pure lineage. Similarly, the people of
northern Arabia, comprising tribes that traditionally looked
toward Syria and Iraq, are seen as inferior, as are those of
southern Arabia, with its historic ties to the tribes of Yemen.
The people of these four regions remain distinct and divided
to this day. Even when people move to major Saudi cities,
many tend to seek out their own regional and tribal kin as
neighbors. Regional racism is a daily fact of Saudi life.

Overlaid on these traditional divisions of Saudi society
are more contemporary ones that result from the kingdom's
haphazard development and faltering modernization since
the advent of spectacular oil wealth in the 1970s. Most Saudis only two generations ago eked out a subsistence living in
rural provinces, but Saudi society has undergone a pell-mell
urbanization over the past forty years with the result that
fully 80 percent of Saudis now live in one of the country's
three major urban centers—Riyadh, Jeddah, and Dammam.
In Riyadh, the kingdom's capital and largest city, there are
first-world shopping malls and third-world slums. Some
royal palaces stretch literally for blocks behind their high
walls that block out the less fortunate parts of Saudi society.
In poorer neighborhoods, some Saudis live in tents beside
barren patches of dirt, where filthy, barefoot boys play soccer on fields demarcated only by piles of garbage or live in
ramshackle tenements often with little furniture and limited
electricity.

Trapped between the wealthy and the poor is an increasingly fearful and resentful Saudi middle class, whose standard
of living has slipped dramatically over the past half-dozen
years. A 2006 Saudi stock market crash, coupled with rising
inflation, has left them treading water and slowly sinking as
they borrow money to try to maintain a lifestyle they cannot
afford. Consider a Saudi schoolteacher who can no longer
afford to buy a car, whose son cannot find a job and who
spends too many hours a week lining up at dysfunctional
government offices supplicating for services that all too often
can be secured only with the signature of a prince or a bribe to
a corrupt bureaucrat. A teacher who wants to be reassigned to

The growing gap between wealth and poverty rankles many Saudis. *Above,* one of the hundreds of Al Saud walled palaces in Riyadh and throughout the country. (KAREN HOUSE) *Below,* Saudi tenements in Jeddah are all too typical. (ROGER HARRISON)

work in a different school district can register with the Ministry of Education and wait three or four years for approval or, as one teacher describes, pay 5,000 Saudi riyals ($1,350) to one of the ubiquitous middlemen who make a living buying and selling approvals that ought to be routinely granted by a functioning government. This teacher in the Eastern Province is typical of an increasingly embittered middle class that no longer sees a path to upward mobility in Saudi society and is bitter at the daily indignities necessary to survive.

Other societies, too, have disparities between rich and poor, between old and new, between liberal and conservative, but in few if any societies are they so pronounced as in Saudi Arabia. These disparities are all the more glaring because Islam preaches equality of all believers. Other societies have social and political systems that at least offer mechanisms to bridge divides. Not so in Saudi Arabia, where there is only one law—Islam—and only one final arbiter of that law—the Al Saud king. Islam itself has become a major source of division as religious leaders offer widely divergent interpretations of Koranic scripture and thus of Allah's will. Meanwhile, the Al Saud, whose legitimacy is rooted in their role as guardians of Islam, far from seeking to diminish divisions in society, continue to exploit them in order to protect and perpetuate their rule. And, like everything else in Saudi Arabia, the royal family itself, as we shall see, is increasingly divided.

So modern Saudis—divided and distrustful and increasingly frustrated over a social contract with the Al Saud that no longer serves them well—maneuver within their maze, most of them neither knowing how to escape from it nor actively seeking to do so while sullenly resenting the ways in which they are trapped.

CHAPTER 5

Females and Fault Lines

I suffer not the good deeds of any to go to waste be he man
or woman: the one of you is of the other.

—KORAN 3:195

Of all the divisions in Saudi society, in none are the battle
lines more sharply drawn than on the matter of the status, role and future of women. The Prophet's first wife was
a successful businesswoman, and his favorite wife led troops
in battle, but today women themselves are the battleground.
The intensifying clash over the role of women in Saudi society is about far more than whether women should be allowed
to drive or, however well shrouded, mix with men in public
places. It is not a war between the sexes, but rather a proxy
war between modernizers and conservatives over what sort
of Saudi Arabia both sexes will inhabit and over the role and
relevance of the omnipresent religious establishment in Saudi
society.

As Arab youths challenged authoritarian regimes across
the Middle East in the Arab Spring of 2011, in Saudi Arabia,
ironically, it was the women, not youth, who had the temerity to confront authority. This challenge amounted to some
dozens of women repeatedly gathering outside the Interior
Ministry demanding the release of their husbands, brothers,
and sons imprisoned for political reasons. Some dozens of
other women staged a succession of "drive-ins" to protest the
continued ban on women driving. Some were arrested; others were ignored. Still, courageous individual women across

the kingdom have continued unannounced to test authority by getting behind the wheel of a car and posting videos of their defiance on YouTube.

It is easy to exaggerate the significance of these small public protests. That said, however, even small acts of public defiance are a remarkable sign of change in a society where all public demonstrations are banned and in which the overwhelming majority of women are totally subjugated by religion, tradition, and family. Driving isn't the most critical issue confronting women. Wasting their talents, which could be used to develop society, frustrates most women far more than not being allowed to drive. Still, it is impossible to overstate the symbolic importance in Saudi society of women driving. If a woman could exercise the freedom to drive, a tether of male control would be severed. Indeed, the whole core premise of Wahhabi Islam—that men obey Allah and women obey men—would be challenged. Fortunately for men, Allah is distant, but unfortunately for women, men are omnipresent. In Saudi Arabia women are the thin wedge of change. The sharp edge of that wedge is the tiny number of women willing to confront authority openly, but behind them is the far larger number of younger women who are deeply albeit mostly quietly dissatisfied with their subordinated status and are taking steps to push social strictures where possible.

In today's Saudi Arabia, the struggle over the role of women is visibly intensifying. Younger women have greater expectations for individual fulfillment than did their mothers, the result of better education and especially of external influences like travel and the Internet. At the same time, King Abdullah, a traditionalist in many respects, has emerged as a relative champion of expanding the role of women, thus encouraging them to press for more freedom. In 2011, he announced that women would be allowed to vote in the kingdom's largely meaningless municipal elections in 2015 and to be appointed to its Potemkin parliament, the Majlis Ash Shura, or Consultative Council in 2013. Many Saudis saw these moves as cynically intended to impress the West while at home providing a new pretext to stall growing demands for election of

Saudi females lead diverse lives. Most remain fully
shrouded in black; a growing number, like these students
at Dar al Hekma College for Women in Jeddah, are
challenging dress and other conventions. (GETTY IMAGES)

members to the Consultative Council. All 150 members now
are appointed by the king, and in January 2013, he appointed
thirty women, or twenty percent of the membership. To be
sure, the king definitely is not issuing proclamations for full
equality of women, but even the modest steps he has taken
on their behalf are dramatic in the context of a society in
which women traditionally have been subservient—and in
the past generation, totally subjugated. Even today, religious
scholars issue fatwas attempting to govern women's menstru-
ation, makeup, and even the length of their nails.

In that environment, the king's call to allow women to
help develop society has made the elderly monarch a hero for
many modern Saudi women—and something of an apostate
to conservative men and women. Here again it remains to be
seen whether the historic Al Saud skill at balancing contending forces will meet the challenge of this controversial issue,

on which both modernizers and traditionalists are marshaling scripture from the Koran to support their deeply divergent positions. "The resistance to change is getting greater, because the change is getting greater," says Madawi al Hassoun, a thoroughly modern woman who sits on a Jeddah business development board and admiringly sports a lapel pin bearing a likeness of King Abdullah. "We pray for his long life," she says. Nashwa Taher, another Jeddah activist and successful businesswoman, says, "We don't want to be equal with men. God created us differently. What we want is an equal right to live our lives, to have a voice, to have a choice." Even these modern Saudi women wear *abayas,* cover their hair with a scarf, and excuse themselves in the middle of meetings to comply with the call to prayer. They are far from bra-burning Western feminists, though sometimes their conservative female opponents portray them that way.

"We feel sorry for the modernizers who have strayed," says Amal Suliman, a *daiyah,* or female religious teacher, who instructs women on the requirements of Islam. "I dream of females leading society, not with their minds but with their behavior." That behavior, she says, requires a woman to pray five times a day, fast once a year, remain unseen always, and obey her husband in all things. "If she does these things, the Prophet Muhammad says she can enter paradise through any gate she wants," says Suliman. Because we are meeting in a public coffee shop with male waiters, Suliman's head and face are completely obscured in black. Only when the waiters retreat does she even slightly lift the bottom of her veil to insert a straw up to her lips to sip orange juice. Even after several hours of conversation, it remains disconcerting to converse with a disembodied voice, and I find myself straining to make eye contact through her black veil but to no avail.

Not only are women divided against each other, they also are divided from the rest of society by the religious establishment that enforces separation of the sexes. To be born a woman in Saudi Arabia is at best to endure a lifelong sentence of surveillance by a male relative and to take no action outside the household without male approval and, most often, male accompaniment. A father controls every aspect of a Saudi girl's life until she is passed to a new dominant male—her husband. At worst, a woman's life is one of not just subjugation but virtual slavery, in which wives and daughters can be physically, psychologically, and sexually abused at the whim of male family members, who are protected by an all-male criminal system and judiciary in those rare cases when a woman dares go to authorities. So it's not surprising to learn that the supplication to Allah that a groom offers on his wedding night is the same he is instructed to offer when buying a maidservant—or a camel: "Oh Allah, I ask you for the goodness that you have made her inclined toward and I take refuge with You from the evil within her and the evil that you have made her inclined toward." Imagine on your wedding day in any other society being equated by your husband to a servant or a beast of burden.

As small children, Saudi girls look like those in the West. In airports and shopping malls, little girls in frilly short dresses or knit tights and T-shirts joyfully jump about their black-draped mothers like little bees circling a hive. But very quickly this vivaciousness is snuffed out, as the cell door swings shut. After age six, a Saudi girl no longer goes to school with boys. By twelve, she can't join her dad at a soccer match, the kingdom's major sporting event, or for that matter any other male gathering. And by the age of puberty, she is expected to swaddle her body in an *abaya,* plus veil her face if she wants to appear a truly devout Muslim. In sum, the religious ideal in the kingdom is that the two sexes never meet outside the home after kindergarten.

A woman is not allowed to drive a car, not because Islam forbids something that didn't exist in the Prophet's day, but ironically because authorities say she might be prey to misbehavior by Saudi men. Nor can she be alone with a man who isn't a close relative, even in a public place—indeed, *especially* in a public place, as this flouts religious tradition against gender mixing. When she shops, she cannot try on clothes in the store, because sales attendants are men. She must first buy the garment and then take it home or to a female-supervised restroom for a fitting. In some conservative homes, she doesn't even eat with her husband but dines only after his meal is finished.

Because most ministries and places of business are staffed only by men, if she wants to apply for a job, pay a telephone bill, or secure a visa to import a maid for her home, she needs a male relative to accompany her. If the men in her life are not enforcing these strictures, self-appointed members of the Committee for the Promotion of Virtue and the Prevention of Vice, the *mutawa'a,* or so-called religious police, will always do so. These men are recognizable by their trademarks of public piety— long beards, shorter than average *thobes* hitting above the ankle, and head scarves devoid of the black *agal,* or double circle of twisted yarn that most men wear to anchor their *shemagh* or head scarf. Such decoration is a sign of vanity and extravagance. The *mutawa'a* patrol shops and streets, on foot and in cars, to enforce their stern standard of proper Islamic behavior.

"A woman is made to feel she cannot survive without a man," explains Salwa Abdel Hameed al Khateeb, an anthropologist and associate professor at King Saud University in Riyadh. As an anthropologist, she has written articles on marriage and family in Saudi Arabia. "My mother told me to respect a man: If your husband says milk is black, you must agree."

To any Westerner, the traditional role of Saudi women remains an enduring paradox. Here is a society in which even according to the words of the Prophet, a mother is the most respected person in a man's life. It is mothers rather than fathers who rear sons in their formative years. In this sense, Saudi Arabia is a more maternal society than most. How is it, then, that these same dutiful sons wind up subjugating their wives to a degree unprecedented in any other society? The answer, of course, is tradition. Traditionally, it is the responsibility of men to safeguard their families from the shame that could result from almost any independent action by a female family member. Therefore the surest way to protect the family reputation is to cloister the family's females. Nevertheless, to any outsider, Saudi women acquiescing in their own imprisonment seems a form of Stockholm syndrome, in which prisoners sympathize with their captors.

Foreign women, too, are expected to adhere to these societal restrictions and are not exempt from harassment by the religious police. Sitting with a Saudi man in the family section of the food court in one of Riyadh's exclusive shopping malls, I was startled by two young religious police who demanded in perfect English, "Cover your head. You are in Saudi Arabia." They demanded my passport—and the identity card of my companion, a government official. The fact that his ministry had assigned him to escort me on this particular day made no difference to the religious police, who were enforcing their edict against mixing of unrelated men and women. I was ordered to my hotel, and my companion was taken to the headquarters of the Committee for the Promotion of Virtue and the Prevention of Vice, who questioned him for nearly an hour before releasing him. (This is just one of the many examples of legal contradictions in the society: a government employee following the instructions of his ministry runs afoul of that same government's religious police.)

If there are limits on a woman's freedom, a foreign female in Saudi also has definite advantages. Only a woman can explore all aspects of the intensifying battle over women's status, including, most important, the views of women. Conservative Saudi women would never talk with an unfamiliar man, but they are happy to speak to another woman. Because foreign professional women in Saudi Arabia are treated as honorary men (by all but the religious police), they have access to both males and females. Indeed, men often take me to meet the women of their household and then, seemingly oblivious to the irony of their behavior, usher me to join a group of men for dinner, leaving their own women isolated behind walls. It is hard not to feel a twinge of guilt when a Saudi wife prepares dinner for her husband, a male guest, and me but cannot enjoy the meal with us. When the food is ready, she knocks quickly on the closed sitting room door but is nowhere to be seen as we emerge to enjoy the food.

Slowly—very slowly—the role of women is changing, primarily due to education. Since the 1970s, women have had access to both secondary and higher education, albeit in gender-segregated classrooms. As women become more educated (60 percent of university graduates now are women), they are pressing for more partnership in marriages and in life. Some even want jobs. They want more opportunities for their children and are prepared to work to help provide them. They want divorces from men who abuse them: one in three marriages now ends in divorce. Since King Abdullah came to power in 2005, he has supported more freedom for women through a range of government declarations.

For the first time, women can obtain a photo identification card, giving them an identity independent from their male guardian, on whose card they previously had been listed. For the first time, they can check into a hotel or rent an apartment without a male guardian alongside them. They can register their own business and even receive a government scholarship to study abroad—so long as they are accompanied by a male relative. To help them secure government services, the king has required all ministries to open sections for women, though some continue to ignore him—yet another example of the petty lawlessness rampant in the kingdom.

More visibly, the king has once again, for the first time since the 1980s, permitted female television anchors who, on camera for all Saudis to see, wear head scarves but neither veils nor *abayas*. And he has named the first woman deputy minister of education, the most senior role ever held by a female in the kingdom.

While none of this may sound revolutionary—or even ambitious—to American women, whose fight to gain equal opportunity in education and the workplace began in earnest at least fifty years ago, it definitely is daring in Saudi society. There is no reliable polling on this issue, but one Saudi business owner offers a microcosmic glimpse of female conservatism. At her company, female job applicants are asked a gating question: Are you willing to work in a gender-mixed environment with your face uncovered? Fewer than 10 percent answer yes.

Most Saudi women, of course, can't work—or they refuse

to work in a mixed environment. Women make up less than 12 percent of the total labor force, the lowest percentage in the Middle East, and an enormous waste of productive talent for the Saudi economy. Most who are working are employed as teachers of other females. While many more women want and need jobs these days, the religious pressure against working in gender-mixed environments means few jobs are available to them. As a result, more Saudi women are starting their own businesses, though the number of female-owned businesses still is less than 5 percent. Despite efforts by King Abdullah, women continue to confront endless obstacles, including limits on their ability to travel, long delays in securing required registrations from often obstinate bureaucrats at the "female sections" of government ministries, and lack of enforcement of the modest new rules and regulations that are intended to help women.

A new survey of Saudi businesswomen recommends above all else the creation of a Ministry of Women's Affairs to monitor enforcement of royal decrees regarding women and to devise a national strategy for their transition into the Saudi economy. Lack of enforcement of royal decrees, of rules and regulations, and even of court judgments is a major problem for all Saudis but especially for women. Given the many religious and regulatory hurdles women face, it is understandable that the majority simply stay home.

One evening at two different social gatherings illustrates how diverse and divided are Saudi women beneath their public uniform of black, which makes all of them, regardless of age or physique, resemble flying crows.

In a wealthy neighborhood of North Riyadh lives the large family of an imam, or religious leader. Approaching the door of the imam's home requires covering oneself in an *abaya* and ensuring that every hair is hidden beneath a black scarf. Anything less would be tantamount to allowing the neighbors to see a loose woman entering the home of a religious leader.

Inside, the women have gathered in a sitting room furnished with heavy burgundy couches and chairs. Pots of coffee and tea rest on a table in the center, along with bowls of dates and trays of chocolates and the ubiquitous box of Kleenex for wiping fingers soiled by sticky dates. The imam's mother, a small woman sixty years of age, presides. She is dressed in a plain floor-length cotton dress with long sleeves and a scarf tightly binding her hair and neck. The younger women, all bareheaded since no men are present, are wearing long skirts but not the high-necked dress of the matronly hostess, indicating that even in a conservative religious family, the young are edging away from tradition—if only in dress. The conversation rapidly turns to family.

"Sometimes people say don't have children as they are expensive," says the imam's mother. "But the more children I had, the more God provided." She has six boys and six girls and twenty-two grandchildren. Most of her daughters have one or more young children on their laps or leaning against their chairs. Still, she teases them and urges, "Why not more children? Get busy." Even in this conservative home, her daughters are university graduates, but they, like their mother, stay home with their children. The grown daughters take turns pouring tea while their young daughters perpetually press trays of sweets on all the women. (In Saudi, sweets precede dinner.)

Over dinner, served in traditional Saudi style on a plastic sheet spread on the floor, the hostess squats on her knees and eats with her right hand, rolling the rice and vegetables into a ball and scooping them into her mouth. Her more modern daughters use forks and spoons. Throughout the meal, the mother dispenses advice on proper Islamic living. "Women shouldn't have two maids," she says. "It is all right to have someone to help with the cleaning, but if you have someone to look after your children, what do you do? You go out. This is wrong. You should focus on your children." These daughters don't smile or snicker to one another as Western daughters well might upon receiving such motherly advice. They listen respectfully and nod obediently.

In this home, religion, not work, is topic number one. The hostess asks God that one day all assembled here will be together with him in paradise. She and her daughters deplore the impact of modernity on the lives of Saudi women. "The prophet tells us not to do what others are doing. If they are going this way, we should go that way," says one of the women, using her cell phone to draw a sharp turn on the floor. "But young Saudi girls watch television, and instead of being proudly different, they do what others are doing, and this is a shame. They cut their hair. They don't wear the *hijab* [scarf] and *niqab* [full-face veil]."

The imam's mother, like many traditional Saudi women, is one of several wives of her husband. His two other wives, she explains, live nearby so he can easily move from home to home. The wives do not mix, but their children do. One of the other guests acknowledges that she too is the second wife of her husband of two decades. "I knew he had another wife," she says, "but what is important is only whether or not he is a good man. Will he treat us equally?" These two wives do not see each other now, though in earlier years their husband used to drop his new wife's baby with the first wife so that the younger second wife could attend university—hardly likely to endear the two women to each other. I ask if any of the younger females shares her husband with another wife, and each emphatically shakes her head no. "But it is not my choice," adds one. "If Allah wills, I accept."

While there clearly are some generational differences in outlook within this family, all the women, young and old, adhere to a way of life that acknowledges the primacy of men and the centrality of Islam. While the younger women are adapting to some changes in society, none seeks to change society.

On the same evening, in a large walled home not far away, another group of women are gathered in a different setting pursuing a very different conversation. These women, while far from revolutionaries, are pushing gently against the traditional strictures of Saudi life and seizing whatever new space society allows women. The hostess, a slim thirtyish woman in white pants and blouse with long stylish dark hair and expensive jewelry, is entertaining a half-dozen friends. There are no clinging children to wrinkle the expensive Western outfits of these women. Nor do any of them share their husband with another wife. Alone among the group, the hostess isn't employed outside the home, as she has four children, including a new baby. The other women include an event planner, an elementary school principal, the owner of a small business, and a trainer in cosmetology. All the women speak excellent English. All graduated from King Saud University in Riyadh, and all have educated mothers who encourage them to work. All have traveled to Europe, and they greet each other with several touches of the cheek before sinking comfortably into plush chairs and couches in this modern Western-style living room. Two Filipino maids circulate silently serving tall fruit drinks, then Arabic coffee, then tea, and finally trays of expensive little sweets.

This scene and these ladies could be anywhere—Paris, London, New York—but for the content of the conversation. In no Western gathering of women discussing social mores would one hear talk of whether and how to shake hands with men. "In a professional situation it is up to the lady whether or not to offer her hand," says Sadeem. "If a woman sticks out her hand with a stiff arm that means shake hands only; if the arm is slightly bent that means one is willing to touch cheeks." It is a largely hypothetical conversation. Most traditional Saudi men, of course, would refuse to shake hands with a woman and would be horrified at touching cheeks, because strict religious believers see touching an unrelated woman as forbidden by Islam.

These working Westernized women who can afford drivers, nannies, and maids insist they like the special, protected role of women in Islam. "Men are supposed to take care of us even if we work," says Hala. "We like our life and our religion." But they also say they want the opportunity to choose their lifestyle. "We want a choice," says the cosmetology trainer. "We want to work or not, drive or not, shake hands or not." In their childhood, before the migration of nearly 80 percent of all Saudis from rural villages into one of three urban centers—Riyadh, Jeddah, and Dammam—people were much freer, they say. A woman's *abaya* was simply a short shawl around the shoulders. Couples mixed over dinners in their homes. Children played all across their neighborhoods and spent the night in each other's homes, something most children aren't allowed to do these days. "In the eighties the country became very conservative," says one woman. "We no longer know what is required by religion."

Certainly Saudi was much freer in the late 1970s for both Saudi and Western women. In those days, most Western women, including me, rarely wore an *abaya,* and I often was invited to mixed-gender dinners in the homes of Saudi officials. Now an *abaya* is essential to avoid unwanted attention, and Saudi women are much rarer than alcohol at dinner, even in the homes of elite businessmen and government officials.

Since Islam underpins all of Saudi society, advocates for more freedom and opportunity for women couch their arguments in the Koran. References to what is required by religion have a far wider resonance with women—and surely with men—than talk of women's rights, since anything Western is suspect as being imposed or encouraged by an alien culture for a sinister reason. So if confrontation—bra burning, marches, and demonstrations—was the predominant tactic of American women demanding equality in the second half of the twentieth century, co-option is the strategy of their Saudi sisters in the dawn of the twenty-first. A group of Saudi women tried confrontation once with very unhappy consequences.

In October 1990, articles began appearing in the heavily censored Saudi press quoting Saudi women expressing alarm that had Saddam Hussein invaded Saudi Arabia rather than Kuwait, they would not have been able to drive their children to safety as Kuwaiti women had done. A month later, forty-seven women driven by their chauffeurs gathered at a supermarket in downtown Riyadh and dismissed their drivers. About a quarter of the women—all of whom had valid international driving licenses—took the wheel, with the other women as passengers, and drove off in a caravan through Riyadh. Within blocks, the religious police stopped the cars and ordered the women out. Regular police officers arrived and took control. The police officers drove the cars with the religious police in the passenger seats and the women in the backseats to police headquarters.

Before their demonstration, the women, all from prominent Saudi families, had sent a petition to His Royal Highness Prince Salman, at that time the governor of Riyadh, begging his brother, the Saudi king, to open his heart to their "humane demand" to drive. They argued that in the Prophet's day, women rode camels, the primary means of transportation, and that "such is the greatness of the teacher of humanity and the master of men in leaving lessons that are as clear as the sunlight to dispel the darkness of ignorance." The women were detained while Prince Salman summoned religious and legal experts to discuss what to do with them. Since all the women were veiled with only their eyes showing, the religious officials found no moral issues, and because the Koran says nothing about driving, and the women had legal international licenses, the women were released. But any celebration of this small victory for women proved premature.

As word of the demonstration spread from family to family (even though it wasn't covered in the Saudi media, and the Internet did not exist), the women, many of whom taught at women's universities, found themselves denounced by messages tacked to their office doors, in sermons at mosques around the kingdom, and by leaflets in the streets entitled "Names of the Promoters of Vice and Lasciviousness." This sort of spontaneous religious backlash is what makes even the Al Saud cautious about pushing reform too fast.

Sure enough, nervous royals quickly caved. Prince Salman's finding was buried. The kingdom's grand mufti, Abdul Aziz bin Abdullah bin Baz, the blind sheikh famous for declaring some thirty years earlier that the earth was flat, issued a fatwa. "Allowing women to drive," the grand mufti declared, "contributes to the downfall of society" by encouraging mixing of the sexes and "adultery, which is the main reason for the prohibition of these practices." And there things still stand, more than two decades later, though there are recurrent rumors that the driving ban again may be reviewed and relaxed, perhaps starting with foreign females, Saudi women physicians, or women over thirty-five. Essentially a Saudi woman is seen as some kind of sexually depraved creature who, if alone in a car, would be rapidly lured into adultery. On the other hand, that same woman being chauffeured around Riyadh by a foreign male driver is considered secure, as she is under the control of a man—the driver. Moreover, that man by virtue of being foreign is seen by Saudi men as merely a sexless extension of the car with no possible appeal to the female passenger. It is just one of the myriad mystifying contradictions of Saudi society.

"The king wants to let women drive," explains one of his close royal relatives. "But he did a poll that showed 85 percent of Saudis oppose women driving. He was shocked; totally shocked. But what can he do?"

Saudi women learned from their aborted drive-in two decades ago. If the religious establishment would use the Koran as a sword against women, then women would use the holy book as their shield—and even occasionally as a sword—against religious officials. When the women of Jeddah, the kingdom's most international city, finally won agreement, a decade after the driving incident, from the all-male chamber of commerce to create a business bureau for women, they named it after the Prophet Muhammad's first wife, thus the Kadijah bint Khuwailid Businesswomen Center.

One of the ironies of strict Wahhabi Islam, which encourages Muslims to return to the original teachings and practices of the Prophet, is that the Prophet's first wife, Kadijah bint Khuwailid, was a successful businesswoman. Indeed, having lost two husbands to death in raids, she hired her distant cousin Muhammad to lead a trading caravan to Syria. She was so pleased with the profits he returned to her that *she* asked the twenty-five-year-old Muhammad to marry her. And she asked him directly to his face, not through a male relative. "Son of mine uncle," she said to Muhammad, "I love thee for thy kinship with me and for that thou art ever in the center, not being a partisan amongst the people for this or for that; and I love thee for thy trustworthiness and for the beauty of thy character and truth of thy speech." He accepted and then agreed to inform her uncle. (She is estimated by Islamic historians to have been ten to fifteen years Muhammad's senior.)

Their relationship apparently was one of great affection and respect. Some fifteen years later, when Muhammad returned home shaking and sweating from his initial encounter with the archangel Gabriel, it was a composed Kadijah who calmed and embraced him. She immediately assured him he was sane. "You are striving to restore the high moral qualities that your people have lost. You honor the guest and go to the assistance of those in distress," she told him. Kadijah became the first convert to Islam.

So long as Kadijah lived, Muhammad took no other wives, even though polygamy was common in Arabia. Once Kadijah died in A.D. 619, he married another ten women before his own death in 632. His favorite was Aisha, the prepubescent daughter of his companion, Abu Bakr, one of the men who would lead the Islamic believers after Muhammad's death. Aisha was only six when she was promised to Muhammad, nine when she moved to his home, and eighteen when he died in her arms. She never bore him a child.

One story recounts how Aisha, tired of hearing the Prophet proclaim Kadijah's virtues, said to her husband, "She was only an old woman with red eyes, and Allah has compensated you with a better and younger wife." The Prophet responded, "No. He has not compensated me with someone better than her. She believed in me when others disbelieved; she held me truthful when others called me a liar; she sheltered me when others abandoned me."

Most of Muhammad's wives were young and beautiful. All but Aisha were widows or divorcees, like the beautiful Zaynab, forty, who caused something of a scandal by divorcing Muhammad's adopted son to marry the Prophet. This marriage violated the ban on a father marrying the wife of a son, but Allah conveniently sent Muhammad a revelation that adoption did not create the same ties as blood kin. Nor did the Prophet limit himself to Muslim women—or to only four wives at a time, as later became the rule for Muslim men. At least one of his wives, Safiyyah, seventeen, was a Jewess who converted to Islam. He also had a beautiful Christian concubine, Mariyah, who bore him a son, Ibrahim, a favorite because the sons he fathered with Kadijah had died.

The Prophet made no secret of his love for women. "It hath been given me to love perfume and women," he said. But he treated his wives with kindness and enjoyed their company. He used to run races with Aisha and her young friends. He allowed all his wives to speak openly to him, including about their jealousies of one another and their wish that at least occasionally he would provide better for them when he passed out the spoils of Islam's military victories rather than keep them in penury. His companion Umar complained to Muhammad that he should demand more respect from his wives. The Prophet laughed as one of his wives promptly told the prickly Umar to mind his own business. "Yes, by God, we speak freely with him, and if he allows us to do that, that is surely his own affair." Muhammad sometimes teased his wives about their jealousy. Entering a room where his wives were gathered one day, he held out an onyx necklace and said, "I shall give this unto her whom I love best of all." The wives began to whisper that he would give it to Aisha, his well-known favorite. Instead, he beckoned to his little granddaughter, Umamah, and placed it around her neck. Clearly the Prophet did not view women as temptresses waiting to lead men astray unless closeted, as his latter-day Wahhabi followers do.

The Prophet, as we clearly see, was not averse to strong women. Women in his day attended mosque, listened to his discourses, and even participated in war. Nusaybah, a woman of Medina, joined other women in providing water to soldiers at the Battle of Uhud, and when Muhammad came under attack, she joined the fray, drawing her sword and shield to protect the Prophet, something Saudi religious clerics do not mention. Similarly, after the Prophet's death, Aisha led an army in a bloody attempt to shape the leadership succession of Islam. She took up arms against the Prophet's son-in-law, Ali, to try to deny his succession as caliph, or leader of the Islamic believers. Some ten thousand men were killed in the Battle of the Camel, so called because Aisha sat astride her camel leading her troops, until Ali's men succeeded in sneaking up behind her and cutting off the legs of her mount. Captured, she later was released to live out her life in Medina, finally dying at age seventy-four.

The independence and forthrightness of Arab women like Kadijah and Aisha were curtailed over the next centuries, as the new Islamic religion conquered most of the area from Arabia to Spain and its triumphant foot soldiers procured captured women as multiple wives and concubines. During the eighth and ninth centuries, women, now plentiful in the harems of elite men, became debased and dependent. Unfortunately for women, codification of Muslim legal thought and practice occurred during this period and achieved final formulation in the tenth century in four major schools of thought that still dominate today. These schools of thought were—and still are—deemed infallible. Thus, legal scholars to this day are obliged to follow precedent, not originate legal doctrine. As a result, women continue to be seen as sex objects whose intrigues can destroy men and disrupt society unless tightly controlled. "Establishment Islam's version of the Islamic message survived as the sole legitimate interpretation . . . because it was the interpretation of the politically dominant—those who had the power to outlaw and eradicate other readings as 'heretical.'" The same is true in Saudi today, where the Al Saud and their senior *ulama* enforce their interpretation of Islam.

As a result, neither of the prophet's strong wives is seen by Wahhabi *ulama* as evidence that women in the Prophet's day played large roles in society and thus should be allowed to do so today. But modern Saudi women cite them and point to verses in the Koran such as Sura 3:195 that indicate Islam indeed does regard women as equal before Allah. "I suffer not the good deeds of any to go to waste be he man or woman: the one of you is of the other."

Suhaila Zein Al Abdein Hammad, the female head of the

Saudi Human Rights Commission, a new organization in the kingdom, is one of the leaders of the struggle to help women gain more rights and responsibilities with the help of the Koran. "Our religious leaders say females are less intelligent than males. It isn't true," she says. "The Prophet consulted always with his wife, Kadijah. His successor named a woman, Al Shifa bint Abdullah, as in effect the first minister of municipalities. She oversaw the market in Medina." What's more, says Al Abdein, Allah himself praised the legendary Queen of Sheba. "He said her governance was good. He wouldn't have done so if he were against women leaders."

It is telling, of course, that the female leaders whom these women cite lived centuries, if not millennia, ago. Today Saudi Arabia has no women in its Majlis Ash Shura, the Consultative Council (though appointments are promised for 2015), and no female ministers. When the kingdom conducted its first experiment with elections in 2005, allowing Saudis to elect representatives to municipal government councils, women were not permitted to vote, let alone seek seats on the largely ceremonial councils. That exclusion held when the elections were repeated in September 2011, though as we have seen, the king has announced they will be allowed to participate in 2015. Only in 2009 did King Abdullah name a female as a deputy minister—and then of women's education, a field composed entirely of women.

Norah al Faiz, this deputy minister, is the daughter of a woman with a third-grade education. She has no royal connections but simply a résumé of rising from humble beginnings through hard work. The eldest of ten children, she graduated from King Saud University with a degree in sociology and in 1979 left Saudi to attend Utah State University while her husband was earning a degree in Texas. Since returning to Riyadh in 1983, she has worked full-time and reared five children. Every summer, instead of relaxing, she has taken some training course abroad to improve herself, she says. This is rare, as the majority of Saudi women still feel they can't leave the country even for educational opportunities.

"I am the first woman, and thus I have more challenges,"

she acknowledges in the privacy of her office after a few months in her new position. "If the first woman fails, it is very bad, so I am working hard to understand this new job and make the right changes." Even though she says she is accustomed to speaking to male audiences, she is treading cautiously in her new job. A sign of how slowly things change: to communicate with the new minister of education, Prince Faisal bin Abdullah, the king's son-in-law, she must sit before her office computer in the Women's Education Building—only a few miles from the minister's office—and communicate via video conference, always careful to block the camera atop her computer so the men don't see her. Yet both the deputy minister and her boss are U.S.-educated Saudis who mix easily with members of the opposite sex; that they dare not flout conservative tradition in their official capacities speaks volumes about the pervasive clout of religious extremists. Ministers who dare stretch the limits of tradition report receiving regular visits from the religious scholars who insist on strict Wahhabi interpretations of Islam.

It's not surprising that women like Al Faiz tread carefully when deciding how much to challenge tradition—and how much to remain bound by it. All over the kingdom, Saudis perform daily a sort of Japanese Kabuki theater, daring to nudge the edges of behavioral norms while trying to appear consistent with tradition.

King Abdullah has tried to stretch the rules and focus the spotlight on women achievers. In 2010 he conferred the King Abdul Aziz Medal of the First Order on a prominent Saudi female scientist, Dr. Khawla al Kuraya, director of the research center at King Fahd National Children's Cancer Center; he was also shown on television and on the front page of Saudi newspapers placing the medal around her neck and shaking her hand, an unprecedented public display of proximity to an unrelated woman. Not long afterward, he attended graduation ceremonies for female nurses, a career that Saudi women only now are tentatively entering, and shook hands with each as she received her diploma. This ceremony, too, was shown on television, including one traditional young woman who declined to shake hands with the monarch. The king responded by saying, "God bless you."

The tug-of-war over women's proper place in society goes on daily, spurred by a small but growing minority of women who actively are pushing for more independence from men and more opportunity in society. Among the most active is Princess Adelah, one of the king's daughters, who uses her prominence to champion change for all women and particularly to support abused women. A casually elegant woman in her midforties, Princess Adelah has joined with activist female physicians, eyewitnesses to the effects of abuse, to create a national program to raise awareness of domestic violence. Again, it may not sound radical, but in a country where public organizations mostly are forbidden, any such association is a sign of change. The group has obtained an order from the king requiring each Saudi city to open a home for abused women, has secured a fatwa from the grand mufti declaring domestic violence a "crime," and most important, is holding public meetings in major cities between women and authorities—police, prosecutors, and judges—responsible for protecting them from their tormentors. The need is great.

At the Jeddah center for battered women, a twenty-nine-year-old with no independent means of support and little education sits shrouded in black to tell a visitor her story, unfortunately an all too common one. A drunken husband's beatings sent her repeatedly to the hospital, until finally a doctor referred her to the shelter. Not all abused women are so fortunate. One female doctor who works with abused women angrily decries the refusal of the all-male judiciary to protect women. She cites a judge who refuses to protect a thirty-year-old whose father sexually abuses her and then, when she complains to authorities, claims his daughter is mentally ill. The woman's stepmother is ready to testify for her stepdaughter, but the judge refuses and further refuses to allow a mental evaluation of the father. Instead, he has ordered the young woman dispatched to a religious sheikh who is to read verses from the Koran over her to drive the devil out.

Persuading judges to render justice is the primary purpose

of the public sessions that Princess Adelah convenes. At one of the public sessions in Dammam, attended by some nine hundred women and sixty men from police and legal organizations, authorities outline how abused women should be treated when they go to the police or a hospital. The women then tell their own stories of how the system really works—or doesn't. There is a huge gap. Or as the princess delicately puts it, "Sometimes we find there is a deficiency in the procedures." Airing grievances clearly is progress, even if redressing them often remains elusive because cases wind up being adjudicated by men.

At another such session in Abha, one judge justified a husband's beating his wife because he agreed with the husband that the woman had spent excessively. There were murmured protests from the assembled women in attendance and more activist outrage around the country when the judge's comment was reported in the press. The judge later apologized. "If a woman can stand up to a judge in public, she can get the courage to stand up to her husband," says Dr. Maha Muneef, who heads the National Family Safety Program, working with Princess Adelah.

"We have the opportunity now to push the wheel further," Princess Adelah says. "We should make an effort to move ahead as quickly as possible. What used to take five years, we can now do in one. Society is more open. And Jeddah and Dhahran are even more open." Echoing a sentiment endorsed by her father, she says that if a woman can help develop her society, she should be encouraged to do so. "We need the help of men who believe in the ability of women. We do not want this to be women against men. It is not a woman's issue but a society issue."

She is convinced that the progress toward greater openness for women in recent years, encouraged by her father, will continue even after he is gone. She acknowledges that the freedoms of the pre-oil-boom days were lost in the 1980s but insists that won't happen again. "We didn't have the experience of fundamentalism in the 1980s, so we thought that might be an answer. But we know better now."

What accounts for her eighty-nine-year-old father's willingness to give women more freedom and opportunity? "Older people are more open-minded," she says. "People had less means to be complicated back then. Life was simple, and men and women shared the work." Ironically, it was oil wealth that made possible the sidelining of half the country's productive population. These days, as government allocation of oil wealth fails to keep up with a growing population and increased public expectations, more and more women hope to get off the sidelines and into the game.

Activist women pressing, however politely, for change can be found scattered across Saudi society, from the soccer field to the riding ring to the chamber of commerce. These women, many of them young, are pushing the parameters of what is permissible in Saudi society. A still small but growing number of young women shun veils and scarves and don jeans and sneakers under their *abayas*. They seek employment as computer programmers, interior designers, filmmakers, artists, and even engineers at Saudi ARAMCO, which has begun in recent years to award women scholarships to study engineering abroad.

Women's sports are officially banned, but young women increasingly ignore the prohibition and play hidden from public view. Here, members of a new women's cricket team are discreetly covered. (ROGER HARRISON)

Women's sports are the latest arena for female activists. Officially, sports for girls are banned. In 2009 Grand Mufti Sheikh Abdul Aziz bin Abdullah al Ashaikh told *Okaz* newspaper he had ordered a university in Riyadh to cancel a women's marathon. A year earlier the governor of the Eastern Province publicly condemned a soccer game between women, played before only female fans, after religious officials complained. A professor at Imam University wrote on an Islamic Web site that allowing physical education classes for women in public schools would be tantamount to "following in the devil's footsteps." All this helps account for why some 66 percent of Saudi women (as opposed to 52 percent of Saudi men) are reported by health officials to be overweight.

Despite this strong religious opposition, women in recent years have been forming soccer, basketball, volleyball, and cricket teams. Some are in schools. More are under the auspices of charities. And some, like Kings Court, a soccer team in Jeddah, are independent. Indeed, Kings Court has won financial and public support from Prince Al Waleed bin Talal, probably Saudi Arabia's best-known businessman and a nephew of King Abdullah.

The girls, whose team logo is a lion's face, began playing soccer simply as a group of friends to avoid the boredom of surfing the Internet or shopping. Reema, thirty-one, the coach, assembled the team after her father died. He had played soccer with her when she was a girl and pushed her to develop her talent. She is a reporter for Saudi television Channel One and coaches the team in her spare time. She organizes the practices, requires each girl who wants to play to obtain written permission from her parents, and is responsible for the young women while at practice or games. "Sometimes I feel overwhelmed with responsibility for the girls," she says.

Reema is a tiny woman with short dark hair and a frail physique. She meets her team for practice at six thirty P.M. on a soccer field surrounded by a high wall, about half an hour from downtown Jeddah. The women arrive with male drivers. Each girl pushes open the sliding steel door to the walled field and, once inside, closes it, leaving the male driver behind to await her return two hours later. Because there are only women at the practice, the girls roll their *abayas,* stuff them into gym bags, and prepare for a round of warm-up exercises in baggy shorts and T-shirts. Before practice begins, Reema dons her *abaya* and disappears into a room to pray the Maghreb, or sunset prayer. One young team member says she joined the team because she likes all sports. She plays beach volleyball in Tunisia every summer. "Even in Saudi Arabia, I lead a European life," she explains. "Not in public, of course, but with my family. I go to the beach here where girls wear bikinis and we go to restaurants with boys every weekend." (There are only a few private beach communities where strict privacy from the prying eyes of the religious police is provided and where liberal, wealthy families can allow their daughters to appear in bathing suits or even to drive a car. For 99.9 percent of Saudi families, however, these restricted areas might as well be on the moon.)

These young women dream of being allowed to play more openly and competitively. Reema is careful to say it is up to the government to decide what happens to women's soccer teams and it's not appropriate for her to express a vision for the team. "But if one day government asked us to represent Saudi Arabia, we would have no problem doing it. I would like to reach that level—a career—if not for me, then for the next generation." She notes that Iranian women wear scarves and long pants and long-sleeved shirts to play soccer. "If they can do it, surely we can do it too."

Since *Al Watan,* a reformist Saudi newspaper, first revealed the existence of the women's soccer team, they have received a lot of publicity on television and in newspapers. "We were the first to take the risk of publicity," Reema says. Indeed, the publicity has brought them denunciations. "Yes we get mail from people who oppose us, but these people represent themselves, not the people of Saudi Arabia," she says. "This is all possible because of God and King Abdullah," she adds, pounding her heart with her fist when she mentions the monarch. "We love King Abdullah. He has a white heart."

If team sports are controversial and still rare for women,

individual sports are forbidden. Alya Al Huwaiti, a Saudi woman in her late twenties, is an eight-time winner at international endurance horse racing for women, but she isn't allowed to compete inside the kingdom. At sixteen, Alya won her first endurance race in Jordan in 1997, triumphing over fifty-two men. She and her horse covered 120 kilometers in five hours and thirty minutes. Since then she has competed in Qatar, Bahrain, Egypt, and Jordan. "Horses are part of our culture," she says. "Women rode in the Prophet's day. But because we are a male-dominated society, they feel threatened by women."

Alya began riding as a young girl, strongly supported by her father and mother. But once she won the race in Jordan, she began getting hostile messages from Saudis. The religious police urged the government to confiscate her passport so she couldn't disgrace the country by riding competitively abroad, and they insisted she wasn't a Saudi. "Nobody supports me here," she says. "I am under a lot of pressure, so sometimes I get very sad, but I keep on." The key to winning an endurance race, she says, is patience. "If you push your horse too much, you hurt him and go out of the race." Her analysis of endurance racing aptly applies to women seeking opportunity in Saudi Arabia.

Paradoxically, Alya tells her story sitting alongside a ring for show horses on the private farm of Prince Khalid bin Sultan, the kingdom's deputy defense minister and son of the late Crown Prince Sultan. The prince owns a sprawling horse farm some forty-five minutes from Riyadh, where he hosts an annual event to display his prize-winning horses and those of other wealthy owners from around the world. It is a unique Saudi gathering, with men and women mixing in a large white tent across the ring from the royal pavilion, which features large gold and brown overstuffed chairs for the prince and his special guests, including Arabs, Europeans, and Americans. At one end of the royal pavilion, elite Saudi women in black *abayas,* including some with uncovered heads, watch the parade of prize stallions, mares, and geldings.

To see Saudi men, women, and children relaxing in a tent,

sipping coffee, eating sweets, and talking to each other and to foreigners is very rare. Alya is dressed in a pink blouse topped by a white sweater and tight jeans stuffed into fur boots. A shiny two-inch-long crystal fish is pinned on her left shoulder. Her long dark hair hangs below her shoulders. There is no *abaya* or even a scarf in sight. Her sister, Sara, who also rides but not competitively, is studying to be a lawyer, even though at present women are not allowed to present a case before the kingdom's male judges. "I am like my sister," she says. "I chose a very difficult career. It is in the family not to take the easy way."

For Alya, this is a bittersweet Cinderella moment. Because she is on the private property of a senior prince hosting an international event, she can sit in her native country and witness Saudi men and women relaxing together in common admiration of Arabian horses. She can dress as if she were outside Saudi Arabia. But she is denied the right to compete in the endurance race hosted by Prince Khalid. Even senior princes have their limits.

Not all women are grateful for the modest changes that undeniably are occurring in the kingdom. Alia Banaja, a businesswoman in Jeddah who heads a technology company she founded in 2002, says bluntly, "We have had some progress in the past five years, but if you compare us to the countries around us, like Qatar and Dubai, we are standing still. They are jumping to compete in the world, so the gap between me and businesswomen in the Gulf is widening."

She grows more indignant as she speaks: "The king didn't give us our rights because he believes in us. He did it because we made noise for three or four years. We should be running, but instead we are looking at the moon and debating whether it is the moon or the sun. So I can't call what has been done in recent years 'progress.'"

Banaja isn't alone in her impatience. Jeddah has a considerable number of such activist, outspoken women who have led the fight for change in their city and, by extension, across the kingdom. One is Manal Fakeeh, a slight, attractive mother of three who serves on the board of the Kadijah bint Khuwailid

Businesswomen Center at the chamber of commerce. "If you want to change society, you have to change the women," she says. The kingdom's wealth is dwindling, she argues, and the new generation must be taught to create wealth, not simply consume it, as earlier Saudi generations have done. Fakeeh clearly is not a typical Saudi mother. She relishes diversity in a society that prizes uniformity. With her Buddhist cook, her pastel-colored *abayas,* and her children in international schools, she obviously fits no norm and takes pride in that. "I'm not advertising an alternative lifestyle," she says. "I am living it."

Women's education clearly has helped create a demand among women for better lives, more independence, and more opportunities to fulfill roles in society beyond breeding children and satisfying a husband. In the 1970s, the kingdom had only a handful of prominent women, mostly doctors. In the intervening decades, more and more women have begun pursuing careers and rearing families simultaneously. The number of women achievers in Saudi Arabia these days in medicine, in academe, and in business offers us some reason to believe they will continue to press forward and in so doing pull the country with them. The sharp edge of the female wedge has been planted, but the sheer density of religion and tradition in Saudi culture means the society remains largely resistant.

Perhaps the strongest sign of things to come isn't even the activists like Fakeeh but the changing lives of young women in a remote and conservative Saudi province like Qassim, where forty years ago parents protested the introduction of girls' education. These days at least some rural parents are permitting their daughters to live without a male chaperone in apartments near Qassim University, to enable them to obtain an education. That, more than any activist sentiments expressed in a Jeddah drawing room, is a sign that times indeed are changing.

The tale of one woman from Al Jouf named Fatima Mansour encapsulates the conflicting currents of traditional female subservience, emerging women's rights, and a monarchy seeking to navigate between the two. In 2005 Fatima's half-brothers took her to court to demand she divorce her husband because he was from a lesser tribe than their family, something the brothers claimed he had hidden from their father. Even though the father had approved the marriage before his death and even though the couple had two small children, the judge annulled their marriage. Fatima, uneducated though she was, refused to comply. Unable to go home to her husband, as that would amount to adultery, she also refused to return to her family, for fear her half-brothers would kill her for what they regarded as bringing shame upon the family.

Instead, she insisted on imprisonment with her one-year-old daughter while she appealed the judge's ruling. She stayed in jail for nearly four years while her husband cared for their son. Her plight gained growing public attention and quiet support from Princess Adelah and eventually the princess's royal father. Four years into the sordid saga, the king asked the Supreme Judicial Council to review the case. Within months, the lower court's decision was overturned, and after more than four years of separation, Fatima, Mansour, and their children were reunited. Fatima's tale, however horrifying, also is uplifting since it indicates that even poor and uneducated women can refuse to accept the status quo when they reach the limits of their tolerance of tradition and of a sometimes cruel social system. It isn't any longer only modernizers who seek more dignity for women.

Over the past half-dozen years, society's attitude has shifted marginally toward greater acceptance of women pursuing higher education, jobs, and even a modicum of independence. Still, when it comes to marriage, to making the critical decision of what male will assume control of a woman's life after her father, most Saudi women continue to wait for others to seal their fate. "Girls wait to be selected like a commodity from a fruit stand," says Fawzia al Bakr, a sociologist at King Saud University and a veteran of the 1990 driving protest who is researching young Saudis' attitudes. "For a Saudi woman, there is no legal age for having no guardian. She is always dependent on some male."

Such dependence remains a fact of Saudi life, but what is new is that increasing numbers of Saudi women so clearly resent it. Saudi women may remain trapped in cocoons, but they are flexing to burst free. This process may well prove liberating for all of Saudi society.

CHAPTER 6

The Young and the Restless

F riday mornings in Saudi are as tranquil as Sunday mornings in the West. Because it is the day of rest and religious observance, shops and schools are closed, the streets are empty of cars, and most people go back to bed after dawn prayers. At midday, men stream into one of the kingdom's seventy thousand mosques to pray and hear the weekly sermon by their local imam. Muslims are required to attend this communal sermon—all except women, who are allowed but not encouraged to go to mosque. They stay home and watch the televised sermons preached in the Grand Mosque in Mecca or the Great Mosque in Medina, Islam's two holiest sites.

Strolling alone down Riyadh's main shopping street on a Friday morning reminds me, in the words of Texas folksinger Kris Kristofferson, "there's nothing short of dying, half as lonesome as the sound, of a sleepin' city sidewalk, Sunday morning coming down." The morning may belong to God, but afternoon along Tahlia Street belongs to rebellious youth. Tahlia is Riyadh's Champs-Élysées, with three lanes of traffic in each direction separating expensive shops and restaurants on both sides. The center median features a row of fake palm trees. At night, the street has a glamorous glitter from tiny lights that encircle the palms. But in the daylight of a hot March afternoon, they are all too visibly a dusty brown.

Young men lounge against souped-up cars parked along the curb as they watch other young men alternately gun their engines and hit the brakes, causing their cars to rock up and down in the bumper-to-bumper traffic of Tahlia Street. Adding to the chaos, boys on four-wheel bikes weave with suicidal abandon among the cars and then up onto the median, lifting the front wheels so high that the bikes are virtually vertical and the riders who cling behind each driver can almost drag the long hair of their uncovered heads on the pavement. Loud rap music—in English—echoes from every bike. Most of the young men are dressed in low-slung jeans or ghetto shorts and T-shirts. Riyadh police, leaning against their green-and-white-marked cars, double-parked every few hundred yards, watch the scene but do nothing to interfere with this display of youthful exuberance, so at odds with the decorous behavior demanded of the young by austere religious leaders, especially in this, the kingdom's most conservative city. The so-called religious police are nowhere to be seen, perhaps because they know this crowd is too large to be thwarted by a few bearded men in short *thobes* armed with thin sticks.

This scene of jaded youth—rebels without a cause—so reminiscent of a 1950s James Dean movie, is just another example of tensions tearing at Saudi society as tradition is challenged by modernity. The young, overwhelmingly Internet savvy, are well aware of the lifestyles of Western youth, but have almost no leisure options available in the kingdom to absorb their youthful energies. Cinemas are banned. Dating is forbidden. Shopping malls are off limits to young men unless accompanied by a female relative. (This is intended to ensure they do not prey on young women in the malls.) Public fields for soccer are few. Concerts are outlawed. Even listening to music is forbidden by conservative religious sheikhs, though this admonition is widely ignored, as the ubiquitous rap music along Tahlia Street underscores. An annual book fair sponsored by the Ministry of Information and Culture is about as close to public entertainment as the kingdom gets. Yet religious fundamentalists in 2011 crashed even that staid event, seized a microphone, and berated the presence and dress of women in attendance.

"Youth want freedom," says Saker al Mokayyad, head of the international section at Prince Nayef Arab University, which trains the oppressive internal security forces, here and

A growing number of young Saudi men defy tradition in favor of jeans and T-shirts. (GETTY IMAGES) However, most young Saudis are reared traditionally, like the robed boy, below, brushing his teeth with a *miswak,* as the Prophet Muhammad did. (TURKI AL SHAMMARI)

throughout the Arab world, that keep citizens under constant surveillance. "A young man has a car and money in his pocket, but what can he do? Nothing. He looks at TV and sees others doing things he can't do and wonders why."

Young people in every society resent authority, reject rules, and seek to exert their independence. But the difference in Saudi Arabia is at least twofold. Because this is a quintessentially authoritarian society, there are many more restrictions and conventions against which youth can rebel. Further, almost any form of youthful rebellion stands in stark contrast to the unquestioning acceptance and unruffled conformity of previous generations of Saudis. In a society with one of the youngest populations on earth, this frustration poses a powerful challenge not just to parents but to the regime and to the religious establishment, from whom the young increasingly are alienated. In a recent survey, some 31 percent of Saudi youth said "traditional values are outdated and . . . I am keen to embrace modern values and beliefs," the highest percentage in the ten Arab countries surveyed. In short, the sedentary Saudi python is having a very hard time digesting its youth bulge.

The youth rebellion takes many forms. Some young people simply show their independence by wearing baseball caps and sneakers or by adopting other Western fashions and habits, though this does not necessarily mean they want a Western way of life. Restlessness leads others to lawlessness, such as beating up teachers, vandalizing property, or using drugs and alcohol. For still others, rejecting encroaching modernism means turning to fundamentalist Islam as the only acceptable means to confront authority both parental and governmental. For a minority of these Islamists, this confrontation leads to extremism and even terrorism. But virtually all Saudi youth, whether attracted by modern mores or by the pull of religiosity, are part of a generation that, unlike their parents or grandparents, is questioning and confronting authority. For a conservative society like Saudi Arabia, this attitude itself is revolutionary—and its manifestations are evident everywhere.

In a society that is usually passive, one young Saudi man confronted conventions and the royal regime by filming a poor neighborhood in Riyadh and posting his dramatic nine-minute film on YouTube in October 2011. The film opened with young Feras Bugnah noting, "We are not in Somalia," as he takes his cameras into the homes of three poor Riyadh families to show unlit rooms, broken beds, and families living on 2,500 Saudi riyals (about $650) a month. Bugnah concludes the film by interviewing the neighborhood imam, who acknowledges that young boys are selling drugs and young girls are sold by their fathers into prostitution to earn money. He asks each family what they want to say to King Abdullah, and each asks only for a home, something out of reach for about 70 percent of Saudis, given the high price of land because previous kings have given most of the state's land to princes or a handful of powerful businessmen who do the regime's bidding.

The film, entitled in English *We Are Screwed,* went viral— some eight hundred thousand Saudis viewed it—before young Bugnah was arrested by authorities, an indication of how explosive the kingdom's housing issue is deemed to be by the government, which promised 250 billion Saudi riyals (roughly $65 billion) for housing in the wake of the Arab Spring upheavals across the Middle East.

A second youth video, *Monopoly,* highlighted the near impossibility of owning a home in Saudi Arabia because a monopoly on landownership by royals and other wealthy Saudis has put the price of land out of reach of a majority of Saudis. It struck a responsive chord in the population. One Saudi went to his Twitter account to call on wealthy countrymen to donate land to the Ministry of Housing so ordinary Saudis could afford to buy homes, and at least one Saudi businessman responded.

Not all angry young Saudis are so constructive. Alienation increasingly is begetting lawlessness among Saudi youth. Newspapers regularly report students beating teachers who dare to give failing grades. One young woman in Jubail, an industrial city on the Persian Gulf, angered that her school headmistress confiscated her camera-equipped cell phone (forbidden as she could snap photos of unveiled classmates), returned to school with her mother to confront the headmistress. When the conversation didn't go as the young woman hoped, she picked up a glass and cracked it over the supervisor's head, sending her to the hospital for five days and earning the twenty-year-old student two months in prison and ninety lashes. More shocking to authorities in a country that forbids demonstrations of any kind, hundreds of Saudi youth celebrating National Day, honoring the kingdom's founding, spontaneously began smashing windows and ransacking shops and showrooms along the Corniche in Al Khobar, a generally modern town comprising a mix of Saudis and foreigners in the country's oil-rich Eastern Province. Such out-of-control behavior once would have been inconceivable. But some of the 225 youths arrested during the rampage essentially excused their behavior by blaming the authorities for failing to provide places for young people to relax and enjoy free time. (A dozen of the teens were flogged for their conduct.)

If boredom is one motivator for lawless acts, another is anger at the government. The Saudi government in 2010 installed in major cities a sophisticated camera system that tickets speeders by automatically sending a ticket to their cell phones. Traffic accidents are the number-one killer in Saudi Arabia. Every ninety minutes someone dies in a traffic accident, and every fifteen minutes another Saudi is left handicapped for life. Traffic fatalities in 2010 totaled more than six thousand, double the number who died in Britain, even though Saudi Arabia's population is less than half that of Britain. Despite the obvious need to enforce traffic rules, the new *saher* system has been repeatedly vandalized by young Saudis, who destroy the cameras or steal license plates from police cars and then repeatedly speed through lights, generating scores of bogus tickets for police officers. Youth claim that the money from fines goes to enrich Prince Nayef bin Abdul Aziz, crown prince and minister of interior, who is responsible for the nation's invasive intelligence agencies. In choosing this target, young Saudis are protesting what they see as both royal corruption and state intrusion into their lives.

Not all youth, of course, act out. Some simply bear their boredom in sullen silence. Two teenage sons of a midlevel government employee describe the ennui of their lives spent studying, praying, and for relaxation, watching movies and playing computer games at home. The brothers, seventeen and fifteen years of age, are wearing jeans and T-shirts, not traditional Saudi dress, as they accompany me to a Jeddah restaurant. To join a foreign woman on a public outing is most unusual, but Jeddah, as a port city with a long history of foreigners mingling with Saudis, is far more liberal than Riyadh, and their father is a U.S.-educated government official eager to expose his sons to a wider world. The elder youth, who just received his driving permit, drives us to the restaurant in his used white Toyota, complaining along the way that wealthy boys his age own new BMWs. A subdued and shy boy, he rises at five to shower and pray. At six fifteen he drives his brother to school before heading for the seven fifteen start at his own school. When classes conclude at one thirty P.M., the boys return home to have lunch with their father and then do homework. "There's nothing much to do after that," says the elder youth. So the young one plays video games on the Internet and the elder watches Egyptian movies on his computer. They are typical of the bored but largely well-behaved majority of Saudi youth who don't like the emptiness of life yet don't know what to do about it.

Asked if they could change one thing about their country, the elder pauses before finally saying he would allow cinemas. The younger answers instantly: "I would allow girls to go to school with boys."

Boys from wealthy families can relax in one of the multiple male sitting rooms of their homes or the well-appointed tents common inside the walled compounds of the wealthy. Young men of more modest means pool their money and rent an *istirahat,* or public house for relaxation, that can be leased by the day, week, or month. They gather there regularly to talk, eat, and watch sporting events and movies—or sometimes engage in less innocent pursuits.

But poor young Saudis have almost no options for entertainment. These bored teenage boys play soccer in the streets or often are attracted by the allure of petty crime. Crime, of course, isn't limited to the poor. Many Saudis who turn to car theft do so not because they need a car or want to sell it for money but simply for excitement. I meet with one young convicted thief at a coffee shop. Mustafa, twenty-five (who declines to give his family name), began stealing cars when he was nineteen even though he says he was earning $1,000 a month working in the National Guard. He and a group of similarly bored friends would select a car they liked, follow it for a few miles, and then bump into it. When the driver pulled off the highway to survey the damage, usually leaving the engine running, one of the boys would jump in the victim's car and drive away, leaving his accomplices quickly to follow. At other times, they would trade excitement for ease and select their victims by surveying a supermarket parking lot for cars left running while the owners dashed in to make a purchase. "Our concentration was on playing with the cars and having fun. It was exciting," he says.

A handsome young man with a large gap between his two front teeth that makes him look even more boyish, Mustafa was caught after a year and a half of joyriding in stolen vehicles and sentenced to ten months in prison and 350 lashes, administered in groups of 50 over seven weeks. "I used to cry and feel sorry for myself," he says. "Prison is for criminals, and I was just having fun. I am not a criminal." While in prison, he began using drugs and once free again supplemented drugs with alcohol. He resumed stealing to help pay for his vices. Soon he and his young accomplices were caught by the religious police. A lack of evidence allowed him to escape conviction and jail, but the incident frightened him enough that he finally listened to a friend's urging that he join Alcoholics Anonymous. Mustafa insists he has been clean for two years and now has a new job as a receptionist in a clinic. "I just wanted excitement, but now I am convinced it is not exciting. But too many young people do this," he says.

Indeed, according to public security authorities, auto theft is on the rise and nearly 80 percent of all cars are stolen by

Saudis between the ages of eighteen and twenty-four. Most use the cars for *tafheet,* or spinning, a favorite after-midnight pastime of thrill-seeking young Saudi men. Groups of young men gather on isolated roads and accelerate their cars, spin them sideways, sometimes overturn them, or more often smash them into the parked vehicles of the scores of other young men who gather to watch. Not surprisingly, those who engage in *tafheet* prefer to spare their own vehicles by using stolen cars. Some 90 percent of stolen cars are found abandoned by thieves after joyriding or spinning, so police often refuse even to look for a stolen car until several days after it disappears. It's yet another sign of the growing lawlessness in Saudi Arabia, as citizens decide which laws to obey and police which ones to enforce. "Young people don't care about laws," says Muhammad al Negir, who works in public security in Riyadh. "Families have a responsibility to help us police their children, but they don't."

Not all or even most young Saudis flagrantly flout society's rules and laws, but even conservative youths are questioning authority. Imam University, named for Imam Muhammad bin Saud, founder of the first Al Saud dynasty in the eighteenth century, is home to some sixteen thousand devout young men pursuing studies, primarily in Sharia, or Islamic law. But here, too, winds of change are wafting. Four young men in their early twenties gather one evening with one of their professors at the home of an Imam University graduate to meet with me, a double no-no. (Mixing with women is forbidden, and for the deeply orthodox, so is mixing with infidels.) All four of the boys have beards, a sign of religious devotion. Three of the four wear their scarves draped across their heads without the black *agal,* the double black circle of cord, to hold the scarves in place, another mark of strict religiosity. These outward signs leave me expecting to hear a very austere interpretation of the responsibilities of young Saudis and strong support for the Al Saud and the religious establishment. But appearances in today's kingdom often are deceiving.

Saud, twenty-one (who declines to provide his family

name), describes objecting when his father tried to enroll him in a Koran course at age six. Three years later his father forced him to go despite his protests. By secondary school, he says, he had become knowledgeable about Islam and, to his teachers' dismay, began questioning what was taught in religion classes. "I don't accept I should be loyal to Salafi," he says, referring to the fundamentalist Islamic thought that underpins Wahhabi teachings. For an Imam University student to say such a thing is tantamount to a Baptist preacher's son saying "I don't accept Jesus as my savior."

Asked to whom he turns for guidance on religious issues—parents or professors or the imam at his mosque—the young man says, "I depend on myself to research an answer. I have no specific sheikh." Again, this independence of mind on religious orthodoxy is something new; the generation of this young man's parents simply accepted religion as dictated by parents, schools, and imams.

The other three young men are more circumspect. While growing up, says one, "my main concern was to obey my parents. There was no discussion. You just obey." For that reason, says another, despite his deep interest in science and his desire to study it, he enrolled in Imam University because his background was religious and his parents directed him toward religious studies. This parental push leads nearly two-thirds of university graduates to earn degrees in Islamic subjects that fail to equip them for work in the private sector, where employers seek expertise like economics, marketing, computer programming, or management.

The young men talk openly about their parents, their rearing, and the doubts—at least briefly—that each experienced about Islam as it was taught in their schools. Listening to even mild doubts about Wahhabi Islam expressed by Imam University students makes me feel almost subversive. The setting is a large, well-appointed living room where the attentive male host repeatedly pours small cups of Arabic coffee and offers cups of sweet tea and bowls of dates. When I unthinkingly set my teacup on top of my Koran to spare the expensive side table, one young man leaps to move the offending cup off the holy book, wordlessly reminding me that no temporal table is as important as the book of Allah's word.

After the young men speak, their professor, a man in his early forties, sums up with what amounts to a shockingly harsh indictment of Saudi society. The country, he says, has turned its focus from religion to money. "We have become consumers," he says. "Everything is for sale. You can buy and sell a fatwa. Sheikhs go on television to advise the people, but all they care about is their television contract. Our social relations are chosen on the basis of whether or not we get a benefit." Even the sacred right of a Muslim to demand punishment of an offender or receive instead "blood money," a payment in cash to the victim's family if it agrees to spare the offender from his required Islamic punishment, is being exploited to earn cash, he says. "We have a bazaar of blood. Greedy people now earn commissions on arranging a deal between the victim and the offender to forgive the offender in exchange for a large sum of money." (This is a Saudi version of tort lawyers in the United States who sue on behalf of victims and take a large portion of any award.)

Suddenly the call to prayer sounds through the night from a nearby mosque, and the men all rise and depart to a tent in the front yard of this large walled home to perform *isha,* the final prayer of the day. The host lingers a moment to end the evening. "These young men are very moderate," he says. "Most Imam University students wouldn't agree to meet a foreigner." What percent would refuse? I ask. "At least seventy-five percent," he says. Pronouncing his own conclusion on the evening, he insists society is changing—as evidenced by these young men meeting a foreign woman. "Usually in society, the old teach the young," he says, "but now with technology the young are teaching the old."

Such meetings always leave me grateful for a glimpse into the evolving attitudes of conservative young Saudis, but at the same time mindful of the enormous gulf between them and young people in the West. However much adherents of so-called cosmopolitanism would like to see all peoples around the globe as similar, Saudis, even Internet-savvy ones, are not at all like Western youth. It isn't just that many young people in the West use drugs, have sex before marriage, and rarely even think about religion, let alone practice any faith. The biggest difference is that Western youth aren't reared in societies that venerate religion or value tradition, so they are free to seek their own paths uninhibited by strong societal or family pressures. Young Saudis, even those resisting authority and seeking some independence, are struggling against the thick walls of religion and tradition constructed brick by brick from birth by family, school, mosque, and government. Even if these values and traditions are rejected, the act of breaking free defines the individual.

This struggle to break free of the strictures of Saudi society is vividly illustrated by several works in a youth art show in Jeddah in early 2011. The show, staged discreetly in a fifth-floor gallery hidden from street view, is nonetheless new, provocative, and for Saudis even daring. One sculpture portrays a gaunt plaster-of-Paris head jerked back by clear plastic tubes that connect the head to a large stone, depicting the controlling connection between authority and youth. The mouth on the upturned head is agape in an anguished scream. Visible inside the open mouth are scores of tiny words representing the messages that parents feed to children from birth—words like *abi* (shame) and *haram* (forbidden). Behind the head is a spigot indicating that youth sometimes can turn off the messages from parents but can never sever the connections that link youthful minds to stone-age authorities. The artist "perceives a culture that suffers from subservience and uniformity through mind compulsion and his art mirrors that view and creates in turn the ultimate defining point of today's generation," the show's printed program says in describing the sculpture.

Nearby is another example of art criticizing authority—this one by a Saudi prince. The painting, entitled *A Witness Who Never Forgot* by Prince Saad bin Muhammad, depicts a young male face staring sternly as cars float in rising flood waters. To indicate the young man is Saudi, the traditional red-and-white *shemagh* is bound tightly around his head, but it also covers his mouth so that it resembles a football helmet more than a scarf. The painting "conveys the societal limitation that prevents one from realizing his personal power and potential," says the show guide. The artist, who lived through the devastating 2009 flood in Jeddah, explains over coffee in the gallery, "The painting is the accumulation of the pain of the city. It is like a bleeding wound. I had to get it out of my system by painting a witness who could never forget." Ironically, a week after the painting went on display, the second devastating flood struck Jeddah and forced the prince to cancel an earlier scheduled meeting with me at the gallery because he couldn't get out of his home. When we did meet a few days later, I asked how he felt living through another flood only fourteen months after government officials had promised "never again." "I am not going to answer that," he says. "It is like pressing on a raw nerve and I don't want to say something I will regret." Even an alienated Al Saud prince has to be careful what he says in words if not in his art.

Saudi youth, whether liberal, traditional, or fundamentalist, share at least three characteristics: most are alienated, undereducated, and underemployed. Unlike their parents and grandparents, who generally express gratitude to the Al Saud for improving their standard of living during the oil boom of the 1970s, young Saudis born in the 1980s and 1990s have no memory of the impoverished Arabia prior to the oil boom and thus express almost no sense of appreciation. Instead, they have experienced a kingdom of poor schools, overcrowded universities, and declining job opportunities. Moreover, their royal rulers' profligate and often non-Islamic lifestyles are increasingly transparent to Saudis and stand in sharp contrast both to Al Saud religious pretensions and to their own declining living standards.

"The government has become that 'other' which is no longer trusted," writes Dr. Mai Yamani, a Saudi sociologist, in *Changed Identities,* interviews with some seventy young Saudis on their attitudes toward social change. In Saudi Arabia, youth are supposed to practice silent obedience. But for this generation of twenty-something Saudis, youthful optimism has been replaced by concern for their livelihoods and contempt for a government that fails to provide. As a result, the young use religion as a sword against authority, confronting their elders and, by extension, the regime for religious and social hypocrisy, Dr. Yamani writes.

Young people in any Saudi city drive past princely palaces that often stretch for blocks and ask how such opulence squares with the Prophet's example of humility and equality among believers. "He is not a perfect Muslim who eats till he is full and leaves his neighbors hungry," the Prophet said in a well-known hadith. How can the Al Saud claim to represent Islam and so visibly violate this basic religious tenet? they wonder. They also hear their religious imams condemn any human likeness as sinful, yet they see life-size pictures of Al Saud rulers in the foyers of every public building in the kingdom. The young also question the sincerity of religious leaders whom they see as sycophantic shills for the Al Saud. In mosques, they hear sermons condemning mixing of unrelated men and women, yet some senior religious scholars endorse King Abdullah's namesake university, where such mixing occurs. Some of those scholars also lecture to mixed audiences when they go abroad.

How can a film festival be permitted one year in Jeddah and banned the next? Why does Jenadriyah, the annual national festival celebrating Saudi culture, allow families to attend one year and ban them the next, forcing men and women to attend on separate days? Why did the kingdom spend a reported $100 million to build the King Fahd Cultural Center and use it primarily for commercial events or rare cultural programs that never focus on Saudi Arabia?

Above all, they see daily reminders of hypocrisy at home. Why, they ask parents, is it permissible to watch a movie on television, yet public cinemas are forbidden? Why is it okay for one hundred thousand Saudi students abroad, at government expense, to mix in Western universities, but not permissible for those same universities to open mixed-gender branches in the kingdom, as they have in other Gulf sheikdoms like Qatar, which would enable many more young

Saudis to obtain a quality education? Why can a young Saudi, however furtively, exchange cell phone numbers with a girl and even video-chat online with her, yet if they dare sit together in public, both risk harassment by the religious police? How can it be wrong for young Saudis, who increasingly meet on Facebook, to hold hands before they are married? "Facebook opens the doors of our cages," says a young single Saudi man in his midtwenties, noting that the social network is the primary way men and women meet in the kingdom. "The young understand it is part of nature to have a boyfriend or girlfriend, and we should not pretend it isn't happening."

One father who has had to field queries from his children counsels patience. "I saw things change in my lifetime," he tells his sons. "I used to go to cinema. Maybe you will see them change in your life too." This father, who like so many Saudis doesn't want to be publicly identified, predicts that cinema will return to Saudi sooner rather than later. "The religious will decide they can make money owning cinemas showing Islamic films," he says. "Gradually we will get cartoons like *Tom and Jerry,* then animated children's movies like *Toy Story,* and finally adult movies like *Ocean's Eleven.*" So religious greed will restore cinema—clearly, cynicism in Saudi isn't limited to the young.

"The young are at a crossroads," says a thoughtful Jeddah-based businessman and father. "They see life in the West, and also the Saudi Arabia of tradition. They need guidance to know how to choose the best of the West, but they don't get guidance. Instead, what they see here is a gap between religion and life. If religion is preached rigidly and practiced another way, it confuses the young."

A number of young Saudi adults are trying to bridge the gulf between religion as preached in the mosque and life as seen on the Internet. It is another of Saudi Arabia's many paradoxes that in a country where religion and state are one, far too often religion and life are separate. Ahmad Shugairi, a Saudi businessman in his thirties, is trying to help young people connect religion and life. "Religion here is just a ritual," he explains, "not a way of life."

For the past half-dozen years, Shugairi has been host of a popular television show called *Yalla Shubaba* (Come On, Youth). He knows something about alienation firsthand. As a young man living in Long Beach, California, he rejected religion and focused on fun. Then at age twenty-two, he abruptly decided to "stabilize" his life. He returned to the kingdom, married, began to read the Koran, prayed five times daily, and fasted during Ramadan. By his own admission, he swung from having no interest in Islam to what he describes as a fixation on the minutiae of religion, engaging like so many Saudis in debates on the proper length of one's *thobe* or beard rather than on the essence of the Prophet Muhammad's message. All this, he says, convinced him that most of his fellow Saudis were corrupt and not living their religion properly. He describes himself as having been perpetually angry and intolerant.

Then, like so many young Saudis these days, he began to watch and listen to religious sheikhs from outside the kingdom on satellite television and the Internet. In his case, they were moderate ones, though the airwaves also are replete with extreme fundamentalist sheikhs. Two moderates in particular caught his eye. One was from Kuwait and the other from Egypt. He began to hold weekly studies of the Koran with a few Saudi friends, and he developed what he calls "a more tolerant, updated, flexible view of Islam."

It is this kinder, gentler Islam that he now seeks to propagate on his television show. "In the past we had two kinds of television—boring sermons from a sheikh, or sports. I want to provide spiritual and life guidance but make it fun. In the eighties religion meant praying in the mosque and reading the Koran. We want to change that so people understand that a religious person is successful and connected to God in this life."

To do so, he sometimes shines a harsh light on Saudis as they are, to encourage them to seek change. For instance, in one show he went to the street to ask citizens to guide him to the nearest public library. None could. But when he asked directions to the closest shopping mall, everyone had a ready answer. He showed the contrast between shopping malls teeming with young Saudis and empty libraries dusty from disuse. He holds up a mirror to the materialism and shallowness of Saudi life, which has made him a popular hero among the young, who see in him the candor and courage so lacking in a culture where appearances, however hypocritical, are everything.

"The old ways of rearing kids won't work anymore," he says, explaining why new efforts at guiding youth are essential. "This age group has enormous energy, and it can either be constructive or destructive, but you can't suppress it. And they are a thousand times more exposed to the world than their parents.

"When I was young," he adds, "if you wanted to meet a girl, you had to drive by, and if you liked her, you rolled down your window and passed your phone number—your family's phone number. Then you went home and sat by the phone to see if she would call. Today, you see a girl, you exchange mobile phone numbers, and five minutes later you can be sitting in Starbucks"—at some risk, of course. While unrelated males and females are not allowed to meet, young people do so surreptitiously but frequently, finding in the thrill of evading the religious police an added excitement to meeting someone of the opposite sex.

Another prominent Saudi seeking to channel the restlessness of alienated youth is Prince Turki bin Khalid, a grandson of the kingdom's late crown prince Sultan bin Abdul Aziz. The young prince has founded a newspaper, *Al Shams,* specifically targeted at young Saudis. "We cover everything from the perspective of the young," he explains. "And we write about human interest, education, new habits, new trends—everything except politics." The paper, with a modest circulation of sixty thousand, runs features on successful young Saudis who the prince hopes will be seen as role models for alienated youth. "We have a big problem with the system, equal opportunity and work ethic," he says, proving that even some royals are well aware of the malaise that grips growing numbers of young Saudis. "If we could solve these things, we could soar, as we have many really smart young Saudis."

Prince Turki was inspired to launch a publication aimed at the young by observing former U.S. president Bill Clinton, who as a presidential candidate successfully courted young Americans through MTV. The prince, a student at Georgetown University in Washington at the time, says he learned that "young people everywhere have more power than they think." The prince sees today's Saudi Arabia as emerging from a "darkroom" into the light. "At first you can't see color until your eyes adjust," he says. "That is what is happening with young people here; we are now seeing colors after twenty years in the darkroom. I don't want alcohol. I don't need cinema, but I want a Saudi Arabia that is colorful, tolerant, and proactive."

Even at Saudi ARAMCO, the national oil company, which is widely acknowledged to attract the best and brightest young Saudis—and which offers them the most open environment in the kingdom—the generational divide is apparent. "The young generation is demanding, impatient, and much smarter than my generation," says Abdulaziz al Khayyal, a senior vice president at the company. "We took whatever jobs were offered because we had no choice. We needed to eat. This generation doesn't need money, so talented young people want to have fun; they want to be challenged and feel they contribute something to their society, not just do what they are told. Today's young want more action."

Saudi ARAMCO, founded and run by U.S. oil companies for more than four decades until Saudi Arabia purchased it in 1980, is a massive fenced city often called "Little America" because its wide streets, low bungalows, and grassy lawns resemble a California suburb. The Saudi ARAMCO compound features its own golf course, schools, cinemas, swimming pools, grocery stores, and library. Until religiosity gripped the kingdom in the 1980s, pork and alcohol were permitted on the premises, and Christmas was celebrated, complete with wise men riding camels to see baby Jesus. No longer. But today men and women continue to mix freely both at work and leisure. Women even are allowed to drive within the compound. Like many Western companies, Saudi

ARAMCO sponsors public service campaigns, including one to discourage driving while using a cell phone.

"I start from the view that talking on the phone while driving is against the law so one shouldn't do it," says Al Khayyal, who is responsible for the campaign's message. His son, on the other hand, tells him that any such campaign simply will look silly, because no young Saudi ARAMCO employee is going to ignore a ringing cell phone just because he or she is driving. "I often ask myself if this youthful exuberance will diminish as they get older or will this young generation be like the sixties generation in the United States and stay demanding and self-centered all their lives," Al Khayyal muses. My conversations with young people of all types across the kingdom convince me that this bulge of young Saudis is very likely to bring the kind of societal change in attitudes that baby boomers forced on America starting in the 1960s. America proved resilient enough to weather that generational storm. With all the entrenched rigidities of religion and regime, Saudi Arabia is unlikely to prove anywhere near as resilient.

Accommodating these rapidly changing attitudes and demands of youth is a challenge even at Saudi ARAMCO, the most international and professional institution in Saudi Arabia. In recent years, the company has begun to allow young women to compete for its coveted College Preparatory Program, which accounts for 75 percent of all new hires at the company. The young women chosen for the program know that, on average, they outperformed men on the standardized test given to all applicants. They understand that they are privileged to be in the program, but none of them exhibits any sense of gratitude to Saudi ARAMCO for giving them an opportunity that they earned just as their male colleagues did.

In a country where young women are kept under constant family surveillance until marriage, these young women live in a dormitory on the grounds of the corporate compound. It is, of course, well supervised but still a big break from tradition. Here they attend classes to prepare for entry into foreign universities to earn degrees mostly in engineering, management, or finance and eventual employment at Saudi ARAMCO in jobs typically held by males. They are taught, among other things, how to manage contemporary social issues such as handling confrontations with foreigners or explaining the *hijab,* if they choose to wear a head scarf when abroad.

At my meeting with a dozen of these young women, they discuss how different their lives are from those of their mothers. Most of their mothers are educated but do not work. The difference, the young women say, isn't the absence of society's rules, which still exist, but rather the willingness of their generation to break them.

"There are even more rules in society now," says one young woman. "But it is no longer shocking not to follow them." Most of these young women nineteen or twenty years of age have had their own e-mail accounts and their own cell phones since prepubescence. They believe opportunities will be much greater for them than they were for their mothers, but only if they persist. "We know the opportunities won't come voluntarily," says one. "As Gandhi said, we have to make our own change, and we will."

It is not just educated and privileged young women who push for more opportunity. In the poor, underdeveloped province of Jizan, in the south of Arabia near Yemen, Salim al Fafi, seventy-five, sits in the front yard of his large home in Faifa, a village atop a three-thousand-meter mountain an hour's drive from Jizan City. Reaching his home in a four-wheel drive vehicle is like climbing a corkscrew. Al Fafi's beard is white, but he proudly points to his youngest son, who at six is the same age as one of the dozen barefoot grandsons darting around his yard. From his mountain perch, he gazes contentedly at a big orange sun setting slowly over the green fields below and says he measures his pleasure by the size of his family: three wives, thirty-five children, and thirty grandchildren. While all the women are kept inside the house, even here in this bucolic, if primitive, world, new demands intrude. His greatest problem: his seven unmarried daughters are pressuring him to get them to school in Jizan so they can receive an education. By contrast, none of his wives who grew up in the village is educated or even thought of becoming so. Because he has no way to get his daughters down the mountain and into the city for schooling, he says he tells them to "just get married and have children." For these young women, life has not yet changed—though clearly their thinking has.

Saudi society, as we have seen, is deeply divided along multiple fault lines—tribal, regional, religious, gender, and more. All these divisions are visibly accentuated among Saudi youth. The gap between the easy riders on Riyadh's Tahlia Street and the devout but questioning Imam University students, between the educated young women at Saudi ARAMCO and the isolated girls on the mountaintop in Faifa, between Lulu's cloistered daughters and Manal's liberated ones, is all the sharper and thus all the more threatening to the future stability of the Al Saud regime. If overall Saudi society was once homogeneous, the current generation of Saudi youth is openly and proudly heterogeneous. The most significant thing they have in common is dissatisfaction with the status quo. Whether, and if so how, to accommodate this pressure from the young is among the most daunting challenges for the Al Saud regime.

CHAPTER 7

Princes

"Please excuse me for rushing," Prince Abdullah bin Musa'id, a nephew of King Abdullah, says, ushering me hastily from his study toward the front door of his home. "I have to finish early today—this is football day." As if to ease the impression of insufficient hospitality, he adds, "If you are free, please come back at ten P.M."

When a Saudi speaks of football, he means soccer, the kingdom's national sport. Saudi soccer games are about the only time reserved Saudis are allowed to shout and show joy. Prince Abdullah, however, is referring to American football, his personal passion. Behind his desk is an autographed football and helmet from his favorite team, the San Francisco 49ers. Every Sunday during the American football season, he hosts a dozen or so male friends to watch Sunday afternoon football live on the four oversize television screens in the basement of his Riyadh home. Given the time difference between the United States and Saudi, these gatherings begin around ten P.M. and last until the early hours of Monday morning. The prince watches football for entertainment but also because he sees in the sport lessons for his country's somnolent, riskless society.

"In the United States, 'we tried' is a compliment," he explains. "Here we focus on failure, not on trying. Saudis don't take risks because we are so hard on failure. But if you don't risk much, you can't accomplish much."

Prince Abdullah took a risk—and failed. He had a dream of transforming Al Hilal, the country's most decorated soccer team, into a profitable, high-performance powerhouse that would win Saudi Arabia admiration throughout the Middle East for exporting something other than religious jihadists. "Soccer is our only entertainment, so we should have the best league, make huge money, and reach youth all over the Arab world," he says. To pursue this dream, he assumed the presidency of Al Hilal determined to use all the modern promotional and marketing strategies of a successful U.S. sports owner. But his royal relatives who control television and franchise rights were unwilling to surrender power even in a sports franchise. So after a few years, a thwarted Abdullah gave up and took up Fantasy Football and watching powerful U.S. football franchises compete. Like many other Saudis who seek change, the prince expresses deep concern for the future of his country and, like those nonroyal Saudis, is resigned that he cannot effect change.

Clearly, it is not just women and young people who chafe at the strictures of tradition and religion but princes as well. Listening to intelligent, creative, concerned Saudis, whatever their gender, age, or birthright, talk about stifled ambitions and straitjacketed lives inevitably makes me feel I am exploring a museum of mummies rather than a living culture. If only Saudis could throw off their centuries-old bindings and be allowed to think and act independently and even organize with others, they clearly would have sufficient enterprise and energy to begin to reverse the sullen social lethargy now so pervasive that even billions of petrodollars have not been able to resolve problems of poor education, overdependence on foreign workers, growing joblessness among Saudis, declining health and health care, and mounting poverty. The fact that most Saudi princes are as powerless as ordinary Saudis to address these problems may seem surprising, but perhaps it should not in a society where seniority trumps enterprise, especially among princes.

Being born a prince still has advantages, but these days the benefits are more akin to those enjoyed by the offspring of elite businessmen or politicians in the West. These younger princes can gain access to an influential minister or businessman more easily than the average Saudi, but they have little access to or influence on the handful of senior Al Saud princes who rule the kingdom through division, diversion, and dollars.

Saudi Arabia's founder fathered forty-four sons and innumerable daughters. Many of his sons were almost as prolific as their father, so the kingdom now boasts thousands of princes—sons, grandsons, great-grandsons, and by now great-great-grandsons of the founder. These princes may be born to rule, but the truth is only a handful ever will. Indeed, this plethora of princes is so large and so diverse that little if anything links them except some Al Saud genes. In no other country on earth is there a royal family on anything like this scale. Collectively, they increasingly are viewed by the rest of Saudi society as a burdensome privileged caste. The monarch sees their diversity, divisions, and demands as just one more problem requiring skillful management, all the more so as the issue of generational succession looms large, now that Abdul Aziz's surviving sons all are in their late sixties or older.

Even in a government that prefers princes for most key jobs in Riyadh ministries and provincial leadership roles around the country, the majority of Abdul Aziz's heirs have no government position. Hundreds of them, to be sure, have quasi-official roles running programs to help the poor or foundations of one sort or another, and many hundreds more use their royal lineage to build businesses through which they obtain land and government contracts worth hundreds of millions and sometimes billions. But the family is so large some princes still can't find a sinecure. Third-generation princes are said to receive only $19,000 a month, hardly enough to lead a princely life, and King Abdullah, since assuming the throne in 2005, has stopped passing out envelopes of money to vacationing family members, has curbed the use of the Saudi national airline as an Al Saud private jet service, and has privatized the telephone company so the government no longer covers free cell phone usage for royals. (The extended royal family, including progeny of Abdul Aziz's siblings, is said to include roughly thirty thousand members.)

So what's a prince to do? Let's look further at Prince Abdullah and also at three of his cousins. All are grandsons of the founder, and none are playboy princes of the all-too-frequent sort so open to Western caricature. Rather they are educated, talented, and serious men. All four understandably are concerned about the future of Saudi Arabia and of Al Saud rule. These four underscore the diversity among princes, yet share a common powerlessness to shape the country's future.

THE FOOTBALL-LOVING PRINCE

Prince Abdullah, the football fanatic, is one of the least aristocratic of the founder's grandsons. A double tragedy in his family helped force this prince to earn his own way in life. The year Abdullah was born, 1965, his older brother, Khalid, was shot and killed for protesting the introduction of television into the kingdom by his uncle, King Faisal—ironically, the very innovation that the prince and his football friends so enjoy today.

A decade later, in an unprecedented act of regicide, another brother, Faisal, assassinated King Faisal. The young man, perhaps angry that the king had banned him from traveling abroad or seeking revenge for his brother's death, entered King Faisal's office with a visiting dignitary. When the monarch reached to embrace him, the young man shot his uncle three times with a small pistol. He was swiftly apprehended and soon beheaded in front of ten thousand spectators. As a result of these two losses, the boys' father, Prince Musa'id, is largely a recluse, leaving Prince Abdullah, his eldest surviving son, to represent his branch in royal-family councils, including the important commission of princes who will select the kingdom's leadership once King Abdullah dies.

Today Prince Abdullah, in his midforties, lives a quiet life on the outskirts of Riyadh in a well-guarded walled estate. His home is a desert-mud color set against bare desert hills. The large but certainly not palatial home resembles the walled house of a wealthy Southern California business magnate. Foreign laborers are busy tending flower beds that create splashes of color in the otherwise monochromatic brown surroundings of home and hills.

Because his father had no money to lend him, Prince Abdullah says, he secured a bank loan to launch a recycling business in 1991. Saudi Paper Manufacturing buys waste paper from the government and then recycles and sells it. After a decade, with the business solidly successful, Prince Abdullah says he got bored and turned to his real passion—sports. Having failed to persuade the government to let him build Al Hilal into a powerhouse franchise, he now watches American football and dreams of owning a U.S. football team. On this particular Sunday night, he and his friends face a wall of four large flat-screen televisions tuned to two National Football League games and two soccer matches. This modern prince is multitasking by also playing Fantasy Football on the computer in front of his knees as he squats on the floor with his friends. This is hardly a beer-guzzling, couch potato crowd. Most of the young men are in their thirties, bareheaded but dressed in traditional Saudi *thobes* and sipping Pepsi, nothing stronger. The food and drinks are laid out by servants, but each man serves himself and returns to his seat on the floor. Abdullah, sitting cross-legged in sports pants, his balding head uncovered, would fit no one's image of an Al Saud prince.

For a member of the publicity-shy royal family, the prince has a most unusual new ambition. Abdullah wants to write a book comparing sports in the United States and Saudi Arabia, to illustrate how sports reflect national character and could be used to change national character. His description of some of the key differences amounts to a damning portrait of Saudi society. American sports stars, he says, rarely make excuses for losing. "They acknowledge the other team outplayed them. But here we make excuses and blame a loss on things beyond the team's control, like the referee wasn't fair." Similarly, he admires the hard work U.S. athletes put into improving their performance and thus that of their team. "Here Saudis prefer not to work if they can avoid

Al Saud princes may dress alike, but they do not think alike. *Clockwise from top left,* American football fan Prince Abdullah bin Musa'id bin Abdul Aziz al Saud (ABDULLAH AL SHAMMARI); astronaut Prince Sultan bin Salman bin Abdul Aziz al Saud (GETTY IMAGES); diplomat Prince Turki al Faisal bin Abdul Aziz al Saud (GETTY IMAGES); religious scholar Prince Abdul Aziz bin Sattam bin Abdul Aziz al Saud. (ABDULLAH AL SHAMMARI)

it. So we don't train hard or try hard." The book remains unwritten.

THE PROFESSORIAL PRINCE

Abdul Aziz bin Sattam, another grandson of the founder, has little in common with Prince Abdullah bin Musa'id, other than his Al Saud genes. Abdul Aziz, a forty-nine-year-old bachelor, is as formal in his dress and bearing as his cousin is casual. He disdains sports, spending his free time either walking in the desert or reading books. His conversation is dominated by professorial explanations of Islam—the religion, the ritual, the law, the hereafter.

His father, Prince Sattam bin Abdul Aziz, was the first son of the founder to earn a U.S. degree—and the only son to marry just one wife. Prince Sattam earned a degree in business administration from the University of San Diego in 1965 and soon afterward became deputy governor of Riyadh, a post he held for nearly forty years before becoming governor in late 2011. His son, by contrast, was educated entirely in Saudi universities. Prince Abdul Aziz earned degrees in industrial relations and sociology and finally a doctorate in government jurisprudence from Imam University, the kingdom's premier institution for religious training.

The prince typifies the generation that came of age in the 1980s on the heels of the attack on the Grand Mosque in Mecca by religious extremists. The country ceased sending students abroad for education and exposure to Western ways and sharply tilted toward pacifying the fundamentalists, allowing the religious establishment to dominate every aspect of Saudi life, especially education. So for most of the two decades between the attack on the Grand Mosque in 1979 and the attack by extremist Saudis on the World Trade Center in 2001, Saudi education was dominated by fundamentalist, xenophobic religious indoctrination that encouraged young Saudis to see the West as decadent and Christians and Jews as infidel enemies of Islam. That is pretty much Abdul Aziz's view.

Abdul Aziz is a man of average height and build, but his rimless glasses give him a bookish appearance, and his stiff demeanor conveys a sense of pride in being an Al Saud prince. His English, learned in the kingdom, is fluent, and his incisive speech reflects a mind honed to precision by mastery of arcane details of jurisprudence and yet stretched to include context by exposure to the study of sociology. Regardless of the topic, the prince answers at length, providing both perspective and detail in a dignified, lecturing tone, as if addressing a class, not an individual alongside him. There is a formality about everything he does or says that makes it impossible to visualize him relaxed in front of a television screen doing something as frivolous as cheering for a football team—and certainly not an American one.

His mind is on serious issues like the future of Islam, not just in Saudi Arabia but throughout the Middle East. The whole region has been in decline for four hundred years, he says, but it is now beginning to turn around. "Over the next thirty to fifty years," he says, "Islam will challenge democracy as a way to live and practice human rights." The change that results in the region, he says, "won't be democracy with an upgrade but a different system," which he can't yet articulate but is confident will emerge. Even after the revolutions in Tunisia and Egypt, the prince insists democracy will not prevail. "Whoever wins from the revolution in Egypt," he asserts, "it won't be the young people who demonstrated in the streets for democracy." Elections as practiced in the West, he insists, are not permissible under Islam, which forbids promising something you don't have or praising oneself. Certainly, adhering to those two restrictions would shut down most U.S. political campaigns.

The professorial prince makes a point of needing nothing from the West. On a recent business trip to Geneva, Paris, and London, his first trip abroad in a decade, Europe offered nothing he wanted—other than books—that wasn't available at home. "I came home with ninety percent of my money," he says, "and only two boxes of books, not the ten or twelve I anticipated buying."

This is doubtless a commentary both on the prince's modest desires and on the rapid rise of Saudi consumerism. Major Saudi cities now offer all manner of modern consumer products not available a couple of decades ago. Indeed, about all that isn't available in Saudi Arabia these days is entertainment, alcohol, and books that the government considers subversive—meaning most political and religious titles, including the Bible, and almost all books on Saudi Arabia.

Like so many royal princes, Abdul Aziz holds no government position. But he isn't completely without influence, as he teaches young judges judicial governance at the Higher Institute for Judiciary Studies. The kingdom is undertaking a $2 billion overhaul of its judicial system to nearly double the number of judges over a five-year period, to create specialization among judges, and thus to produce a legal system more compatible with international obligations on Saudi Arabia as a member of the World Trade Organization since 2005. (Judicial governance is the study of the laws of religion as they apply to the judiciary.)

In the wake of the September 11, 2001, terrorist attacks on the World Trade Center and the Pentagon, the kingdom has been under pressure to revise its education curriculum to eliminate condemnation of Christians and Jews and also to downplay religious education in favor of knowledge that helps the flood of young Saudis emerging from high schools adapt to a global economy and secure jobs in Saudi Arabia. But Prince Abdul Aziz argues that more, not less, religious education is needed.

"If you say terrorism is bad, you must *show* the terrorist in Islamic law why that is so," he insists. "Ignorance doesn't help anything. In the eighties the government said, 'Don't talk about jihad, stay out of politics.' Now the government says, 'Stay out of religion.' But you must teach Islamic law and religion even more now. Everyone is fighting for the hearts and minds of the young. But they have their own minds. So we have two choices: let them all develop their own religion, or teach them the right religion so when they encounter ideas on the Internet, they can assess them correctly." His conclusion: "The only way to combat extremist ideas of religion is for government to teach the right religion." The right religion, of course, is Salafi, or the pure Islam of the so-called rightly guided caliphs, who led Islam immediately after the Prophet's death fourteen hundred years ago.

That, however, is easier said than done when young Saudis actively using the Internet can select from a range of religious scholars' views at the touch of a keypad. "Yes, the young search the Web," he acknowledges, "so the religious leaders can't wait in a classroom for young people to come and ask them questions. They have to get their views out there. This is the role of government—to support a way of life and put it out there for people to adopt. To be correct, you have to be legal. To be legal, you have to be Islamic. To be Islamic will mean you have to be conservative." And that's that.

Beyond a nimble mind, Abdul Aziz exhibits an intriguing devotion to conservative tradition shared by few other third-generation princes I have met. He seems to enjoy the anachronistic family traditions and is happy to share them. He recounts how a cousin a few days older than he encouraged Prince Abdul Aziz to enter a room first. Abdul Aziz's father, witnessing this break with tradition, quickly corrected the younger men. "I am only fifteen days older than my brother, Ahmed, and I enter in front of him," Prince Sattam told his son. In other words, stick with tradition. Abdul Aziz says his father, Prince Sattam, governor of Riyadh since 2011, kissed the hand of his older half-brother, Prince Salman, who preceded him in that post, each time the two met during the forty years Prince Sattam served as Prince Salman's deputy governor. Similarly, at formal occasions, Prince Sattam understands that his nephew, Prince Saud al Faisal, the kingdom's foreign minister, sits above him because Saud is older. Tradition means predictability, and predictability means that everyone royal or otherwise knows his or her place in society.

The Al Saud's place is to rule, and the people owe them their loyalty. Asked if the populace obeys out of loyalty or necessity, the prince responds with an Islamic juridical answer: "If the ruler is ruling by Islam, even if he got there illegally, he must be obeyed."

THE ASTRONAUT PRINCE

King Abdul Aziz conquered Saudi Arabia riding a camel. Nearly fifty years later, in 1985, his grandson Prince Sultan bin Salman rode into space aboard the U.S. space shuttle *Discovery*, becoming the first Saudi, the first Arab, the first Muslim, and the first prince to travel in space.

This rapid transition from camel to spacecraft illustrates the breathtaking pace of modernization in Saudi Arabia. When Prince Sultan was born in 1956, Riyadh was a poor town of eighty thousand inhabitants. Today the city, governed for nearly fifty years by his father, Prince Salman bin Abdul Aziz, is a sprawling metropolis of 5 million people with traffic jams, two towering skyscrapers, shopping malls, spas, health clubs, and of course, those Western icons, McDonald's, Kentucky Fried Chicken, and Dunkin' Donuts.

Prince Sultan is the eldest son of a father widely seen as a future king of Saudi Arabia if only because, at seventy-four years of age and in relatively good health, he is expected to outlive his older full brother, Crown Prince Nayef, who is ailing. Prince Sultan, who, having circled the earth, came home to found and lead a Saudi commission on tourism, is a charming, gregarious man thoroughly at ease with Western people and modern ways. And thanks to his role in promoting tourism, he is one of the few Saudis who knows his own country, since most Saudis prefer to stay close to home in their prescribed places inside the Saudi labyrinth or, if they venture out, to travel abroad, where they can take a break from the rigid social and cultural confinement of their country.

Prince Sultan, fifty-six, is seen inside Saudi Arabia as one of the stars of the generation of grandsons. Tall and lanky, he has retained the fitness he achieved as a fighter pilot in the Royal Saudi Air Force that led to his selection as an astronaut.

Some twenty-five years after his historic flight, the prince sits in the large earth-toned living room of his walled compound in Riyadh, remembering the past and outlining the future he seeks for Saudi Arabia. At the time of his selection by NASA as a payload engineer aboard *Discovery,* the kingdom was in the grip of a wave of conservatism, led by its senior religious authority, Sheikh Abdul Aziz bin Abdullah bin Baz, a blind religious scholar who believed the earth was flat because that was how it felt under his feet. When Americans landed on the moon in 1969, Sheikh Bin Baz had issued a fatwa entitled "On the Possibility of Going into Orbit," warning Muslims that they must not believe what infidels said without proof. "We cannot believe anyone who comes and says, 'I was on the moon' without offering solid scientific evidence," he wrote.

Prince Sultan recalls going to see the sheikh for, among other things, advice on fasting during the holy month of Ramadan when he would be in space. The elderly sheikh advised the young prince that he could forgo the fast while in space and make up those days later back on earth. But Prince Sultan decided to fast and pray in space at the required intervals by keeping his watch set to the time in Florida, location of *Discovery*'s launch. Given the speed and frequency with which his space capsule would orbit the earth, he recalls telling the sheikh, "I am seeing sixteen sunrises and sixteen sunsets daily, so is Ramadan over for me in two days?" The religious cleric enjoyed the joke.

Praying was more problematic than fasting. Prostrating in the direction of Mecca proved doubly vexing. The space capsule moved so fast that no sooner could Mecca be located than it was already behind the capsule. Moreover, kneeling in a weightless atmosphere was impossible. So the prince made an accommodation to reality: "I prayed strapped in my seat."

Upon his return, he paid a visit to Sheikh Bin Baz to thank him for his advice on fasting and prayer. The prince says the cleric grilled him about what he saw, and Prince Sultan described the round earth below. "He didn't ask about the shape of the earth," recalls the prince. "I think he already knew by that time that the world is round."

Some twenty-five years later, the prince says the trip into space changed him forever. He recounts what he had said in a speech a few months earlier: "On the first day in space, we all pointed to our countries. The third or fourth day, we all pointed to our continents. By the fifth day, we were only aware of one earth."

Back on this earth, however, things move slowly. The prince's task of developing a tourism industry is hampered by a host of challenges. Most foreigners can't get even get an entry visa, and those who can aren't allowed to visit the kingdom's two primary attractions, the holy cities of Mecca and Medina, unless they are Muslim. In every city, foreigners risk harassment by the omnipresent religious police, unless they adhere to the strict dress and conduct codes imposed by the conservative religious establishment. On top of all that, young Saudis whom the prince hopes to help with new jobs don't want to work in a service industry like tourism. Being the eldest son of a powerful senior prince who may well one day be king hasn't yet helped Prince Sultan overcome any of these obstacles.

Like many grandsons of the founder, Prince Sultan is Western-educated and open-minded but unable to significantly change the conservative, closed-minded habits of the majority of Saudis, especially his powerful, elderly uncles. He insists that the new generation will be different because they are more aware of the world and more comfortable in it; and that terrorism, an export of the kingdom, is a diminishing phenomenon. "There is no doubt that in the struggle we all are living today against terrorism, we as humans will win. Yes, technology is being used for terrorism now. But at the end of the day, the new generation will use technology to know each other, and they will be comfortable with each other all around the world." He points to his five-year-old daughter, noting, "She is much more adaptable than I was at her age."

Indeed, Hala is a self-confident little girl, steeped in both Saudi etiquette and American culture. She bounces into the room wearing pajamas and white fluffy slippers. Immediately, she holds out her hand and touches her cheek to mine several times in a traditional Saudi greeting. "Do you want to know the names of my shoes?" she asks. Without pausing, she answers, "This one is Bugs and this one is Bunny." Sliding down the couch to escape the reach of her father, she continues her chatter. "I'm not four anymore. I'm five—almost six. When I was three or four, I was very shy, but now that I'm five and a half I make friends easily." Her father hugs her and dispatches her to bed.

"We can't continue to live in Saudi Arabia and feel alive only somewhere else," he says, observing that Saudis go abroad to relax rather than spend vacation time in their country. "People need to be able to live in their country and have fun, to love it and enjoy it." That Saudi Arabia, however, still seems a space voyage away.

THE DIPLOMAT PRINCE

Prince Turki al Faisal is not only one of the most recognizable royal princes in the West but also one of the most respected. A grandson of the founder, he is also a son of the late King Faisal, admired by Saudis for his austere lifestyle and his role in launching the process of modernization in the kingdom. King Faisal is probably best known in the West, however, for imposing a crippling oil embargo in the wake of the October 1973 Middle East war and creating long gas lines in the United States.

Prince Turki, sixty-seven, shares the famous Faisal family face—a hawkish, unsmiling visage—so familiar to Saudis, who see photos of the late king hanging in every public building and frequent news photos of his three prominent sons: Prince Khalid, governor of Mecca; Prince Saud, the foreign minister; and Prince Turki, retired from a long career of public service. Turki served as director of intelligence for twenty-four years, followed by appointments as ambassador to Great Britain and then the United States. The prince now is chairman of the King Faisal Center for Research and

Islamic Studies, founded in 1983 to promote expanded dialogue among Muslims, Christians, and Jews.

The prince reportedly is out of favor with King Abdullah for abruptly resigning as ambassador to the United States in December 2006 after only fifteen months in the job. That resignation was prompted by intrafamily intrigue that pitted him against his cousin, brother-in-law, and ambassadorial predecessor, Prince Bandar bin Sultan, who continued to meddle in high-level Washington affairs after being replaced by Prince Turki. Their power struggle to play point man in the all-important U.S.-Saudi relationship was a rare example of internal family infighting becoming public. Such factionalism and friction are not infrequent within this family, but it almost always is camouflaged from public view.

Regardless of the state of the prince's intrafamily relations, these days, with his vast international experience, he is clearly another of the kingdom's wasted assets. With the region in revolution, this wise diplomat spends his time welcoming a succession of foreign academics and policy consultants to the King Faisal Foundation to deliver lectures; traveling to speak to international audiences; writing in prominent global newspapers; and occasionally watching his son Abdul Aziz race Formula One cars.

The prince began his international learning as a fourteen-year-old student at the Lawrenceville School in New Jersey in 1959. He recalls being lonely and wanting to go home for the Christmas holiday break. He wrote his father seeking permission to visit, but the late King Faisal's response wasn't what he hoped. "We miss you too but you are there for an objective," his father wrote. "Patience is required for the best things in life and it won't be long until summer. Tomorrow comes more quickly than you think."

Recalling his father's continual efforts to teach his sons by example, Prince Turki now says, "Fortitude, endurance, and patience: these were my father's example." He acknowledges he has been less austere with his own sons. Upon graduation, the prince ambitiously enrolled in Princeton University, majoring in engineering. The coursework proved too challenging. "When I failed at Princeton, my father said to me, 'I am not going to say you have to finish your education. You have to finish studying for your sake, not mine.'" The chastened prince continued undergraduate studies at Georgetown University, where he washed dishes at Clyde's, a popular Georgetown bar, then pursued additional study in Great Britain and returned to the kingdom to be appointed an adviser in the royal court in 1973. Four years later he replaced his uncle as head of the General Intelligence Directorate, Saudi Arabia's CIA. In that post, the very young prince was instrumental in working with the United States to help funnel Saudi money and U.S. arms to mujahedeen fighters in Afghanistan after the Soviets invaded in 1979.

Prince Turki, like other sons of King Faisal, exudes quiet dignity. At his desk or in public appearances, he wears a *bisht,* the soft flowing cloak atop a man's *thobe,* which gives a more formal look. Indeed, Prince Turki is simultaneously formal yet friendly, conveying warmth with his candor and with eyes that smile even when his face doesn't. He is at ease discussing international politics or Saudi customs and history. All his adult life he has made a special effort to educate the West on his country, his religion, and his family. Given his deep knowledge of both his country and the West, he is adept at explaining them to each other.

Prince Turki insists the kingdom is changing and modernizing—and no longer just from the top down, as when his father imposed television, and education for girls. "In the fifties to the nineties change happened vertically, with the leadership initiating it," he says. "Today change happens both vertically and horizontally, through dialogue, the media, and social networking."

Asked what kind of Saudi Arabia he expects to see a decade from now as a result of these avenues for change, Prince Turki gives a politically correct response: "I hope to see a thriving country that is open to everyone on an equal basis and where meritocracy is the rule." Is this really possible without tensions flaring between moderates and traditionalists? "No society ever progresses without disruptions," he says. "Look at the United States with a civil war, a struggle over civil rights and women's rights. One of the kingdom's accomplishments is that it has so far avoided major upheavals."

And so far it has also avoided any serious change. With revolutionary upheaval all around Saudi Arabia, intractable problems at home, and aged, infirm rulers, maintaining stability now requires more than exploiting differences to divide and conquer. It requires learning how to bridge these deep divides among all Saudi citizens, including youth, women—and even a surplus of sidelined princes.

CHAPTER 8

Failing Grades

For him who embarks on the path of seeking knowledge
Allah will ease for him the way to paradise.

—PROPHET MUHAMMAD

Illiteracy has never shamed Saudis. No less an exemplar
than the Prophet Muhammad could not read or write. For
nearly two decades, the Angel Gabriel spoke Allah's revela-
tions to Muhammad, who repeated them to his followers. As
with Muhammad, hear and repeat is the foundation of all
Saudi education.

To this day, the concept of educational inquiry is barely
nascent in Saudi Arabia. Students from kindergarten through
university for the most part sit in front of teachers whose lectures they repeat back to them like echoes. Small wonder,
then, that schools are just one more tool for constricting and
controlling the minds and lives of Saudis.

Public education in the kingdom did not begin in earnest
until the 1960s. At that time, only 2 percent of Saudi girls
and 22 percent of Saudi boys attended any sort of school. As
a result, even today, it is common for cabinet ministers and
successful businessmen to be the sons of illiterate parents.
Since those days Saudi Arabia has spent hundreds of billions
of dollars on education and today spends a larger share of
gross domestic product on education than does the United
States. Yet the results can only be called catastrophic. In
comparison with students around the world, Saudis repeatedly perform at or near the bottom. Nearly half of the king-

dom's schools are in run-down rented buildings. Native Saudi male teachers in K–12 come from the bottom 15 percent of their university classes. This helps explain why almost half the kingdom's higher education faculty is imported, mostly from other Muslim countries. Better-qualified men choose more lucrative careers, and highly qualified women are not allowed to teach male students. Altogether, in oil-rich Saudi Arabia, good education is one thing money cannot buy.

Saudi Arabia's failed education system matters for reasons that go far beyond wasting good minds. In a country where more than 60 percent of the population is under twenty years of age, the result is a huge pool of uneducated young men who are not qualified for the jobs they seek and a similarly large pool of better-educated young women who are not permitted to take jobs for which they are qualified. As a result, excluding the Saudi military, there are more than twice as many foreigners employed in the kingdom as Saudi citizens. More alarmingly, unemployment among twenty- to twenty-four-year-olds is an astounding 39 percent—45.5 percent for women and 30.3 percent for men. (The official unemployment rate is said to be 10 percent.)

The implications of these sorry statistics aren't just educational and economic—they also involve national security, always the predominant concern of the ruling Al Saud family. These millions of uneducated and undereducated, unemployed and underemployed youth make up the pool within which the extremists trawl for recruits, with their line and lure that the Al Saud are selling out Islam to the West. Sadly, that line did not disappear when Osama bin Laden's body sank into the Arabian Sea.

For all these reasons, education has become a high priority for the regime, with money the least of the obstacles. Education spending has tripled this decade. At 137 billion Saudi riyals ($37 billion) in 2010, it now accounts for more than 25 percent of the country's annual budget. To underscore his determination to reform the kingdom's failing education system, King Abdullah named his nephew and son-in-law, Faisal bin Abdullah, a Stanford University graduate, as the new minister of education in 2009 and appointed the first-ever Saudi woman of ministerial rank, Norah al Faiz, as deputy minister of education. To encourage modernization in higher education, Abdullah ordered construction of the first ever co-ed university, which he placed under the management of Saudi ARAMCO to keep it free of influence from his own moribund Ministry of Higher Education.

All these efforts at reform, however, have simply intensified the battle between traditionalists and modernizers over education. For the religious establishment, controlling education is at least as important as controlling women because education is a key instrument for perpetuating a devout, conservative Islamic society. Most Wahhabi religious leaders see education as simply an extension of religion and want it to consist of mostly Islamic theology and history. Indeed, to some of these religious purists, studying science, foreign languages, or anything about the rest of the world is not merely irrelevant but also distracting and even dangerous, luring Saudi youth to worldly wickedness.

In the West, God is virtually unmentionable in public schools, and in America at least, even perfunctory school prayer is banned. By contrast, in Saudi Arabia all the public schools are religious, and the state mandates daily intensive studies of the Koran, beginning in first grade and consuming roughly half the school day. At the elementary school level, religious studies average a total of nine periods a week, while math, science, geography, history, and physical education combined average only twelve periods a week. In a Western country, a devout family might opt to put its child in a religious school to avoid a purely secular education. In Saudi Arabia, the child of a more secular family that chooses a private school still is required to spend much of the school day studying Islam. Indeed, Saudi educational policy states that one of its objectives is to promote the "belief in the One God, Islam as the way of life, and Muhammad as God's Messenger."

As a result of this educational philosophy, supported by parental and societal pressure, most Saudi students, even university graduates, choose education in soft subjects like religion, sociology, and Islamic history rather than the academic disciplines and practical skills that would equip them to compete in the private sector, where real jobs are available, rather than in the stagnant public sector. Worse yet, most Saudi students emerge even from college or university having learned how to memorize rather than how to think. In Saudi Arabia, religion is not a matter for deliberation and debate, in the classroom or anywhere else. It is Allah's word that must be learned and then lived. Tellingly, the entire subject of philosophy, in which questions would be the core of a curriculum, is banned in Saudi.

Saudi schools weren't always so fundamentalist. Tewfiq al Saif, a businessman in Qatif, contrasts his education in the 1960s, a time of relative relaxation, with the education his son received in the 1990s—and still would receive today. The father recalls his Jordanian-born teacher making him master the Koran, including the prevailing Wahhabi view that Shias (the minority sect in Saudi but the majority in Qatif) are heretics. Because young Tewfiq was a Shia, the Jordanian teacher told him, "Just write it, you don't have to believe it."

When his son attended school a generation later, his Saudi teacher taught that Shias are heretics and ordered the boy to go home and convert his parents to Sunni Wahhabism. Al Saif eventually sent his son abroad for education, but the majority of Saudi families aren't so fortunate. The fact is that all too many Saudi students emerge from school knowing little more than the Koran and believing not only in the tenets of their own religion but also that most of the rest of the world is populated by heretics and infidels who must be shunned, converted, or combatted.

In Saudi Arabia, the religious establishment does not merely exert a powerful influence on education; education is its wholly owned subsidiary. Education began with boys memorizing the Koran with religious scholars. It was not until 1951 that public education (still only for boys) began to be available in what then were big villages like Riyadh and Jeddah, and even then the teachers were mostly religious scholars. Any family seeking a better-rounded education for its sons sent them abroad, primarily to Cairo or Beirut. At that time, Prince Faisal bin Abdul Aziz, who was viceroy of the Hejaz (later King Faisal), was confronted by angry religious leaders, who accused the schools in Jeddah, the largest city of the Hejaz, of teaching magic (chemistry) and atheism (physics). Faisal called the director of education before the religious leaders and asked if he was indeed teaching chemistry and physics. "Yes," he said. "I have to teach those subjects to get students into Cairo and Beirut universities." The wise prince said to the director of education, "Don't teach chemistry. Teach the nature of substances. Don't teach physics. Teach the nature of things." Faisal crossed out the titles on the sheaf of handwritten teaching materials his education director held and wrote in the new ones. The religious leaders departed, pleased with their prince's devotion—and Saudi boys continued to learn chemistry and physics under a new name.

In the 1960s, when Faisal became king, he championed the creation of public schools across the kingdom for boys—and also girls. The largely illiterate nation had few qualified teachers, so the government dispatched emissaries abroad, mostly to Egypt and Jordan, to recruit teachers with substantive skills who also were devout Muslims. A hallmark of King Faisal's reign was an effort to create an Islamic alliance in the Middle East to counter the Arab nationalism of Egypt's president, Gamel Abdel Nasser. When Nasser, a nationalist strongman and sworn enemy of Saudi Arabia, turned on his country's conservative Muslim Brotherhood, King Faisal welcomed those religious conservatives into Saudi Arabia as scholars and teachers, reinforcing the fundamentalist hold on the young Ministry of Education, founded in 1954 under his predecessor and half-brother, King Saud. It's a grip that has yet to be broken.

Throughout the 1980s and 1990s, King Fahd, who served as the kingdom's first minister of education, as we have seen, gave the religious establishment free rein to dictate what went on in educational institutions—and nearly every other aspect of Saudi life. By 1991, when U.S. troops entered Saudi to help evict Saddam Hussein from Kuwait, the beehive of fanatics bred during the preceding decade turned on the royal family—and on the religious establishment that supported the Al Saud. These radical Islamic critics saw the established religious scholars as tools of the Al Saud and the Al Saud as lackeys of the American infidels. In short, King Fahd (and the royal family) was hoist on his own petard.

The rulers imprisoned some of their critics and bought off others, believing they had suppressed extremists, but in reality these radical religious fundamentalists simply went underground, only to erupt with deadly attacks on the United States on September 11, 2001, and, of much more direct concern to the Al Saud, bombings and other terrorist attacks inside Saudi Arabia in 2003.

Belatedly awakened to terrorism's threat, the royal family in recent years seriously has sought to combat extremism to protect itself. Curbing extremism, they realize, requires changing the educational system both to teach a more tolerant version of Islam and to prepare Saudi youth to qualify for jobs. Even the king, however, has found it hard to institute reforms that significantly challenge the entrenched religious-educational bureaucracy.

"Invading a country is easier than changing educational curriculum," the late Ghazi al Gosaibi, a confidant of King Abdullah, quipped when asked why the king couldn't make more progress with his education reform agenda. Gosaibi, a poet and novelist whose day job for nearly forty years included various ministerial and ambassadorial posts, was an outspoken intellectual almost always out of step with the kingdom's religious conservatives. His books, often critical of regimes in the region and the lack of freedoms in Saudi, were banned in that country until just a few weeks before his clearly impending death from cancer in 2010. "I always referred to Abdullah as the 'loyal opposition,'" he once told me, "because in the eighties Abdullah wrote a long memo to the king describing how poor Saudi education was."

Abdullah finally got his chance to try to reform education

once he became king in 2005. He announced a 9-billion-Saudi-riyal ($2.4 billion) project to transform the way the kingdom's 5.5 million students are taught. This so-called *tatweer*, or reform project, was set up outside the educational bureaucracy. Some fifty boys' and a like number of girls' schools were selected to serve as models. Teachers were sent to retraining to help them abandon memorization methods in favor of teaching students critical thinking aimed at solving problems.

To get an idea of what, if anything is changing, I visit a *tatweer* school in Buraidah, a town in central Arabia so conservative that parents there protested the introduction of girls' schools in the 1960s. In the 1980s, Buraidah still was so insular I was not permitted to visit; religious fundamentalism was ascendant there and across the kingdom. Even now my translator and I are met at the guarded checkpoint to the city and followed in marked cars by agents of the Ministry of Interior and the Ministry of Education to "assure our security"—and keep track of our movements.

At the school, a group of young Saudi women dressed in native costumes is singing the national anthem. This in itself is a bit of a reform, because Wahhabi religious scholars object to any celebration of nationalism as being in conflict with their view that believers belong only to the *umma*, or community of believers, which transcends borders and polities. (In an effort to build national identity among Saudis, King Abdullah has insisted on celebrating the kingdom's founding on September 23, 1932, with a national holiday, even though religious leaders oppose any holiday other than celebrations marking the end of Ramadan and Hajj.)

This token innovation, followed by readings from the Koran, sadly is paralleled in the classroom. While teachers point proudly to their new electronic "smart boards," most, on this day at least, are using them only as props, not for pedagogy. Indeed, as far as I can see from visiting half a dozen classrooms, education, notwithstanding expensive new gadgetry, still consists largely of the old memorization—hear and repeat. The educational process seems as ritualized as the ceremonial tea and dates graciously offered by the school principal.

A second *tatweer* model school in Riyadh is somewhat more promising. Tatweer 48, located near King Saud University, is attended by the upper-class offspring of university professors. Principal Moddi Saleh al Salem proudly observes that this is the only *tatweer* girls' school in Riyadh. The girls, all dressed uniformly in gray floor-length jumpers and gray-and-white-striped blouses, are a world apart from the reticent young women in Buraidah. There the English teacher read her class a word from the text, and in unison the girls repeated it. Here, in a tenth-grade English class, girls are asked to come to the front of the class in teams of four to present clever video scripts they have written and produced to supplement a chapter in their text on how to order in a restaurant. Each team of girls is composed, confident, and at ease presenting to a classroom of forty fellow students plus their school principal, Al Salem.

One particularly lively foursome discusses how to set the table. As their chosen narrator describes how to lay the plates, silverware, and glasses, her narration is illustrated on a screen behind her by a video that her group created with pictures pulled from the Internet. "If you are serving more than one wine," the narrator continues reading from her script, "start the glasses from the right. Just remember L E R D—left for eating and right for drinking." The teacher glances toward me, clearly chagrined that a visitor should hear her students discussing how to serve forbidden alcohol, yet she can't hide her obvious pride in the quality of their spoken English, which, after all, is what she is responsible for teaching.

Under the umbrella of reform, the kingdom also has begun an even more controversial revamp of curricula to enhance math and science and to curb extremism in religious teaching. A committee that included government-selected religious scholars rewrote religion textbooks at government behest to encourage more tolerance of other religions, or at least to curtail teaching of intolerance against Christians, Jews, and Shia Muslims. For instance, the new religion textbook recounts how the Prophet visited a sick Jewish neighbor even though that man had thrown garbage at the Prophet's front door. The new textbooks, which will be introduced into all Saudi schools by 2013, also define *jihad* as something only the ruler can declare rather than as an obligation on every Muslim, as asserted by Al Qaeda and fundamentalist religious scholars who support it.

Predictably, conservatives accuse the Ministry of Education of kowtowing to the West and undermining Islam, while modernizers see the textbook changes and the three extra hours of math and science a week as window dressing, completely inadequate to improve students' preparation for the job market or to prepare them to practice a more tolerant Islam. Moreover, whatever the changes in curricula and texts, teachers are largely the same religious conservatives and are free to say what they will in a classroom.

"When you close the door, the teacher can always put the book aside and talk," acknowledges Dr. Naif H. al Romi, deputy minister of educational planning and development, who helped lead the curriculum reform. "But that is true everywhere, not just in Saudi. With thirty thousand schools and half a million teachers, it is very hard to change a system quickly." By contrast, in the tiny adjacent Gulf state of Qatar, which modernizers often cite as an education model, there are only two hundred schools.

It is all too common for students to correct their parents' religious habits based on lessons learned at school. One father complains that his daughters tell him he isn't allowed to pray at home but only in a mosque. So says their teacher. Similarly, the teacher, aware that these preteen girls have a male Arabic tutor at home, tells the girls they are too old at ten and eleven to be alone with an unrelated male. A female professor at King Saud University, who wears a scarf but not a face veil, complains that her daughter's teachers have turned her into a one-girl Gestapo on the necessity of her mother's veiling whenever she leaves her house. Realizing that even modest reform of Saudi education will take at least a generation, King Abdullah has sought to shortcut the process. In 2006 he began offering scholarships to male—and more surprisingly, female—students to go abroad for university studies. While Saudis came to the United States in the 1960s and 1970s for university education, in the 1980s and 1990s the government, responding to the dictates of religious conservatives, stopped providing scholarships to study abroad and reduced sharply (from 10,000 in 1984 to 5,000 by 1990) the number of Saudis who could get an education outside the kingdom. After September 11, that number shrank still further (2,500 in 2003), as visas dried up and Saudis feared going abroad. Determined to reverse that trend, King Abdullah launched his scholarship program, which in 2011 funded more than one hundred thousand Saudi students studying in the United States, Europe, and Asia. Almost all are expected to return home, creating a new cadre of educated Saudis. Whether they become a force for change upon their return, or don the mental blinkers of tradition along with their *abayas* and *thobes*, remains to be seen.

To try to jump-start reform in higher education at home, the king established the King Abdullah University of Science and Technology, KAUST, at a cost of 10 billion Saudi riyals (nearly $4 billion), the country's first co-ed university, created from scratch in only three years. With Saudi ARAMCO, the kingdom's most efficient institution, in charge, the pristine new university opened on schedule in September 2009 with some six hundred students from around the world, including Saudis of both sexes. The founding president is Choon Fong Shih, a Singaporean and the only non-Muslim university president in the kingdom. Dr. Shih, a world expert in non-linear fracture mechanics, earned his doctorate at Harvard and taught at Brown University.

A non-Muslim president and the mixing of men and women are remarkable innovations for Saudi Arabia. Equally jarring is the juxtaposition on campus of a mosque alongside a movie theater (the only cinema in the kingdom outside those on Saudi ARAMCO property). On campus, most students are dressed in modest Western attire. The Saudi women on campus, however, wear long black *abayas,* albeit without veils covering their faces. All the students receive full scholarships and pursue graduate studies in science with state-of-the-art laboratory facilities.

"Throughout history, power has attached itself, after God, to science," the king said at opening ceremonies for the new university, some eighty kilometers outside Jeddah." Humanity has been the target of vicious attacks from extremists, who speak the language of hatred, fear dialogue, and pursue destruction," he added. "We cannot fight them unless we learn to coexist without conflict—with love instead of hatred and with friendship instead of confrontation. Undoubtedly, scientific centers that embrace all peoples are the first line of defense against extremists." It might have been Barack Obama or David Cameron speaking.

Notwithstanding the king's noble sentiments, it took a tense confrontation with religious conservatives and the sacking of a prominent sheikh to protect the king's "dream of more than twenty-five years." While his intercession on KAUST was at least a small victory for reform, the king cannot intervene in every issue in every school and so, day in and day out, the religious-educational bureaucracy remains largely impervious to reform. Whether the issue is who teaches or from what textbooks, what makes up the curriculum or what actually is taught in the classroom, reform still exists more on paper than in practice. By one estimate, fully 70 percent of the three thousand supervisors who directly oversee public schools around the kingdom are conservative Salafis, a more politically correct term for Wahhabis, whose priority is not educational reform but religious orthodoxy. Even at the university level, where reforms began and where reform arguably should be easiest, the obstacles are many and the results few.

"There is no critical thinking even in university," says one political science professor at King Saud University in Riyadh. "Students just memorize and repeat. All they want is a diploma and a job in government. They don't care about their country or about the Arabs or about freedom." A sociology professor at the same university similarly laments the lack of curiosity among students. "Students aren't curious; they don't read so they have no background or knowledge with which to discuss issues," he says. "I asked my students after the earthquake in Haiti where is Haiti. Most guessed Africa."

Some Western students might make the same mistake, but what these Saudi professors really are fighting is the result of the years of mindless memorization among students and, more broadly, the intellectual inertia of a conformist society that values neither curiosity nor independent thinking. Many books are banned, libraries often are locked, and at any rate volumes are not permitted to be taken home from most of them.

There also are physical restraints to reform. The regime is seeking to make up for decades of neglect by funding the construction of more than 1,200 new schools across the kingdom in 2010 and completing construction of another 3,100 already under way. The funds are available, but ironically, given the vast size of this country, the land often is not. In or around population centers, much of the open land is owned by various princes or a few wealthy families who are holding it for future development and profit. So in many cases there literally is no available land on which to build a school. One might think royal princes would donate land or that the regime that gave it to them might demand some of it back. So far, neither has been the case.

On a visit to Hail, a poor province, King Abdullah is reliably said to have been told by the provincial governor, one of his nephews, that there was no available land on which to build public facilities. The king, surveying a vista that included much open land, asked who owned it all. The answer: the defense ministry, a decorous way of saying the land was owned by the then minister of defense and royal half-brother, the late Crown Prince Sultan. The next day, by prearrangement, the governor, this time in the presence of both King Abdullah and Prince Sultan, again raised the issue of land to develop his poor province. King Abdullah coyly inquired, "Who owns all this land?" Prince Sultan, put on the spot, responded to the king that the land was "all yours" to dispose of. So Abdullah graciously accepted, and the governor got his land. Again, it is a nice example of what happens when the king personally intercedes, but by definition it is a rarity in a regime where even the king has to balance his priorities with those of his powerful half-brothers and their sons.

If reforming education in general faces multiple obstacles, educating girls should logically face even more. Yet here arguably more progress has been made than in any other area of Saudi educational reform. In 2002 religious police infamously allowed fourteen middle school girls to burn to death inside their Mecca school just after classes began one morning. The girls who tried to flee the burning school were forced back inside by the religious police because the girls were not fully covered in *abayas* and veils.

The national outrage that followed gave Abdullah the opportunity to remove girls' schools from the supervision of religious authorities and put them under the Ministry of Education, which already controlled boys' schools. Girls' schools, at their creation in the 1960s, had been put under the control of the General Presidency for Girls' Education, an autonomous government agency controlled by conservative clerics, as a compromise to calm public opposition to allowing (not requiring) girls to attend school. Now a new wave of public criticism emboldened Abdullah to reverse that decision, yet another instance of the Al Saud bending back and forth with prevailing winds.

Change of control, while progress, doesn't necessarily mean substantive change. For example, in many girls' schools, particularly those in rented buildings, safety inspectors—who invariably are male—are not permitted to enter the schools at any time the girls are present to inspect or enforce safety standards. Moreover, female students, much like medieval nuns, are locked inside their schools, and access is controlled by elderly male guards outside the high walls that surround all schools. The girls arrive in the morning and enter the school through a narrow portal, which then is locked behind them. When school is over, the door is unlocked, to allow the girls to be picked up by drivers or parents. At one such school I was conducted inside in the company of several senior women administrators of education for a tour. At the conclusion of the visit, the group knocked on the locked door to leave, and no one responded. The male caretaker had left his post. Phone calls finally produced him a few minutes later, but had there been an emergency inside, the students would have been trapped until either the female principal inside or the male guard outside unlocked the door. The tendency of elderly guards to wander off on personal errands during school hours has led some parents to propose that schools be safeguarded instead by professional security companies, but so far tradition prevails.

Despite all the limitations and the continued segregation, there are areas of small progress for young women. Women's education clearly is better off under the control of even a religiously dominated Ministry of Education than under the direct control of religious authorities. The appointment of Norah al Faiz to head women's education is a significant step, even if she is proceeding cautiously.

There are some outposts of outstanding education in the kingdom. Ahliyya School in Dhahran, founded in 1977 by Khalid al Turki, a successful businessman, and his Ohio-born American wife, Sally, is one. A private K–12 school, Ahliyya, with tuition of $6,500 a year, attracts mostly well-off students. Most of the girls are daughters of Saudi ARAMCO employees. During a visit with twenty senior class students, the most articulate and impressive women I encountered on visits to a dozen schools and universities in the kingdom, all said they had traveled to the United States, some 80 percent had visited European countries and 30 percent had visited Asian countries beyond Saudi Arabia. All intended to have careers and children simultaneously. Their teachers spend five weeks each year being trained in the latest methods to stimulate students to learn, not just recite. The girls have been taken abroad to compete with other international students in a Model United Nations debate, something unheard of for public school students. "The fact we wear long black robes doesn't mean we can't think," says one young woman. "Things are changing fast," she adds. "Five years ago my parents said I could never go to the United States to university. Two years ago they said maybe I could go with my brother. This year they said I could go alone." Why the change? "Society has changed to accept more things for women," she says matter-of-factly. And in her little corner of Saudi society, it has.

Another sign of progress: even a few law schools have opened for women in recent years. Although females still are not permitted to appear in court as lawyers, dozens of girls flocked to Riyadh's Prince Sultan University law school when it opened in 2006. Maha Fozan, a freshman in this first group of law students, enthusiastically predicted in 2007 that by the time she graduated, women would be allowed to practice before a judge, not simply prepare legal arguments for their male colleagues to present. "The time has come. Society needs women lawyers. King Abdullah is behind us, so things will change," she insisted with youthful certitude.

Sure enough, in this case optimism seems not to have been entirely misplaced. In late 2009, Maha, the articulate young woman whose confidence had visibly grown in the intervening years of her law studies, said emphatically, "I am going to have a career in law just like I planned." Indeed, the minister of justice, another new appointee of King Abdullah, says he is evaluating a regulation to allow women to represent female clients before the kingdom's male-only Sharia judges. The minister, Muhammad Abdul Kareem al Eisa, forty-six, not only agrees to meet me but also expresses support for the idea of women lawyers in courts. "A woman is allowed to speak in court and represent a woman now, but she isn't yet licensed as a professional lawyer," he says. "This is now under study, and I hope it will be completed and women will soon be licensed as professional lawyers." Nothing happens quickly in Saudi Arabia, surely nothing as fundamental as changes to a judicial system under complete control of the religious establishment. In 2012 a Justice Ministry directive allowed female lawyers to be licensed but practice in court remained elusive.

Some other career opportunities also are opening these days for educated women, who traditionally have been limited to the fields of education (teaching only girls) or medicine (treating mostly women). A sprinkling of female university graduates now can be found in business, interior design, computer technology, and marketing, though these women represent only a token presence in overwhelmingly male workplaces. If a glass ceiling still limits career women in the West, concrete walls still block most in Saudi Arabia.

Saudi Arabia remains an almost entirely segregated society where men and women don't mix at the water fountain—or almost anywhere else—so job opportunities remain restricted. For example, a young woman university graduate is offered a position in a small interior decorating firm that employs two men and one woman working in adjacent but separate offices. The young woman's mother expresses fear that if her daughter takes the job and joins the other young woman in the female section, at some point the men and women will encounter each other in their work, and that encounter will be glimpsed by one of the omnipresent religious police, who then could arrest the young people for immoral mixing. "This will ruin my daughter's reputation even though she is doing nothing wrong," the woman frets. "I don't want her to risk her life for this job."

Such concerns are common to all women in the society, however well educated they may be. Only in the rarest of workplaces, such as the offices of multinational firms, can women function alongside men, and even at these offices there are occasional raids by religious police. The one institution exempt from all these conventions and restrictions is Saudi ARAMCO, which since its founding has operated as an innovative and international island in the largely stagnant Saudi sea. KAUST is now a second island. The government has made it clear that these islands—like foreign embassies in Saudi Arabia—are off limits to the religious police.

Whatever educational problems exist now, the government is going to have to run fast just to stand still, given the geyser of young people erupting from Saudi schools. The kingdom's 5.5 million students will increase 20 percent to 6.2 million by 2022. At present, some 140,000 young men (and a similar number of young women) graduate from high school each year, but fewer than half gain admission to a Saudi university—even though between 2002 and 2006 the kingdom opened sixteen new universities, bringing the total to twenty-four public universities. The Princess Nora University, a massive campus for fifty thousand women, opened in 2011, making twenty-five. Private universities, located primarily in major cities, jumped from one to eight.

Of course quantity alone is not sufficient to meet the country's need to train graduates for jobs in a global knowledge economy. "Families put kids on a track to get grades, not to develop as individuals," says Dr. Muhammad al Ohali, deputy minister of educational affairs in the Ministry of Higher Education and the man in charge of crafting Saudi higher education reform plans for the next twenty years. "Knowledge these days expires quickly, so we have to find a way to set the fire in students to want to learn." Prince Faisal bin Abdullah, minister of education and King Abdullah's son-in-law, adds, "The king's message is that oil is not our first wealth. Education is. We have to develop the people now."

Easier said than done. Stephane Lacroix, a Saudi expert at the Institute of Political Studies in Paris, sums up the battle over education in Saudi Arabia: "The education system is so controlled by the Muslim Brotherhood, it will take twenty years to change—if at all. Islamists see education as their base so they won't compromise on this." As with the struggle over women's role in society, the tug-of-war over education continues, with the religious still pulling the greater weight.

CHAPTER 9

Plans, Paralysis, and Poverty

Be not like the hypocrite who, when he talks, tells lies;
when he makes a promise, he breaks it; and when he is
trusted, he proves dishonest.

—PROPHET MUHAMMAD, SAHIH BUKHARI,
VOL. I, BK. 2, NO. 32

Land at any Saudi airport and proceed to baggage claim.
The men offering to handle your luggage are from Bangladesh, India, or Pakistan. Exit the airport for a taxi, and
your driver almost surely is Pakistani. Arrive at your hotel, and
the guard who performs the obligatory security check on the
taxi's trunk is probably from Yemen. The doorman who greets
you is Pakistani, and the smiling men behind the check-in
desk are Lebanese. The waiter offering coffee in the lobby is
Filipino, as are many of the men who will clean your room.
So you have been in Saudi Arabia for more than an hour and,
except at passport control, have yet to encounter a Saudi.

One of every three people in Saudi Arabia is a foreigner.
Two out of every three people with a job of any sort are foreign. And in Saudi Arabia's anemic private sector, fully nine
out of ten people holding jobs are non-Saudi. To the extent
that there is enterprise in the kingdom, it is almost entirely
imported.

Visit any middle-class Saudi home, and you are likely to
see one or more young men of the family, some educated
and some not, hanging around, with little prospect and often
little interest in finding a job. Second, you are even more

likely to see a number of young women of the family, almost surely better educated and more ambitious, who are unable to enter a workforce that offers them precious few opportunities. Third, the family is likely to employ one or more foreigners to do much of the work within the household and to provide almost every service required in daily life, from a ride in a taxi, to tutoring for children, to shopping at a department store.

Saudi Arabia, in short, is a society in which all too many men do not want to work at jobs for which they are qualified; in which women by and large aren't allowed to work; and in which, as a result, most of the work is done by foreigners—Pakistanis, Indians, Filipinos, Bangladeshis, and others—who compose the a majority of the labor force. Most of these 8.5 million foreigners are treated as second-class citizens; their lives are controlled by a sponsoring employer, who must give permission for them to change employment. Essentially they are indentured servants for the period of their contracts.

On the surface, the entire kingdom functions like a grand hotel. Saudi citizens check in at birth, remain isolated in their rooms, take little pride in caring for their surroundings, and merely demand the services provided by the hotel's foreign employees, who are paid pitifully low salaries from the government's bountiful oil revenue. After all, one in every four barrels of oil sold on the world market comes from Saudi Arabia. In 2011, thanks primarily to huge oil revenues, the kingdom's GDP totaled $560 billion, ranking Saudi Arabia number twenty-four among world economies. But this is misleading. Try as it might, with multiple five-year plans over the past thirty years, the kingdom has failed to diversify its economy beyond oil, which creates few jobs for the ever-expanding slick of young Saudis. As a result, on a per capita income basis, the country ranks number fifty-five, between the Seychelles and Barbados. So over the past thirty years, the five-star Saudi hotel has deteriorated into something more like Motel 6 for most Saudi citizens, while royals and some elite business families continue to enjoy a penthouse lifestyle.

Looking forward, the single healthy dimension of the Saudi economy—oil—cannot be counted on to fuel economic growth far into the future. Oil will continue to gush for some years to come, of course, but Saudi reserves are steadily being depleted, and no significant new discoveries have been found to replace them. Some energy experts are convinced that current reserves are substantially lower than those officially claimed by the Saudis and that the depletion rate is substantially faster. Beyond that, domestic consumption of oil is rising rapidly, reducing the amount the kingdom will have to export for revenue in future years.

Indeed, declining oil for export and rising domestic spending to maintain political stability mean the kingdom's expenditures will exceed its oil revenues as soon as 2014, say experts at Jadwa Investment, a large financial institution in Riyadh. "By 2030, foreign assets will be drawn down to minimal levels and debt will be rising rapidly," these experts predict, unless the kingdom takes decisive steps to reverse the trend of domestic consumption and spending, which are outpacing oil production for export. As a result, the Saudi regime is under ever more pressure to diversify the economy while it still has time and while oil revenues still are there, to invest in other sources of long-term economic growth. The fading of the finite resource has broader implications for Saudi Arabia's relationship with the United States, as we shall see in chapter 15.

Oil is one Saudi addiction; imported labor is the other. This dependence on foreign workers is the most glaring current symptom of a dysfunctional Saudi economy. The effects are widespread unemployment among young Saudis and all-too-pervasive poverty. Not only is unemployment among young Saudis fully 40 percent, but 40 percent of all Saudi citizens live on less than 3,000 Saudi riyals ($850) a month. Those twin sad statistics, all the more glaring in a society that flaunts so much wealth, are precisely the sort that led to protests and revolutions across much of the Arab world in 2011. In Saudi Arabia, a nervous regime reacted in its usual fashion by doling out hundreds of billions of riyals in new handouts to every sector of society, from the military and religious establishments to students, the unemployed, and the poor. While the king's new spasm of welfare spending may have bought time, it did nothing to alter the structural causes of unemployment, poverty, and declining standards of living for the Saudi middle class.

Quite the opposite. The king's decision to institute a minimum wage for government jobs, offer two-month bonuses to government workers, and create an additional 126,000 government jobs (60,000 to beef up security forces and another 66,000 for teachers and health diploma holders) will together give young Saudis even less incentive to prepare and compete for productive jobs in the private sector. With this latest largesse, public expenditures have tripled since 2004, while the private sector's contribution to non-oil GDP has stagnated. Until productivity increases in the private sector, per capita income in Saudi Arabia will continue to lag, holding down the standard of living for most Saudis. Indeed, adjusted for inflation, real per capita income has been stagnant since the middle of the 1980s at roughly $8,550.

High birthrates, poor education, a male aversion to manual labor or service roles, social strictures against women working, low wages accepted by foreign labor, and deep structural rigidities in the economy, compounded by pervasive corruption, all have led to a decline in living standards and to the toxic and intransigent unemployment problem among young Saudis. Many of these young feel their future is being stolen from them, that their lives will not be as prosperous as those of their parents.

Imported labor in itself is not a sign of economic sickness. A full-employment economy that imports labor to further spur productivity and growth—a Singapore, for example—benefits both its own citizens and the expatriates it employs. In Saudi Arabia, it is the opposite. An unproductive economy with widespread unemployment is importing labor to perform functions that its own citizens are neither educated nor enterprising enough to perform. Even the minister of labor acknowledges that Saudis aren't qualified for the jobs they want and refuse the jobs for which they are qualified. So while the private sector created some 2.2 million jobs between 2005 and 2009, only 9 percent of those went to Saudis, who prefer the short hours and job security of government employment, which all too often is unproductive and therefore a drag on the economy.

Over the past decade, the government has announced one plan after another to "Saudize" the economy, but to no avail. The foreign workforce grows, and so does unemployment among Saudis. Once again the latest five-year plan calls for reducing unemployment among Saudis to 5.5 percent by 2014, but almost certainly that goal will not be achieved. The previous plan called for slashing unemployment to 2.8 percent only to see it rise to 10.5 percent in 2009, the end of that plan period. Government plans in Saudi are like those in the old Soviet Union, grandiose but unmet. (Also, as in the old Soviet Union, nearly all Saudi official statistics are unreliable, so economists believe the real Saudi unemployment rate is closer to 40 percent.)

The net effect is a society that, however tranquil on the surface, seethes with discontent. The unhappiness is not confined to unemployed young men or to subjugated women but extends broadly across the Saudi middle class who, however divided by region, tribe, or religiosity, share a common frustration with economic stagnation, the declining standard of living, and lack of opportunity for their children. Even traditional Saudis reared in an environment of acquiescence and obedience are increasingly cynical about the pillars of Saudi stability, the Al Saud and its religious establishment. At best they view them as out of touch with the plight of normal people; at worst they see them as self-serving and corrupt.

In any Western democracy, such broad social discontent would be reflected first in public opinion polls showing the leadership with, say, only 30 percent public approval, and then in elections that would result in changes in leadership. In Saudi Arabia, there are no reliable opinion polls, and there is no way of replacing leaders. So society seethes, the Al Saud tinker, and little changes as the one-dimensional Saudi economy continues to stagnate rather than evolve into a more diversified and productive one.

Sadly, it is fair to ask whether this is the way the Al Saud regime prefers it. A modern and diversified economy would have to be accompanied by a much more open, enterprising, and diverse society, one over which the Al Saud and the religious establishment inevitably would have fewer levers of control. Since the days when Abdul Aziz dispensed clothes and food to those who came to his palace, keeping people dependent on the royal family has been a tenet of Al Saud rule. To the ruling family, political control trumps economic competitiveness. But decades of rapid population growth, coupled with the people's near-total dependence on government largesse, have smothered enterprise and left the Saudi economy unproductive and uncompetitive. Now, as in the days of King Abdul Aziz, the Saudi rulers claim to offer security and prosperity in exchange for political obedience and social conformity. These days, however, both ends of the tether binding Al Saud and Saudis are fraying.

Yes, in recent years the Chinese Communist Party has succeeded in unleashing enormous enterprise and global economic competitiveness while retaining ultimate political control. The Al Saud, however, are neither as confident nor as competent as China's rulers, and Saudis are not nearly as enterprising as Chinese. While the long-impoverished Chinese people were hungry enough to sacrifice to build a modern economy, the largely government-supported Saudis have been listless enough to expect one to be delivered to them. So, sadly, the more apt comparison is to the old Soviet regime, where decrepit leaders presided over a dysfunctional economy and an increasingly sullen society until the country's collapse in 1991.

One may well wonder why a country with oil revenues in nominal dollars that ranged from $39 billion in 1978 to $285 billion in 2008 (down to $215.3 billion in 2010, when prices fell from 2008's historic highs) couldn't over three decades create an economy that functions at or near full employment. The ironic answer is that oil wealth actually has inhibited economic development. Given its plentiful oil revenues, the kingdom hasn't, at least until very recently, seriously focused on becoming competitive in any other economic sphere.

Every five-year plan since the first one in 1970 has called for diversifying the economy beyond oil, but oil is still supreme. "At least 85 to 90 percent of treasury still is oil or oil related," says Khalid al Falih, the Saudi Arabian CEO of Saudi ARAMCO.

Nearly 60 percent of Saudi gross domestic product is generated by a monopolistic public sector that includes government-owned entities such as Saudi ARAMCO, Saudi Arabia Basic Industries Corp. (SABIC), and the Royal Commission at Jubail and Yanbu, which dominate the petrochemical industry. Even today manufacturing accounts for only about 10 percent of Saudi GDP, and 65 percent of that is petrochemicals, which are competitive in world markets thanks largely to cheap Saudi oil and gas feedstocks.

In Western countries, wealth is generated by the private sector and taxed by government. In Saudi Arabia, wealth is generated by government-owned industries (largely Saudi ARAMCO) and flows to the private sector, which depends on government for contracts and subsidies to sustain its production. Because the regime prefers mammoth government projects, private capital can find little in which to invest productively. So while precise numbers are not available, most experts believe a majority of Saudi private investment is parked abroad.

The megaprojects that the government favors and funds almost invariably suffer from long delays and large cost overruns. A 2011 survey of three hundred project managers and supervisors found that 97 percent of government projects are not completed on time, and a staggering 80 percent of them exceed budget. "The most dangerous aspect of the matter is that most of the project supervisors, who are government officials, do not find any fault with the delay and do not have to worry about the immensity of such a national waste," says Turki al Turki, an expert in development and management of projects, who conducted the survey.

One such project, King Abdullah's much-ballyhooed (as the world's largest women's university) new Princess Nora University near Riyadh, was budgeted at 6 billion Saudi riyals and wound up costing nearly 30 billion, according to a knowledgeable Al Saud prince. *Arab News,* the kingdom's major English-language daily, reported that the university was budgeted to cost 15 billion Saudi riyals ($4 billion) when construction began in October 2008, but it actually had cost 20 billion ($5.3 billion) by the time it opened in May 2011, a 33 percent cost overrun in just over two years. Whatever the precise numbers, not surprisingly, Saudi citizens are angered at the enormous scale of such government waste of the public patrimony.

To transform this subsidized economy into a productive one that creates jobs, the government will have to allow a more competitive industrial base to develop that leverages both foreign technology and investment. Despite a lot of rhetoric about developing a "knowledge" economy, little has been achieved. One sad snapshot of Saudi competitiveness: the number of Saudi patents registered in the United States between 1977 and 2010 was a grand total of 382, compared to 84,840 from South Korea and 20,620 from Israel. (But thanks to Saudi ARAMCO, the originator of most of the Saudi patents, the kingdom is far and away the largest patent holder among Arab countries.)

The kingdom now has yet another plan—its ninth formal five-year plan—to diversify beyond oil and boost job creation. The plan is called Vision 2020 and aims to double the size of Saudi Arabia's manufacturing sector to 20 percent of GDP. "We want to move from inherited wealth—oil—to acquired or created wealth," says Dr. Khalid al Sulaiman, deputy minister of commerce and industry, who was in charge of the latest plan. (He resigned that post in June 2010 to become vice president for renewable energy at the King Abdullah City for Atomic and Renewable Energy.) The plan acknowledges that the kingdom must make progress on many fronts at once, including reducing government red tape that hinders the start-up or expansion of businesses.

Just lending more money to start new businesses won't be enough unless the kingdom finds a way to spur innovation and technological competitiveness. While the government in the 1970s was successful in creating giant petrochemical industries because of cheap oil and gas feedstocks and because it could provide the huge capital needed to launch such an industry, what is needed these days is not just capital but technological innovation, entrepreneurial spirit, and creative minds, all three in short supply in Saudi Arabia.

If planning equaled progress, Saudi Arabia would already be an economic dynamo. In addition to the new Industrial Development Strategy, or Vision 2020, it has developed a new five-year National Science and Technology Innovation Plan, backed by $2.2 billion, to encourage innovation. A Higher Education Plan, or Horizons, is working its way through the government approval process to reform university education to produce graduates who are not simply unquestioning robots but rather inquiring and innovative entrepreneurs. The Saudi leaders of these three plans are as impressive and dedicated as any country could muster. All three hold doctorates from U.S. universities and exude commitment to their plans' goals. But the chasm between planners and people remains deep and wide.

Beyond government plans and projects, Saudi Arabia has a private sector where a handful of big business names like Bin Laden, Olayan, Zamil, Mahfouz, and Al Rajhi dominate the service sector. This sector is led by construction and real estate, both heavily dependent on government spending, which again is dependent on oil revenues. Most of these big-business families, whose fortunes were made largely through connections to the Al Saud, have diversified their holdings beyond the kingdom so their personal wealth is no longer as heavily dependent on government contracts.

If proximity to government—or more crassly, payola to princes—once ensured wealth, scarce managerial talent now determines the fate of large Saudi businesses, which increasingly must compete in a global economy to survive. This puts a premium on hiring and retaining qualified human talent. Indeed, government, once the driver of economic growth, now is seen by most Saudi businessmen as a roadblock to growth because of its glacial decision making and endless red tape.

For at least the past five years, government and business have engaged in a tense tug-of-war over who is to blame for rising youth unemployment. Private-sector businesses employ roughly nine expats for every one Saudi. The government's mandated "Saudization" of businesses has set annual goals for hiring Saudis in various economic sectors. Because government controls visas, it technically can deny Saudi businesses a new supply of expatriate labor. Yet in 2009 the government issued nearly one million visas, double the number issued in 2005, bowing to business pressure at the expense of Saudi employment. For their part, many businesses complain they can't invest to grow the economy without qualified labor, and Saudi labor all too often isn't properly trained or committed to a strong work ethic. Training new hires on the job, businessmen argue, reduces a company's productivity, raises costs, and thus hampers international competitiveness.

This "Saudization" campaign has become yet another government roadblock that businessmen seek to circumvent by bargaining for expat visas with officials who control visa approval—or simply by buying them from corrupt officials, princes, or other businessmen who acquire visas for ghost workers and sell them to the highest bidder. For instance, a business procures more visas than it needs for a project, then sells the surplus to other businesses in need of quick labor or to individuals who want to bring a relative to the kingdom. Corruption is open to all. Visas can fetch $1,500 or more. Of course, occasionally those who purchase a visa discover it already has been sold and used by someone else, and they are left holding the bag, as they cannot report the crime to authorities without implicating themselves.

A whole new business has developed in recent years, in which the Saudi sponsor of foreign workers allows those workers to run businesses established in his name and pay him a fee from their profits—a complete reversal of the sponsor running a business and paying the workers from its profits. This illegal conduct, especially rampant in the construction industry, allows Saudi businessmen to earn money while doing nothing, but it fails to develop business acumen or to provide jobs for young Saudis. Again, this is just another example of the rampant disregard for rules and regulations by a growing number of Saudis, who seem bent on grabbing whatever they can from their country and justifying their conduct by telling themselves that their royal rulers aren't fairly sharing the national oil wealth.

This corrupting and corrosive influence on the economy has done nothing to increase Saudi employment. If the private-sector workforce in 2006 totaled 4.8 million foreigners and fewer than one million Saudis, three years later the foreign workforce had increased by 30 percent to 6.2 million, while the Saudi workforce remained largely static. All that has increased is corruption. A survey by the Riyadh Chamber of Commerce in 2005 showed that 77 percent of businessmen felt they had to "bypass" the law to conduct their operations, and businessmen say it has only gotten worse.

A Saudi prince insists that "eighty percent of the corruption is simply because government doesn't work, so people pay bribes to get services. Government grew too fast, and we didn't have proper management, but we will change that." Saudis' patience with unaccountable government, however, is wearing thin.

Another roadblock to faster economic growth is the social and religious prohibition on employing educated women. Some 60 percent of university graduates each year are women, yet the Saudi labor force is only 12 percent female. Most of those women are employed as teachers or doctors. While some young women are beginning to push into careers in computer technology, interior design, nursing, and cosmetology (as we saw in chapter 5), their numbers remain small because the religious establishment—and therefore many families—remains opposed to the mixing of men and women in the workplace.

More recently, the government has begun talking about allowing women to teach kindergarten-age boys, which undoubtedly would improve the teaching as well as employ qualified women. Enter the religious scholars. Women surely cannot teach in a boys' school, where they would encounter male teachers. But the religious establishment objects even to little boys attending school with little girls and sharing their female teachers. Thus female teachers for boys are permitted only in private schools. Meanwhile, most Saudi men don't want to teach school at all, so yet another occupation is filled by foreigners.

Whatever the complex of its causes, high unemployment is producing disillusionment among young Saudis. Government wealth isn't created by taxing the enterprises and incomes of Saudi citizens but rather comes from oil. In the eyes of most young Saudis, that oil revenue is simply buried treasure, and they expect to get their full share.

Unlike the generations who grew up before the oil boom of the 1970s, this young generation has never known harsh deprivation. As a result, the young feel little if any gratitude to the ruling Al Saud family for providing free education and health care and cheap gasoline, water, and electricity. These they feel they deserve. Instead, they resent what they don't have, by comparison with the ostentatious opulence that oil has funded for the royal family and some of the privileged private elite. "Ask not what you can do for your country but what your country can do for you" is the mentality of most Saudi youth.

Saudi optimists argue that so long as global oil prices remain anywhere near current levels, the regime can survive all sorts of economic inadequacies and inefficiencies. That proposition, however, now is being tested.

A 2008 color photo of a Saudi Gulf War veteran and his wife and nine children living in a tent in Mecca, the holiest site in Islam, speaks volumes both about poverty and about the failure of government and individual Saudis to live up to the teaching of their religion to care for the poor. *Arab News* ran the large photo prominently atop page three. The veteran of the war to liberate Kuwait described how he had become destitute when rising inflation made earnings from his taxicab insufficient to cover rent and food. As a result, he gave up his house for a tent. "I pity my children," he told the newspaper. "Sometimes they faint because of heat and insect bites." (The following day the newspaper carried another story—the account of an anonymous Saudi donor who had stepped forward to give the veteran a home.)

In addition to government programs for the poor and unemployed, there also are a number of efforts by prominent private citizens to create jobs to lift Saudis out of poverty. Abdul Latif Jameel, a wealthy Jeddah businessman, funds scores of job training centers around Saudi Arabia to teach the poor simple skills like cooking, sewing, and retail sales. But in another Saudi paradox, the primary obstacle to creating jobs is the government itself. The grandiose new programs that the government announces with regularity are largely propaganda and increasingly are seen as such by cynical Saudi citizens. Whenever one grand plan fails, government spinners all too often react by announcing a new one, under a newly designated government agency, with a new acronym, a new headquarters, and of course, a new budget.

Gone is the General Organization for Technical Education and Vocational Training, created in 1980. It has been replaced by the Technical and Vocational Training Corporation (TVTC). But little of substance has changed. The TVTC has sole responsibility for promoting vocational education in the kingdom. The Higher Education Ministry, which runs the kingdom's twenty-five public universities, and the Ministry of Education, responsible for the 5.5 million Saudi youth in both public and private schools K–12, are the other two major institutions responsible for preparing young Saudis for the world of work. The latest five-year development plan provides for spending a whopping 350 billion Saudi riyals (some $100 billion) on education and training between 2009 and 2014, a sign that the government is eager at least to be seen as reversing its poor record for educating and training youth.

The kingdom's amply funded training programs don't work well for many reasons, including a shortage of Arabic-speaking trainers. A visit to the new High Institute for Plastic Education, one of the kingdom's eighty vocational training centers, some forty-five minutes outside Riyadh, is illustrative. Everything is state of the art, including a new

$19 million building equipped with nearly $40 million of the latest plastic fabrication equipment from Germany, but the center is staffed by experts from Japan, the Philippines, Indonesia, and India, none of whom speak Arabic. It is the same at a center that instructs auto mechanics, and at another seeking to train electricians. Even if the trainers could talk to the students, most of the young Saudis appear too sullen and lethargic to want to learn. Many of the trainees appear to be interested only in the government stipend they receive for showing up.

If training Saudi men raises a number of complex issues, training women is even more complicated. For men, at least, statistics are available showing the kingdom's need for electricians, plumbers, mechanics, and auto repairmen. But no such data exists on requirements for female employees—or even what jobs women will be allowed to hold in five years. Teaching is saturated, and 250,000 women are waiting for available teaching jobs. How many women might be willing to work in gender-sensitive fields like marketing or accounting, where men now dominate, isn't known; nor is it clear what roles Saudi society might allow women to fill in the future. One sign of how badly women want to work: some 25,000 women applied for 480 places in technical training colleges in Riyadh, Al Hasa, Tabuk, and Buraidah.

It will take more than training to persuade Saudi men to take jobs that involve manual or menial work, even though many unemployed Saudi men are qualified for little else. The majority of the 8 million foreign workers in Saudi Arabia serve as maids, nannies, drivers, sales personnel, cooks, and waiters—all jobs Saudis shun as unsuitable. From Saudi homes to shop counters to factory floors, these foreign workers from India, Pakistan, Bangladesh, and elsewhere keep the wheels of the Saudi economy turning. A much smaller number of skilled technical and managerial talent from Asia and the West do jobs that few Saudis are yet capable of doing. In sum, few of the expats are contributing special skills and expertise to the Saudi economy; almost all are doing less specialized jobs that Saudis would be fully capable of doing themselves.

Indeed, the influx of foreign menial and manual workers, rather than contributing to the Saudi economy, winds up being a drain. These workers exist at a subsistence level and remit the bulk of their collective earnings to their families in their homelands rather than use it to fuel the Saudi economy. Remittances from expat workers surged 20.3 percent in 2009 to 94.5 billion Saudi riyals (roughly $25 billion), an 84 percent increase from 2005.

In the dusty expanse of industrial warehouses that stretches many miles between Dammam and Al Khobar, in the kingdom's Eastern Province, is Zamil Steel, begun as a joint venture in 1977 but now entirely owned by the Zamil family, a band of twelve brothers, all educated in the United States in the 1960s. As the oil boom began, the brothers returned to the kingdom armed with education and a determination to take advantage of government loans to enrich their families and help develop their country.

Yet more than three decades later Zamil Steel's 6,200 employees are only 25 percent Saudi. That's because the majority of the work involves hot, grimy manual labor like welding, which Saudi men spurn. To meet government goals of "Saudization," Zamil Steel pays beginning Saudi welders 2,300 to 3,180 riyals ($620 to $850) a month, plus an additional $135 transportation and housing allowance beyond that paid to foreign laborers.

Zamil Steel builds warehouses and hangars as well as towers for high-voltage lines and cell phones, selling 70 percent of the output inside the kingdom. A tour of the factory floor finds few Saudis on duty—the bulk of the workers are from India and the Philippines. Such foreign laborers generally come on contract for two or three years, work for low wages, live in substandard dormitory housing, and work ample overtime, both to earn more and because there is nothing to do with their off time other than sleep.

Abdulrahman al Zamil, chairman of the Zamil Group, is one of the kingdom's most colorful and outspoken businessmen. A wiry elderly man with piercing eyes and a white goatee and mustache, Zamil has a no-nonsense, bottom-line view of "Saudization." "When you build a building you get insurance," he says. "Saudization is insurance for us. But businessmen are selfish and want to look for a low-cost foreign worker. Without jobs, Saudis will wreck our nation."

The Zamil Group, established by Abdulrahman's father as a modest trading company in Bahrain in the 1930s, grew to global scale with sixty sectors of business in some sixty countries employing twelve thousand people, thanks to rapid industrial development and easy government credit in Saudi Arabia in the 1970s. Zamil recalls the family's first loan from the Saudi Industrial Development Fund, for 1 million Saudi riyals, to launch an air-conditioning business in the Eastern Province. "My brother wanted to see the cash and carry it to Al Khobar so he took it in a bag by airplane. We never thought he might crash and we would lose it all."

Despite his own difficulty with recruiting Saudi laborers, Zamil keeps trying and pushes his business colleagues to do the same for their own self-interest in Saudi stability. By Zamil's reckoning, 74 percent of the estimated 8 million foreign laborers (7 million legally and at least 1 million illegally) in the kingdom are engaged in retail and services, so this is the place, he argues, to focus and force "Saudization." But this idea quickly runs afoul of cultural and religious obstacles. Saudi men do not want service jobs, while women are not permitted to work in most retail shops, where they would come in contact with male sales clerks and customers.

A visit to a large Riyadh department store, Al Haram, underscores this dearth of Saudi employees in the retail industry. The store, a cut above Western megastores like Wal-Mart but still offering moderate prices, has 150 employees, only 25 of whom are Saudi. All the Saudis are either cashiers or managers. The store manager, Ali al Qahtani, a Saudi, insists that even if a Saudi asked to work in sales (and none has, in his five years at the store), he would not permit it. "I would put him at reception or cashier," he says, "because Saudi society wouldn't accept a Saudi sales person." Indeed, a Saudi intellectual who lives in the kingdom but travels often to Europe and the United States recounts his embarrassment at being served by a Saudi waiter in a restaurant. "It is begin-ning to happen now," he says of the rare Saudi who takes a menial service job. "But I didn't know what to do, it was so embarrassing."

In 2006 the government unveiled a plan to allow Saudi women to work in lingerie shops, where women must buy intimate apparel from foreign males, generally from India, Bangladesh, or the Philippines. This idea quickly ran afoul of the cultural prohibition against mixing genders in the work-place. Women standing behind the counter to sell lingerie would mix with both male sales personnel and with Saudi men who might seek to buy lingerie, or so postulated the reli-gious scholars supported by many conservative Saudis. Thus the plan was abandoned. For inexplicable reasons, Saudi women standing in front of the counter buying lingerie from men is somehow religiously acceptable. (Saudi society sees foreign men more as furnishings than as real men who might tempt Saudi women.)

Six years later, the government finally set a January 2012 deadline banning male salesclerks in lingerie shops. This came only after a royal decree was issued making lingerie shops a women-only working environment, guaranteeing that female and male sales clerks would not be mixing, and after the Ministry of Labor threatened to close lingerie shops employing males. Some 28,000 women quickly applied for these sales jobs according to the Ministry of Labor. Change comes very slowly in Saudi and, as is often the case, only after the king's involvement.

In 2011 when poor women were hired as cashiers in the large supermarket chain Panda, once again religious opposi-tion surfaced. This time, however, a campaign was launched on Facebook to *support* Panda's hiring women. Within months, the grand mufti issued a fatwa banning women cashiers. "It is not permitted for a Muslim woman to work in a mixed environment with men who are not related to them, and women should look for jobs that do not lead to them interacting with men which might cause attraction from both sides," the fatwa said. The fact that religious police feel free to threaten female workers whose employment is promoted by government policy is clear evidence of the absence of rule of law and of a country at war with itself, in which the Al Saud rulers are too insecure to enforce their own decisions.

If microeconomic change is difficult, implementing grand plans across the broader economy is even harder. For all the good intentions of the often Western-educated economists producing the five-year plans, the economy on paper bears little more resemblance to the real one than did the Gosplans to the old Soviet Union. The real economy is a bewildering (at least to outsiders) combination of a feudal fealty system and a more modern political patronage one. At every level in every sphere of activity, Saudis maneuver through life manipulating individual privileges, favors, obligations, and connections. By the same token, the government bureaucracy is a maze of overlapping or conflicting power centers under the patronage of various royal princes with their own priorities and agendas to pursue and dependents to satisfy.

Almost all economic decisions are made by the regime in Riyadh, including decisions on where to locate megadevelopment projects, hospitals, and universities, regardless of the priorities of local provinces. Because the regime has prevented the emergence of any independent organizations such as labor unions or interest groups of any kind, the regime is able to make these decisions with little input from society, but paradoxically, it is then constrained in its ability to execute them. In the absence of such associations, over the decades informal networks have grown throughout the bureaucracy that prevent efficient execution of decisions. Various princely, bureaucratic, and business interests compete for advantage, sometimes simply by blocking or at least stalling government decisions they can't change. The state has "fundamentally reoriented Saudi society, making it dependent and at the same time fragmenting it," writes Steffen Hertog, an expert on Saudi economy at the London School of Economics, explaining this gulf between government pronouncements and actual economic achievements.

The Saudi economy is neither a free market nor an effectively managed one. Most Saudis have no concept of openly competing for education or jobs or, for that matter, marriage partners. Everything is negotiated and arranged. Similarly, most businesses of any size are so dependent on government contracts and on regulated and protected markets that genuine competition is a rarity here too. On the other hand, the layers of bureaucratic control hardly produce an efficient planned economy. Business and government, wealth and power, are inextricably intertwined. The result, however, bears no resemblance to the *chaebol* system of South Korea, where the intertwining of government and big business has produced focused and dynamic economic growth and the twelfth largest economy in the world.

A rare Saudi with initiative—for example, an educated young man seeking to start a small business—has to complete innumerable applications and documents at multiple layers of multiple ministries, which invariably requires seeking favors from various patronage networks and accumulating obligations along the way, most probably including having to hire less-than-competent dependents of his patrons. Then, for any business of any size, government contracts, not private competition, are the financial lifeblood. So this means more patrons, more favors, and more obligations. Not surprisingly, Saudi businesses that can compete outside the protected Saudi market are few. Similarly, only rare Saudis are willing to leave the protective networks of their homeland to seek competitive careers abroad. (While many attend foreign universities, most return home with their degrees to seek government employment.)

When government programs fail Saudis, their recourse invariably is patronage. For instance, buying a home in the kingdom is virtually impossible, even for upper-middle-class people, given the exorbitant price of land and the dearth of home financing. (Islam forbids charging interest on loans.) To resolve the housing problem for members of the armed forces and the National Guard, on which the royal family depends for its protection, both King Abdullah (who until recently headed the National Guard) and the late Crown Prince Sultan (who also served as minister of defense) both provided heavily subsidized or free housing to the military. It is yet another form of patronage available to some, but not a general solution to the critical housing problem facing most Saudis.

While the government claims that 60 percent of Saudis own a home, informed private estimates put that number at more like 30 percent. The government's Real Estate Development Fund (REDF) dominates the housing market, providing 81 percent of all loans for housing. But the estimated waiting period to secure an REDF loan is *eighteen* years, due to pent-up demand. As part of King Abdullah's effort in 2011 to ensure that regional unrest didn't engulf Saudi Arabia, the government raised the maximum loan from 300,000 to 500,000 Saudi riyals, but the average price for a small free-standing home in Riyadh is 1.23 million Saudi riyals (about $328,000), leaving a huge gap for the buyer to fund. Since most state and private-sector employees earn less than 8,000 Saudi riyals a month (or $25,000 a year), housing is simply out of their reach. Lower-income Saudis can't turn to older homes to solve their problem, because almost no secondary market in housing exists in the kingdom. Construction is so shoddy that homes rarely last more than thirty years.

As revolutionary winds swept through the region, King Abdullah announced the government would spend 250 billion Saudi riyals to construct half a million homes for Saudis, and he created a new Ministry of Housing, yet another example of creating new bureaucracies to solve old problems. But the exorbitant cost of land, the low wages, and the difficulty in procuring mortgages almost guarantees continuing housing shortages and rising complaints from middle-class and young Saudis priced out of homeownership.

In sum, the Saudi economy, like Saudi society, is ossified and becoming more so. Its many webs of patronage and multiple layers of bureaucracy evolved over the years to accomplish some purpose or another, but rather than enable, they increasingly disable Saudi citizens in their daily lives. To buy stability, the regime slathers on more money, smothering private initiative and private enterprise, thus further diminishing the living standards of Saudis and increasing their anger, which then necessitates another dose of money. And so the cycle repeats itself. The Saudi system is inflexible and, to many, impenetrable. Saudis spend too much of their lives seeking favors, begging permissions, and facing innumerable frustrations. The arteries of the body politic are clogged, and no one, not even a well-meaning and supposedly absolute monarch, can unclog them.

This Saudi system, where personal loyalties once upon a time lent subtlety and suppleness to everyday life, over the years has become rigid and thus brittle. The old system of loyalties no longer is suited to the demands of a growing population or the requirements of an economy that must expand to create jobs. The new bureaucratic structures superimposed upon the old networks are blocking rather than facilitating progress. Saudis are frustrated and fearful that whatever they get from the various networks of patronage is less valuable than what others are getting. To the extent that information, whether fact or rumor, spreads through the tame press and untamed Internet, more transparency simply produces more envy and anger.

An ossified system can give the appearance of great stability. The Soviet Union in its final decades, for all its shortcomings, was seen as nothing if not stable. The widespread assumption was that its leadership was in firm control. In the end, the system proved to be brittle. The geriatric leadership that commanded communism, for all its purported power, proved incapable of making its own system function. Its leaders could pull the levers of power, but nothing much moved. By the time Mikhail Gorbachev arrived and began trying to salvage the system with some modest reforms, it was too late, and the hollow structure imploded.

The Saudi rulers still have time to unclog the arteries, and they surely have plenty of money for stents and surgeries— but is there a daring doctor among them who can perform the necessary life-saving operations? All indications so far are no. Just as Soviet power passed from an old Brezhnev to an infirm Andropov to a doddering Chernenko, the Saudi royal family continues to pass the crown from one aged son of its founder to the next. The line of succession leads to more old men in their eighties. The youngest of the surviving sons already is in his late sixties, and he is more than a dozen living brothers down the royal line. King Abdullah seems aware of some of the problems facing the kingdom and surely desires to reform the system enough to save Al Saud rule. But even his sincere, albeit far from sweeping, reform efforts of the past decade have brought only limited changes to the economy, the role of women, the control of the religious establishment, and the behavior of his royal relatives—all too many of whom continue to view the country's land and oil revenue as theirs, not that of Saudi citizens.

The halting progress of King Abdullah's modest reforms, while impressive by past Saudi standards, is a sobering reminder of how difficult economic and political change in the kingdom will be, even if the royal family can select a ruler with the vision and longevity to launch and sustain a serious reform program. King Abdullah has brought a measure of glasnost, or candor, about social problems, but not yet perestroika, which would require structural economic reform and some opening of the closed political system. Encouraging and educating the population to depend more on its own initiative and less on the government risks unleashing forces that the regime fears it may not be able to contain. Yet if substantive reform might threaten the regime, so surely will the absence of significant reform. The dilemma for the regime, in a nutshell, is picking which poison to swallow.

Outcasts

The one who looks after a widow or a poor person is like
a warrior in the cause of Allah, or like him who performs
prayers all the night and fasts all the day.

—PROPHET MUHAMMAD, SAHIH BUKHARI,
VOL. 7, BK. 64, NO. 265

If Saudi Arabia's middle class is frustrated by a dysfunctional economy that isn't creating jobs, by a declining standard of living, and by diminished opportunities for their
children, another group of Saudis would see such concerns as
luxuries. They are the Saudi poor. They live in impoverished
rural villages or, more often, in the slums scattered through
the industrial wastelands on the fringes of big cities. They are
largely invisible, not just to visitors but even to most other
Saudis.

All societies have economic disparities, but in no other
does the contrast between the very rich—the princes and
their powerful business partners—stand in such glaring contrast to the very poor.

Surprising as it may seem in a land of bountiful black gold,
shiny new skyscrapers, and a first-world standard of living,
fully 40 percent of Saudi families live on less than 3,000
Saudi riyals (about $850) a month. The very poor, some 19
percent of Saudis, live on less than 1,800 Saudi riyals ($480) a
month, according to a 2003 survey by the Ministry of Social
Affairs. As the Saudi population has exploded over the past
thirty years, with a birthrate of 4.8 percent in 1970 and an

average family size of 6.6, the number of those living in poverty continues to rise. (As education has increased, the birthrate has fallen sharply in the past decade, to 2.4 percent in 2010.)

While $850 a month sounds abysmally low, in Saudi Arabia the government provides free health care (admittedly often slow and low quality), free education, and subsidized water and electricity. Furthermore, gasoline costs only about fifty-three cents a gallon, one-fifth the average price in the United States and less than one-tenth the average price in Europe. The poor and even many middle-class families exist on rice and chicken, both relatively cheap staples. And housing, the major shortage in the kingdom, can be affordably obtained by sharing a room with extended family. Government social payments coupled with charity help the truly poor survive. Still, daily life for the poor is a constant struggle.

Many Saudis were unaware of this poverty in their midst until then crown prince Abdullah, briefed on the Ministry of Social Affairs survey, brought the issue into public view by paying an unprecedented personal visit to the shanty homes of poor Saudis in southern Riyadh. His nationally televised tour shocked many Saudis, who never venture into neighborhoods of such squalor or see filthy, barefoot children. Abdullah's visit led to a spurt of government spending to assist the poor and efforts to draft a so-called National Strategy for Social Development and Plan for Poverty Elimination. As so often is the case in Saudi Arabia, this grand plan sits unfinished. Meanwhile the number of poor continues to grow.

Not surprisingly, women represent a high proportion of the poor. Most of them are women without a husband. Umm Turki, a chubby woman with dark skin and sad eyes, has a husband but might as well be a widow; her husband is serving a five-year prison term for selling drugs, so he contributes nothing to her or their three small sons, who live a short commute from his prison on the outskirts of Riyadh. Her home is completely bare except for a large bed that she and the three boys share. To hide their father's criminality from the boys, she tells them he is traveling. Each month she spends some of her meager money on a taxi to visit him and provide a phone card so he can call the boys to maintain the myth that he is away on business.

Umm Turki means "mother of Turki," her eldest son. (Women are all known as mother of their firstborn son.) She receives 1,700 Saudi riyals each month (roughly $500) in government welfare called "social security." She spends half of that on transportation to get her children out of this poor neighborhood to a better school thirty minutes from their home. Even the very poor want better education for their children. Transportation for her children and money for her husband—who threatens to divorce her unless she gives him 500 riyals a month, with which, she fears, he buys drugs in prison—pretty much consumes that meager welfare payment. To feed her children, she works as a security guard at the girls' section of the school she considers too rough for her sons to attend. A neighborhood Pakistani grocer allows her to buy food on credit and waits for her to pay when she saves a few riyals or receives charity from individuals.

Despite her poverty, she welcomes visitors and brings out a plastic pot of hot Arabic coffee and another one of hot tea along with a small dish of dates. Sitting cross-legged on the floor of her empty living room, she lays out her sad and austere life with no self-pity. Born in southern Saudi Arabia, the poorest part of the country, she came to Riyadh with her husband, hoping to separate him from his drug habit. Instead, he was arrested and imprisoned. She kept his arrest secret from her employers at school for fear of losing her job. One night as she returned from visiting her husband in prison, another security guard at the school reported her to school authorities for coming home late. Confronted by authorities on her religiously inappropriate late-night travel, she pleaded, "I need this job. I can't beg at the stoplight or do wrong to earn money. It is not my way." The school retained her.

Her home is in an alley of dirty buildings in a grimy industrial region of southern Riyadh, nearly an hour's drive from the gleaming skyscrapers of the central city. Inside her front door is a lavatory for washing before prayer. Like her living room, her tiny kitchen is bare but for a small refrigerator and a butane burner for heating food and water. There is no table or chairs. The cell phone always in her hand or on her lap is the only trace of modernity.

As Umm Turki speaks, her boys, ages four, eight, and nine, who have been scuffling with one another in the adjacent room, suddenly grow quiet. Clearly they hear the pain in their mother's voice, even though they cannot see the tears in her eyes. Locked into this limited life by her inability to afford more than the occasional taxi to prison to visit her husband, Umm Turki nonetheless seems largely oblivious to her poverty. "It is my reality," she says. She once traveled through the wealthy neighborhoods of northern Riyadh but was frightened by what she saw. "I saw women with their faces uncovered. I was so shocked, I feared an earthquake. I am very religious. I don't like to see things like that, so I fled."

Not all the poor are as stoic as Umm Turki. In the Al Aziziyah district of southern Riyadh, a divorcee sits alone, cross-legged on her floor, hunched in anguish like a round black boulder. In her late fifties now, she divorced her husband more than a decade ago, only to lose her eldest son two years later when his car hit a camel. Her other son refuses to visit her or provide her any help, a stinging rebuke in a country where the mother-son relationship is almost always among the closest in life.

Indeed, there is a hadith from the Prophet Muhammad on the love due one's mother. A man asked the Messenger of Allah, "Who among people deserves that I be most dutiful to?" The Prophet replied, "Your mother." The man asked, "Then?" "Your mother," the Prophet replied. "Then?" asked the man. "Your mother," responded the Prophet for a third time. "Then?" "Your father," said the Prophet.

As the divorcee recounts the woes of her life in the gathering darkness of her sparse room, she lifts the black shawl that covers her head and chest to wipe her eyes and nose. "I pray to God to return my son," she says. "Perhaps my son is punishing me for divorcing his father." Without a husband or son, she is largely confined to this apartment, going out only to attend Koran classes in the neighborhood. Clearly regretting her divorce, she says she advises her daughter, who lives far away in northern Saudi Arabia, to stay with her husband regardless of what he does. "Even if your husband burns you, stay with him," she advises her daughter.

As dusk arrives and the apartment turns dim, she continues to sit in the dark rather than turn on the small fluorescent lights on her wall. Although she lives what can only be described as a depressing life, essentially a prisoner in her home, surviving on government welfare, she says she is better off than she was as a child in her hometown of Hamis Mushait, in southern Arabia. "Life is better now," she says without hesitation when asked to compare her childhood with the life she now lives. Certainty about even a miserable existence, compared with the uncertainty that poor Saudis faced before government social programs were instituted mostly since the 1960s, has left older Saudis like this woman grateful to the Al Saud.

Next door lives a widow who is similarly deprived but much less resigned to her fate. At thirty-four, the widow is responsible for five children all under fifteen. Her husband died four years ago in a car accident also with a camel. "My life with my husband was good," she says. "I felt on top of the mountain. Now I feel like I am falling, and no one helps me. I just keep falling and falling."

The widow, who asks to remain nameless, is literate and clearly intelligent beyond her tenth-grade schooling. Dressed in a long blue-and-white cotton shift with long dark hair pulled up in a ponytail, she exudes a strength and determination that is at odds with that of most other poor women I met. She sheds no tears telling her story and voices a determination to find some way to get a job and escape her current situation—no thanks to government, she makes clear. Asked if her life is better than when she was a child, she immediately and emphatically says, "No!" Knowledgeable about life in other Gulf sheikdoms, she wonders why Saudi Arabia, with all its wealth, cannot provide the standard of living of its Gulf neighbors. (This is a growing refrain among Saudis, as the Internet and more openness in the press reveal to them life beyond their borders.) She laughs, recounting her visit to a dentist at one of Riyadh's large clinics, where she was told to come back for treatment in one and a half years. She clearly has developed a strong cynicism about government.

Asked what she would like to do when she completes her home study of English, she cheekily responds, "Be prime minister." (The title is now held by King Abdullah.) Her children laugh at the absurdity of a woman occupying a prominent government position. What would she do if she were prime minister? "I would look after the people," she says. "If they knew anything about us, they would too, but they don't know. Without *wasta* [connections], you can do nothing in this country. Even a cook in the palace of the king is better off than we are. He is seen. We are unseen."

Umm Muhammad, forty-six and a widow, refuses to be unseen. Seven days a week she stands from noon to ten P.M. outside the Al Merjan Mall in Jeddah, in temperatures that in summer rise regularly to 120 degrees Fahrenheit, selling cheap items from her small stand to earn the money to support her seven children. She is a tiny woman swathed entirely in black. Only her eyes are visible through a narrow slit in her veil. Her hands are hidden in black gloves, even though the temperature on this spring afternoon already is approaching 100 degrees, made more stifling by the rain-forest humidity of Jeddah.

Like so many poor women, Umm Muhammad is widowed and uneducated—her father refused to allow her to go to school. But unlike most poor women, she is determined to support her family without government help and to maintain her independence. She insists she takes nothing from the government and that neither her elderly father nor her brothers help her. "I don't want people to see me as weak," she says. "I want to prove I can take care of myself and my family. I want my children to be proud of me for looking after them and not leaving it to others."

Umm Muhammad has demonstrated enormous grit and

perseverance to get to this point. After her husband died, she sold small items like *ouhd* (the incense so popular with Saudis), scarves, and *abayas* in her neighborhood. When that didn't produce sufficient earnings, she began to sell in front of a Jeddah shopping mall to be nearer to large crowds. But shop owners complained of her presence, and the municipality responded by forcing her to stop selling near the mall. Determined to find a way to maintain her business, she went to the Kadijah bint Khuwailid Businesswomen Center at the Jeddah Chamber of Commerce to ask for help. Basmah Omair, director of the center and a tireless advocate for women, helped Umm Muhammad secure a loan from Bab Riqz Jameel, a charity funded by wealthy Jeddah businessman Abdul Latif Jameel, which provides loans to the poor for small entrepreneurial businesses. The chamber of commerce also helped secure permission from the municipality to build behind the Al Merjan Mall a group of small stalls with shaded covers where Umm Muhammad and other poor street sellers now operate. One small victory for women and for entrepreneurship.

Umm Muhammad says she earns each day about 50 Saudi riyals' ($15) profit. With her monthly rent totaling 750 Saudi riyals or some two weeks' profit, she says she can't afford to give herself a day off as she would lose one-seventh of her weekly income. "I would like to relax sometime, but I don't have a chance," she says. If she could have one wish, "it would be to own a home." She has learned to read by using her children's schoolbooks and continues to hope she can secure government permission to open a car repair shop. Her late husband taught her to repair car engines, but so far the municipality of Jeddah has refused to grant permission for her to open such a business because she is a woman. The authorities seem oblivious to the fact that she could earn more and in greater privacy than she does selling items outside a shopping mall.

Poverty, of course, is not confined to women. Abdullah is forty years old and has subsisted all his life on government welfare—either his parents' social security or food and board in prison. Unemployed and uneducated when his father died, he began to steal cars to escape the boredom of home and his responsibilities, as the eldest son, for his mother and seven siblings. His family lived on social security from the Ministry of Social Affairs. He began supplementing their small government allowance by selling stolen tires, tape decks, and used cars. Soon he began to use the income he earned for "special things" for himself. Special things, he finally admits, is a euphemism for alcohol and drugs.

One day he stole a car and let a friend use it for joyriding. Unfortunately for Abdullah, among the joyriders was another Saudi man who recognized the car as belonging to a friend of his. He and his friend followed the driver of the stolen car to Abdullah's home and held him until the police came. After a brief interrogation, Abdullah was jailed and sentenced to two years in prison and four hundred lashes. It wasn't his first time in prison (he was in and out several times over the past decade), but he insists it will be his last. At forty, he now has his first job ever—as an expeditor, someone who carries papers to different ministries to secure the endless permissions that tie up the daily lives of every Saudi who doesn't have either influence to circumvent the permissions or money to pay an expeditor like Abdullah.

"There are a lot of unemployed men like me who suffer from nothing to do," he says, with no hint of irony that there are plenty of jobs he could do if he were only willing, jobs that doubtlessly would pay much better than his position as an expeditor. But his willingness to do a job that keeps him going in and out of ministries and office buildings rather than one that would pay better but require physical labor simply underscores the resistance of Saudi men to manual work.

Despite government welfare programs and grand plans for larger ones, charitable giving by individuals and organizations remains a mainstay of helping the poor in Saudi Arabia. And most of the poor feel no compunction—or much gratitude—at receiving charity. The poor often regard the rich as simply lucky in receiving more of Allah's bounty than they have and therefore obliged to share it.

Indeed, the Koran repeatedly reminds believers that giving charity—especially in secret—is pleasing to Allah. "O you who have believed, do not invalidate your charities with reminders [of it] or injury as does one who spends his wealth only to be seen by the people and does not believe in Allah and the Last Day." Elsewhere the Koran assures believers that Allah knows what they give in secret. "If you disclose your charitable expenditures, they are good; but if you conceal them and give them to the poor, it is better for you. Allah with what you do is acquainted." The Bible, of course, includes the same admonition when it tells Christians not to let their right hand know what their left hand is doing when it comes to charity.

Still, the sense by Saudi citizens of a right to the wealth of others is different from the mind-set of most poor people in the West. "People in this society are accustomed to taking, not giving," says a Saudi sociologist, who asks to remain anonymous. "It is in the culture. Bedouins were nomads. The chief took care of the whole tribe. Now government takes care of people. If you govern with money, you need to pass out a lot of it to maintain power." Indeed, as noted earlier, in March 2011 after revolutions in several Arab countries, King Abdullah doled out nearly $130 billion, on top of a $150 billion annual budget for the kingdom, to every sector of society including handouts to the very poor. This spending didn't even pretend to be an economic stimulus but was merely a handout.

While most of the poor live in urban areas simply because more than 80 percent of all Saudis have moved to the country's three largest cities over the past few decades, a number of those remaining in rural areas are very poor. The most destitute people I met were near Hafr al Batin, a city of six hundred thousand near the Kuwait border and home to a large Saudi military installation, King Khalid Military City. On the outskirts of this squalid, crime-ridden city are hundreds of poor outcasts called *bedoons* (nationless people). These people left the impoverished kingdom before the discovery of oil to seek livelihood in Iraq and other places and then returned over the past few decades in hopes of securing a better life. But the kingdom doesn't recognize them as citizens, they say, so their children aren't permitted to attend school; nor can the men work because they lack citizenship papers or visas. These people live in wooden shanties scattered in barren dirt fields. There are no roads, few cars, and in many cases no electricity. When I visit there one night, the landscape, lit only by moonlight, makes this poor village look abandoned. Several of the men and a few boys welcome me to one shanty, an open room with a rug and a lone electric bulb. Most of these people subsist on charity or on occasional earnings from someone willing to hire them for day labor despite the lack of proper papers. Meanwhile they continue to strive to establish citizenship to secure some prospect of escaping this truly subsistence living. My guide for the visit, Mekhlef bin Daham al Shammary, a human rights lawyer who helps them, was arrested six weeks after our visit for "annoying others" and remains in prison. I can't escape the irony that while the Saudi government supports the right of return for displaced Palestinians to their homeland, so far these displaced Saudis get no such moral, much less material, support from their government.

By contrast, life in the tiny village of Al Athlah, in impoverished southern Arabia, seems almost a paradise. The village is half an hour from Jizan, the capital of the province of the same name. Once we leave the main highway, we travel down dirt roads, past mud brick homes, piles of garbage, and barren fields. Most of the four hundred citizens in this dusty rural village are related to the local imam, who has been issuing the call to prayer five times a day for half a century and also preaching the weekly Friday sermon at the mosque. The old man doesn't know his age but estimates he is about ninety. His *thobe* is short, his feet bare, and his face thick and leathery. His long white beard is orange from the henna he has used to dye it. By his count, he has ninety children and grandchildren living in the village; his youngest son is ten and his eldest is sixty. He has just built a new home in preparation for marrying another wife.

Once he held three jobs—school custodian, farmer, and

imam. In his old age, he has cut his workload to two jobs, lopping off work at the local school. He still rises before dawn to call the faithful to prayer, before turning his attention to farming and herding his camels and sheep. He recalls riding a donkey for twenty days over some four hundred miles to make his first pilgrimage to Mecca as a young man. Still, so insular is his life that I am the first Westerner he has ever met. He is incurious; all that matters to him is in this tiny village—mosque, herds, and family.

The family now has electricity, so they no longer go to bed at sunset. And thanks to a grandson who works for the provincial governor, there is a car, cell phones, and even a flickering television. But the old man expresses a preference for an even more austere life. "Life was better in the past," he says. "Camels, sheep, a simple life. I am strong now because of that simple life." Indeed, he still drinks milk directly from the teat of his cow and continues to eat *khader,* a traditional regional dish made from maize, milk, and sugar, for breakfast, lunch, and dinner. The family, a roomful of aunts and uncles, sons and daughters, boys and girls, share three spoons and the bowl of *khader,* which has the consistency of overcooked oatmeal and tastes like sawdust sprinkled with sugar. Also on the menu is bread made from baked *khader* and grilled fish eaten with the right hand. It is this austere rural life that so many Saudis have fled, but this extended family clearly still savors it.

There is another pool of poverty in every big city, consisting of foreigners who do the most menial jobs and live at a subsistence level in factory dormitories or filthy tenements. Visiting one of these tenements, where the stairs are littered with broken glass and stained with spilled liquids and urine, conjures up Calcutta, not Jeddah, the kingdom's most urbane city. Below even this threshold of poverty are the totally indigent—for example, imported South Asian maids, who have fled cruel households to live under bridges and beg money from passing motorists, or East African pilgrims, who stay illegally and beg for a living after performing hajj. All, of course, are Muslims.

Saudi poverty probably does not represent a direct threat to the Al Saud. The Saudi terrorists who attacked America on 9/11 and the ones who have launched similar attacks in Saudi Arabia are mostly the embittered sons of the Saudi middle class who turned first to radical Islam and then to terrorism to vent frustrations. But the poor represent a different sort of threat. They stand as a mute reminder of the pretense of the regime and the religion it claims to represent. Yes, "the poor are always with us" can be said in any society. But no other regime so wraps itself in religion and bases the legitimacy of its rule on living by the dictates of the Koran. Individual royal princes sponsor numerous charities and hand out money to individual supplicants, but the ineffectual government they run has proved incapable of making any serious dent in the country's poverty problem. Islam preaches compassion for the poor, the widows, and the orphans and calls upon all believers to offer charity to those who are less fortunate. The Prophet Muhammad lived a humble, even austere life, sharing what he had with those who came to him and often visiting the poor. "He is not a perfect Muslim who eats his fill and lets his neighbor go hungry," the Prophet said in an often-quoted hadith. Based on that admonition, the Prophet would not feel much at home in modern Saudi Arabia.

CHAPTER II

. . . and Outlaws

A Muslim is the one who avoids harming Muslims with
his tongue and hands.

—PROPHET MUHAMMAD, SAHIH BUKHARI,
VOL. 1, BK. 2, NO. 10

Imagine Saudi Arabia as a stagnant pond. Nothing is transparent in the murky waters. The surface is littered with
the detritus of a dysfunctional society—unemployed men,
frustrated women, angry youth, forgotten poor, inadequate
education, and an immobile economy. All are obstacles for
the Saudi leadership. But another sort of social debris floats
beneath the surface, more immediately menacing than the
rest. These are the Saudi terrorists, once admired and supported by the Al Saud and their countrymen as Islamic
jihadists when they murdered infidels, but now, when they
threaten the regime, branded as outlaws.

They blasted to global attention on September 11, 2001.
In the wake of that attack, a shocked world discovered that
fifteen of the nineteen mass murderers were Saudis acting
under the aegis of Al Qaeda.

September 11, however, was not the beginning of Saudi
jihadism. During the 1980s, thousands of young Saudis had
joined their countryman, Osama bin Laden, in waging war
against Soviet occupiers in Afghanistan; others in the 1990s
demolished a U.S. military barracks in Saudi Arabia and
bombed two U.S. embassies in East Africa; and still others
attacked the USS *Cole* in Yemen. In the years following their

successful destruction of the Twin Towers and damage to the Pentagon, these jihadists turned their terror on sites in the kingdom itself. Only at that point did the Saudi regime focus serious attention on its homegrown terrorists.

Some of these young Saudi terrorist recruits are rebelling against a rigid and repressive society and gravitate to terrorism to escape boring lives; others turn to terrorism in an attempt to impose even harsher religious repression on a society they see becoming corrupted by infidel influences. Some of the Saudi terrorists thus are motivated by an extreme version of fundamentalist Islam and others more simply by hatred of America, the West, and the Al Saud, whom they see as American lackeys. Some, like most of the 9/11 terrorists, are the alienated sons of middle-class families, while others emerge from the urban or rural poor. While their backgrounds and motivations may differ, all the young terrorists seem to share contempt for the society they see around them in Saudi Arabia and a yearning for more meaning in their lives.

No one, including the vigilant and technologically sophisticated security services of the Al Saud regime, knows for sure how many active or incipient terrorists there are inside the kingdom. The regime knows the number it kills or arrests, the number it holds, and the number it claims to have rehabilitated since starting in 2005 a much-touted program to reform them, but it does not know how many Saudi terrorists now are biding their time behind the walls of Saudi homes and mosques. No doubt they are there— as Prince Muhammad bin Nayef, who heads the antiterror strategy, found out firsthand.

Even as the prince was receiving Western accolades in 2009 for the success of the kingdom's antiterror campaign, he narrowly escaped assassination by a homegrown terrorist. The "reformed" terrorist asked Prince Muhammad to receive him in order that he might help facilitate the surrender of a group of Saudi terrorists in Yemen. Muhammad, who meets regularly with young extremists he hopes to convert, agreed. His guest cleverly came to the prince's home on a weekend, thereby avoiding the intensive security at the kingdom's fortresslike Ministry of Interior, where the prince works. Muhammad's bodyguards patted down the visitor but failed to detect plastic explosive hidden in his rectum. Seated beside Prince Muhammad, who offered tea, the terrorist dialed his friends in Yemen on a cell phone and handed it to the prince to arrange the supposed surrender. No sooner had the prince greeted the men on the other end of this deadly conversation than his guest exploded, his body blown into what investigators later counted as seventy-three pieces. The largest piece, an arm, hit the ceiling and fell on the floor in front of the prince, who miraculously was barely scratched. The prince, still holding the phone, could hear the terrorist cell in Yemen cheering *"Allahu Akbar"* at his presumed death. The assassination attempt later was posted on YouTube by the terrorist cell.

The Saudi regime, belatedly focused on its internal terrorist threat, still is inclined to blame the West for the problem. In the regime's view, the West spawned and continues to spawn Saudi terrorism by its covert war against the Soviets in Afghanistan, its invasion and long occupation of Iraq, its war against the Taliban in Afghanistan, and especially its backing of Israel against the interests of the Palestinians. As is so often the case, the Saudi regime finds it easier to blame external forces than to acknowledge its own culpability. But if some of these external events were germs that set off a fever, it was Saudi Arabia that provided the petri dish in which the germs fed and spread. For most of the past three decades, the Saudi regime allowed religious fanatics to set the rules and thus produced a rigid society offering no political, social, or cultural outlets for youthful energy and frustration other than jihad. Not surprisingly, bored, frustrated, and only in some cases pious Saudi youth had little resistance to the blandishments of Osama bin Laden and other jihadist messiahs. To these alienated youths, violence offered an opportunity for action and meaning now and for paradise later.

Khalid Sulayman al Hubayshi, born in 1975 in Jeddah, is typical of the young Saudis who turned to terrorism to escape boredom and find purpose in life. Now in his midthirties,

Khalid spent more than a decade on the run as a fighter in the Philippines, Afghanistan, and Pakistan, and then as a prisoner of the United States in Guantánamo and of the Saudis in Riyadh. He then underwent so-called "rehabilitation" at the hands of the Saudi government and gained his freedom in 2006.

Khalid fit the profile of Saudi terror recruits—a young high school graduate from a middle-class family. Always politically aware, he says, he began reading newspapers at age ten. When he finished high school, he studied power systems and earned a certificate with a 4.8 out of a possible 5 that helped him secure a job at an electric company in Dammam, some 720 miles from his Jeddah family. "I missed my family. I didn't like my life," he recalls, "so I decided to become religious, though my family never had been very religious. I bought videotapes of jihad. I liked the idea of doing good for others. I liked the real jihad—helping other Muslims get freedom—so I went to the Philippines to help the freedom fighters there."

In Mindanao he met other Arabs who gave him the idea of training in Afghanistan, where the Taliban had just won control of Kabul. So off he flew to Islamabad and drove into Afghanistan. "I spent two months training on everything from a pistol to antiaircraft plus mines and explosives," he says. "You feel this is the real life. You discover something in yourself. Every day is new. No regularity, like at work."

During his time in Afghanistan and Pakistan in the mid-1990s, Khalid fraternized with a plethora of high-profile terrorists, including Abu Zubaydah, still in Guantánamo prison, and Osama bin Laden, now dead. "When you stay more, you see more. When you see more, you see mistakes. You see they aren't all honest. Some are looking for money, some for power, some for fun, and only some are there out of belief."

With this new awareness, Khalid decided to return to Saudi Arabia. Because his passport had been confiscated earlier by Pakistani police, he flew to Yemen, got a fake identification, and walked across the border into the kingdom. He had told his father he had been in Malaysia and Turkey spreading Islam. He told his mother something closer to the truth: he had been in Bosnia for jihad. "My mother supported me," he says. "She supported my brother when he married an American woman, and she didn't question me about my jihad." She helped him hide the truth from his father.

Remarkably, he returned to his old job in Damman without any questions being asked about his absence of more than three years. But soon he felt drawn again to the excitement and purpose of jihad, so again he fled Saudi Arabia for Afghanistan, using his brother's passport to exit the country. Thus, he found himself in Kabul on the night of September 11. "I got in a taxi and heard on the radio that a plane had hit the World Trade Center," he recalls. "Everybody was cheering, including me, because at last something big had happened. It was sunset in Kabul. At eleven P.M. we got a videotape from Al Jazeera. When I saw people jumping out of the building, I began to ask, 'Is this religiously right?' I could not show doubts in front of the group, or I would be killed."

When the U.S. bombing of Afghanistan began, Khalid fled from Kabul to Jalalabad to Tora Bora as the American strikes succeeded in breaking the Taliban's hold on city after city. He recalls Osama bin Laden telling him and the other fighters to be patient. "He said the bombing would get worse but that the Americans will lose the war as it is far away." After another six weeks, Bin Laden reappeared to order all the fighters to leave Afghanistan, saying supplies were running out. "He did nothing for us," Khalid says with bitterness. As Khalid and the others sought to enter Pakistan, the Pakistani police rounded them up for jail and then turned them over to the Americans. "It was the worst night of my life," he says. "We never thought it would end like this. The Americans punched and kicked us, and a Marine jumped on me with his shoes and broke my middle finger." But at least after the near starvation in Tora Bora, Khalid relished the U.S. military's MRE (Meals Ready to Eat). After two weeks of intermittent interrogation at least ten times each night, his U.S. captors shaved his head, dressed him in an orange suit, covered his eyes with goggles, and put him on a plane that he hoped was bound for Saudi Arabia but instead terminated in Guantánamo. "On the plane they gave us the best apple I ever ate and the best peanut butter and honey sandwich."

He is philosophical about his time in Guantánamo, where he soon told his captors the truth about his activities in Afghanistan because his friend Abu Zubaydah already had done so. "Most of the people I knew in Afghanistan are dead, so I was lucky to be in Guantánamo," he says. He used the time there to read U.S. Civil War history and came away with an admiration for the American work ethic. "I learned from the guards about hard work," he says. "We thought in Tora Bora standing guard for two hours was hard work. The guards in Guantánamo worked twelve hours."

These days Khalid has a new Toyota Corolla, a job, a new wife, and a baby daughter, all thanks to the Saudi regime's commitment to rehabilitating terrorists in hopes of quelling extremism, which the regime clearly sees as a threat to its survival. Upon Khalid's arrival in Riyadh from Guantánamo in 2005, Prince Muhammad bin Nayef greeted Khalid and other returnees with a handshake. "You are our children," Khalid recalls the prince saying. "We hope you learn from what you did. We are going to take care of you, get you married, get you a job. We aren't perfect, but we are a family. If you see a mistake in Saudi Arabia, don't blow up the house. Let's talk about it."

Khalid, who tells his story in fluent English in the lobby of the modern Hilton Hotel in Jeddah, could be any of the professional Saudi men who frequent Western hotel lobbies. His white *thobe* is immaculate. He is clean shaven with short black hair barely visible beneath the red-and-white scarf that he adjusts constantly to ensure perfect placement. He recounts his life's story and his prolonged foray into terrorism with intelligence and evident enjoyment, as a thirty-something American man might fondly recount his wayward college days. He smiles often and conveys a desire to get on about life after a decade of what he now says were futile efforts to help fellow Muslims. "I was angry in Guantánamo. I wanted to kill Americans. But then I realized I wasn't innocent." His U.S. interrogators wanted to know why he and others turned to terrorism. "If you are someone with no job, no family, and you find someone who says 'I have the way,' it is easy to follow," he says, though he had both a job and a family. (Saudis often fail to see the obvious contradictions in their conversations.)

Khalid excuses himself to go pray in the corner of the Vienna Café, where he has been telling his story for nearly five hours. When he returns, he recalls one of his American guards at Guantánamo telling him upon release that he didn't blame Khalid. "'If I had grown up like you, I might be here too,'" he recalls the American saying. For the first time, Khalid shows emotion. "I will never forget this," he says, his voice choking. "If you grow up in Saudi Arabia, you are for sure affected by the religious atmosphere."

Other young Saudis who chose jihad and wound up in prison in Guantánamo or Saudi Arabia say they were motivated not by religion but by a desire to escape abusive fathers—or fathers too busy to give them any attention. Khalid al Bawadi, thirty-two, says he went to Afghanistan in his early twenties to escape a father who beat him and his eight siblings as well as both his wives. "I tried to defend my mother and brothers, but we suffered too much," he says in a meeting arranged by the Prince Muhammad bin Nayef Care Center in Riyadh, which seeks to rehabilitate young jihadis whom the center calls "beneficiaries" because they benefit from a second chance extended by the Saudi government.

A shy young man who clearly isn't as worldly as Khalid, Al Bawadi says, "I was not religious. I hadn't memorized even one line of the Koran. I just used religion as an excuse to justify leaving Saudi Arabia to find independence and adventure." Al Bawadi departed via Bahrain for Afghanistan just two months before September 11. When the U.S. attacks on Afghanistan began in the wake of 9/11, he, like Khalid, was shunted toward the Pakistan border, where he was arrested and then imprisoned at Guantánamo for six years and six months before being freed in 2007. "Muhammad bin Nayef met us here in Saudi and told us, 'Forget the past. You are born today,'" recalls Al Bawadi. Like other beneficiaries, Al Bawadi was given a job and a car and help in securing a wife. He is currently working at the chamber of commerce, pursuing a high school degree and focusing on his young son. "The whole experience is like a bad dream. I don't want to have enmity for America. I want to get some benefit from it."

What did he learn from six years in Guantánamo? Surprisingly, two things that are absent in Saudi Arabia: respect for the rule of law and punctuality. "There were rules, and everyone had to obey them, and they were applied fairly to everyone," he says. "This was something new." His second lesson from prison, says Al Bawadi: "Everything happened with precision. Showers, lunch, everything had a time, and everything occurred on time. This also was new." (In Saudi Arabia time is an elastic concept, and rules are made to be broken by those in charge.)

Muhammad Fozan, another "beneficiary," says he was arrested even before he could reach his jihad destination— Iraq. His family informed the government of his disappearance, and he was nabbed at the Saudi border as he returned from seeking training in Syria and was sentenced to three years in a Saudi prison. Muhammad illustrates another piece of the Saudi terrorist profile: young men who receive little time or teaching from their fathers. One of twenty-three children from his father's two wives, Muhammad was a high school dropout with no religious piety. "I smoked. My father had no beard. We were not religious," he says. "I traveled a lot, and God knows what I did when I traveled." His induction to jihad came when he saw a report on Al Jazeera television showing an American soldier in an Iraqi mosque killing a wounded man. "I snapped," he recalls. "After that moment I couldn't sleep. My life went upside down. I decided to go help the Iraqis and asked a relative in Mecca to facilitate my trip to Iraq. If I had slept through that report, none of this would have happened to me."

Like so many other rehabilitated beneficiaries, Muhammad insists the idea of jihad was out of his mind even before he entered the Prince Muhammad bin Nayef Center for Counseling and Care. And like Khalid al Bawadi and Khalid Sulayman al Hubayshi, he doesn't seem truly to accept responsibility for his decision to pursue jihad. "I was tricked into jihad," he says. "When the government showed me the right way, I repented. Some people say to me, 'You benefited a lot—a wife, a car, a job.' I say everything the government gave me isn't worth one night in prison."

Like Khalid al Bawadi, Muhammad has found something he admires about America. Holding his new iPhone in his hand, he displays a photo of his new baby boy. "This is the best thing America ever made," he says, holding the iPhone aloft for emphasis.

The inescapable conclusion from the stories of these young Saudi men who chose the path of jihad largely for escape and to find some purpose in their lives is just how ordinary they are. They obviously aren't terrorist leaders. They are the willing foot soldiers bred by a society that protects the young from learning to think and judge issues for themselves by wrapping them in a straitjacket of religious rules that, as often as not, they see prominent Saudis, including religious officials and royal rulers, violate. Accustomed to following without thinking, the young are susceptible to the siren song of jihad as a route to authenticity in life and paradise in death.

Belatedly, the government is trying both to rehabilitate those who chose terrorism and to moderate religious extremism, to prevent yet more young Saudis from straying down a path that threatens not just Western lives but also the Al Saud regime's survival. For the past half-dozen years, the government has pursued these twin goals of rehabilitation and prevention and clearly has managed to curb the number of terrorist attempts inside the kingdom. But it is far less clear what progress has been achieved in the hearts and minds of young Saudis, all too many of whom are undereducated, unemployed, bored, and frustrated.

Senior government leaders can't bring themselves to acknowledge the government's own role in spawning terrorism. Prince Muhammad, the English-speaking deputy minister in charge of combating terrorism, insists in a midnight meeting at his ministry that terrorism was imported by Egyptians in the Muslim Brotherhood who began coming to the kingdom to work in the 1960s. He expresses no regret for the Saudi government's own generous financial and political support of fundamentalist Islam in the 1980s inside the kingdom, and then throughout the Middle East and beyond. For him, the battle seems to be more a military challenge than one of changing the mind-set of young Saudis, admittedly much more difficult. As we conclude our meeting in 2007, he points to a photo of two of his security officials dressed in camouflage carrying on their shoulders a dead comrade. They have a look, he notes, that is grim but proud. "So long as they have that look on their faces, we will win," he says—grimly and proudly.

Not necessarily. "If you just cut the weeds, they will grow back," says Jamal Khashoggi, a journalist who covered Osama bin Laden's rise and then was editor of the *Al Watan* newspaper, until he was fired in 2010 for running afoul of the government's unpainted red line on investigative journalism. "The government has won the military battle but not removed the roots," he says. "It is wishful thinking that an anti-extremism campaign will work when this country was founded on puritanical Islam. We have to grow out of this, like England had to grow out of the Church of England with an archbishop who could veto whatever he opposed."

At the Interior Ministry's Ideological Security Directorate, Dr. Abdulrahman al Hadlag is in charge of tracking terrorists' efforts to recruit young Saudis. Despite ever improving technology and deeper cooperation with Western security agencies, especially the U.S. Central Intelligence Agency, he acknowledges that the task gets harder, as the terrorists too use technology and information to stay one step ahead. For instance, the government banned objectionable books, but the terrorists turned to posting their documents and writings on the Internet as well as using the Internet to recruit. As a result, the government now is paying religious clerics and scholars to visit jihadi Web sites and participate in the debate, in an effort to dissuade impressionable young Saudis.

The government monitors mosques, schools and universities, Internet chat rooms, religious lectures, and all phone communication in Saudi Arabia. Still, with Internet usage by young Saudis growing at a rapid rate (from half a million to nearly 10 million users between 2000 and 2010), along with the number of radical Web sites, from roughly fifteen in 1998 to thousands now, the opportunity for the young to become seduced by terrorist recruiters expands exponentially. Al Hadlag says most of the radical Web sites are hosted in the West and cannot be shut down by the Saudi government, so the government tries to block them. Roughly 35 percent of Saudis' requests for Internet sites are blocked, he says, but most of those blocked requests, he adds, are for pornography; only 2 percent are for radical Web sites. Extremists, he says, have new ways to get around Web site blocks. Furthermore, the extremist theoreticians have issued fatwas allowing radical recruiters to do whatever it takes to appear "normal" and thus avoid detection. For instance, he says, fatwas endorse extremists trimming their beards, wearing Western clothes, and even carrying pornographic magazines in their luggage to avoid appearing religious and arousing suspicion.

Terrorism requires men, money, and mind-set, Al Hadlag says, so the government is focusing on all three. On the first, the government approach is ruthlessly to kill the leaders and to treat the foot soldiers and their families as victims, offering these young Saudi terrorists cars, education, jobs, and wives. Obviously, money is plentiful in Saudi Arabia, where cash is as ubiquitous as credit cards are in the West. "It is common for men to have seven thousand Saudi riyals [roughly $1,800] in their *thobe* pocket at any given time," says Al Hadlag, "so it is hard to control who gives donations to whom when three million people pass through Mecca for Hajj every year and return around the world." But he insists that despite America's continued criticism of Saudi Arabia for insufficient efforts to control terrorist financing, the kingdom is doing all it can. "Please tell us what else we can do," he says.

Mind-set is the hardest issue to tackle. "A mind isn't a building you can destroy," he says. "Nor can you see what is inside the mind." To understand and reprogram the minds of terrorists, the government created the rehabilitation center. It is a thirty-minute drive from Riyadh and largely hidden from public view. A right turn off the highway at a Lebanese restaurant takes one down a poorly lit road that soon ends at a large complex of buildings, surrounded by a high wall topped with barbed wire. Inside are dormitories where the "beneficiaries" live and then three public buildings: a large tent for receiving visitors, an adjacent house for dining, and a tent used for art therapy. The men, who live here for four to six months, also have a library and sports facilities and meet regularly with religious sheikhs and psychologists. Ironically, such facilities are unavailable in the wider society, where the young lament the dearth of anything to occupy their time.

That isn't the only irony. Here the "beneficiaries" are encouraged to talk openly and discuss candidly their religious, social, and family issues. But, in the larger Saudi society, individuals—especially the young—are trained to hide their feelings, to act and think in harmony with the social norm, to listen and obey. Here the young beneficiaries are taught not to trust that a religious appearance signifies a righteously religious man. Yet, ironically, Saudi society is built around the concept that appearance is reality. What is unacceptable isn't what you do in private but how you appear in public. Furthermore, beneficiaries are encouraged to take responsibility for their decisions, actions, and lives, which is at odds with the larger societal stricture of just-do-as-the-religious-say and subsume individual responsibility to social conformity.

Nowhere is the irony more pronounced than in the art course that is part of the rehabilitation program. Awad al Yami, who is head of art therapy, was educated at Purdue University and received his Ph.D. in art therapy in 1995 from Penn State. "Art in Saudi Arabia is typically devoid of human beings or living things," says Dr. Al Yami. "The idea isn't expression but appreciation of the perfection of Allah's creation." Here, however, the idea of art *is* expression—to find out what is in the minds of those undergoing rehabilitation. Even the bearded religious sheikh who works with the so-called beneficiaries waxes positive about art. "It is expression that helps vent feelings and discover the beauty in life through imitation of beautiful things," he says.

Al Yami points to a painting of a brown road with a black sky; in between are telephone poles with lines strung to connect them. "Those poles and lines are like bars showing this man's mind is still in prison," he says. He points to another drawing of a blue sky with a sun in the left corner and in the center a brown tent with a fire in front of it. "This man is ready to welcome me in for a talk," he explains.

Al Yami tells the story of a group of prisoners who painted a mural on the wall of the rehabilitation center. It depicted a man squatting on a black-and-white cell floor with his knees drawn to his chest and his feet shackled. Above him outside the cell was a flame with the words "Make your imprisonment a candle that lights your life." The prisoners went home to see their families, as they are allowed to do regularly during their stay in the rehabilitation center. When they returned, they wanted to destroy the painting by tearing down the wall, he says, a sign of their hostility to prison. Finally they agreed to whitewash it. First they blotted the shackles, then the admonition to use their prison time wisely, and finally they whitewashed the entire mural. Dr. Al Yami insists this was a sign they wanted to erase their prison lives and rejoin society. What the West has to hope is that the rehabilitation process is more than a whitewash. Only Allah, of course, truly knows what is in the minds of rehabilitated young terrorists.

The idea of individual expression—through art or anything else—is truly foreign to Saudis. So this intense effort to listen to young Saudis who chose terrorism and to encourage their honest expression is one that might pay far greater dividends in prevention if applied to the society as a whole. That thought, however, is not on the minds of the Al Saud.

As government efforts to monitor and eliminate terrorism have gained ground, terrorist recruitment has simply gone underground. "When radicalism goes underground, it becomes ever more difficult to study," says Thomas Hegghammer, author of the thoroughly researched book *Jihad in Saudi Arabia: Violence and Pan-Islamism Since 1979.* Fluent in

Arabic, this senior fellow at the Norwegian Defense Research Establishment studied almost eight hundred Saudi militants and their paths to terrorism. Unlike in the 1980s and 1990s, when Islamic leaders like Bin Laden and Ayman al Zawahiri (the Egyptian medical doctor who is one of the leading architects of contemporary radical Sunni Islam) could recruit followers openly, Hegghammer writes, recent recruitment is more private and subtle, leading many recruits to believe the decision was their own.

"No one recruited me in Mecca," one young detainee told his captors. "I met a man who told me about the idea of *Jihad* . . . He gave me money and put me on a plane to the Arab Emirates first going to Pakistan. He didn't train me or anything like that. He just gave me the idea about fighting," Hegghammer quotes him as saying.

Because mosque sermons now are monitored, radical sheikhs and other religious zealots engage individuals in Mecca during Hajj or Ramadan, or during semi-informal religious group meetings, such as religious camps or evening assemblies of young men in *istirahat,* rented guest houses, where the young (and sometimes Saudi families) can gather in privacy.

While the regime has expended enormous resources to eliminate or convert terrorists inside the kingdom—both because security in exchange for loyalty is the implicit pact between the Al Saud and Saudis and because the regime feels directly threatened by terrorists—the government has been far less forceful in combating terrorism against Western infidels, which for now is the primary focus of Al Qaeda. In the past, Bin Laden and Al Zawahiri and other leaders have argued over how much to focus on the "near enemy" (corrupt Arab regimes) and how much to focus on the "distant enemy" (the West's infidel regimes). Al Zawahiri favored the former and Bin Laden the latter.

Al Zawahiri, who went to Saudi Arabia in 1984 after he was freed from an Egyptian prison for playing a supporting role in the murder of Anwar Sadat, often is called the "brains" of Al Qaeda. A jihadist from age fifteen, he is dedicated to reestablishing an Islamic caliphate by eliminating both the corrupt Islamic leaders and the Western infidels who preserve their leadership.

"Liberating the Muslim community, attacking the enemies of Islam and waging a *jihad* against them require a Muslim authority, established on Muslim territory, that raises the banner of *jihad* and rallies Muslims around it," he wrote in one of his many exhortations to the faithful, this one entitled *Knights Under the Prophet's Banner.* "If we do not achieve this goal, our actions will be nothing more than small-scale harassment and will not bear fruit—the restoration of the caliphate and the departure of the invaders from the land of Islam."

Islam's enemies, as defined by Al Zawahiri, are Jews, Christians, and Muslims who associate with them, especially the Saudi royal family. Relying on the Koran's words "Take not for friends unbelievers rather than believers," Al Zawahiri builds the case for separation from Jews and Christians. "God said: 'O you who believe! Take not into your intimacy those outside your ranks.'" In this verse, according to Al Zawahiri, "God prohibited believers taking unbelievers, Jews, and heretics as advisers or from trusting them with money. It is said that you must not speak to anyone whose creed or religion is different from yours."

Because the Al Saud regime ultimately depends on the United States for its protection and preservation while presiding over Islam's two holiest sites, the Saudi regime is a key target of international jihadists. "We saw the noblest of dynasties placing itself in the service of American interests while claiming to defend monotheism; we saw impious imams imposing secular constitutions, judging on the basis of positive law and rushing to normalize relations with Israel, while supervising *Quran* memorization competitions," Al Zawahiri writes, in a clear reference to the Al Saud family.

As for the United States, its sin is not only supporting the Al Saud regime but believing in and promoting democracy. "Democracy is a new religion," he writes. "In Islam, legislation comes from God; in a democracy this capacity is given to the people. Therefore, this is a new religion based on making the people into gods and giving them God's rights and attributes. This is tantamount to associating idols with God . . . Sovereignty in Islam is God's alone; in a democracy, it belongs to the people."

The Saudi regime walks a fine line between discouraging extremism—to assuage its American protectors and to protect itself—and openly attacking this radical reading of Islam, since the regime's legitimacy rests on protecting and propagating puritanical Islam. Small wonder then that only in 2010, some seven years after bloody attacks by terrorists began inside the kingdom, did the grand mufti of Saudi Arabia issue a fatwa condemning terrorism and declaring "any act of terrorism, including providing financial support to terrorists, is a crime." Even then his focus seemed as much on protecting the reputation of Islam as on protecting innocent victims from terrorism. "Terrorism is criminal and spills the blood of innocents," Sheikh Abdul Aziz bin Abdullah al Ashaikh acknowledged, according to the Saudi Press Agency. "It attacks security, spreads terror among people and creates problems for society." He went on, however, to deplore its damage not so much to the victims of terrorism as to Islam's reputation: "It is necessary to fight the attempts of some to attach terrorism to Islam and Muslims with the goal of distorting the religion and assailing its leadership role in the world." But what of the victims?

Efforts to plot terrorist attacks continue inside Saudi Arabia and around the world, though in recent years most have been disrupted before their successful execution. While Bin Laden is now dead, Al Zawahiri remains at large, presumably along the Afghanistan-Pakistan border. Anwar al Awlaki, a young English-speaking imam and terrorist leader born in Las Cruces, New Mexico, and residing in Yemen, skillfully used the Internet to recruit and radicalize young Muslim men in the West to murder their fellow citizens, until a U.S. drone attack killed him in 2011. But the deaths of Bin Laden and Al Awlaki have not ended the threat level—or tension—between Islam and the West.

While many in the Islamic world and in the United States perceive a clash of civilizations, Islam is and historically has been far too divided to support this simple analysis—unless the West were to do something seen as so hostile to Islam that radicals could rally the wider Islamic world into a convulsive backlash against it. Terrorist leaders like Bin Laden and Al Awlaki surely sought to incite such an act. Dr. Al Hadlag, the Saudi official monitoring the ideological strategies of terrorist groups, says Al Qaeda would like to do something inside Saudi Arabia that would prompt the U.S. military to return to the kingdom. (All U.S. forces withdrew to other Gulf countries in August 2003.) He believes one target is Abquiq, the site in eastern Saudi Arabia through which Saudi oil passes for processing en route to the coast for loading on ships for export to the world. The destruction of Abquiq would cripple Saudi oil exports and thus, terrorists calculate, could trigger massive U.S. intervention—with or without Al Saud invitation—to protect vital Saudi oil facilities from further terrorist attacks. In 2006, terrorists drove two explosive-laden cars through a side gate at the facility, but both were blown up by security guards at the gate, according to Dr. Al Hadlag. More terrorist cells, picked up inside Saudi Arabia since, also have targeted oil facilities.

Osama bin Laden, before his death, continued to call for Islamic unity as a prerequisite for defeating the West. "The only way of repelling the [infidel] invasion is through the combined efforts of all Muslims," he declared in his definitive 1998 Declaration of Jihad Against the Americans Occupying the Land of the Two Holy Sanctuaries, "so the Muslims must ignore what divides them, temporarily, since closing their eyes to their differences cannot be worse than ignoring the capital sin that menaces Muslims."

Islamic extremists like Bin Laden and some of the Westerners most fearful of them think in terms of "Islamic civilization," but is there actually such a thing? Islam is widely spread across vast areas of the world, including large and largely secular societies like Turkey and Indonesia as well as theocracies like Iran. Moreover, since its inception under

Muhammad in the deserts of Arabia, Islam has been divided within itself. Three of the first four caliphs who succeeded the Prophet were murdered—two by fellow Muslims—and deep divisions persist today not just among Shias, Sufis, Ismailis, and Sunnis but also within Sunni Islam, as is so evident in Saudi Arabia today. The Arabs are merely a modest component of global Islam, and Saudi Arabia is only a small sector of the Arab world.

Saudi Arabia, however, remains the spiritual center of the Islamic faith and, on a more mundane level, the world's leading petroleum producer. All the forces dividing the Muslim world can be seen in microcosm here—radical imams and moderate ones, rich royals and rootless youth, radicalization and Westernization, fundamentalism, modernism, and terrorism. So while Saudi Arabia is only a small part of the Islamic world, how these forces play out here will have a greatly disproportionate influence on the outcome of the worldwide war against terrorism.

CHAPTER 12

Succession

Of all the pressing problems facing the Saudi regime, the prickliest—and the one that has the potential to shape the kingdom's response to all others—is royal succession. The elderly sons of Abdul Aziz, who have ruled sequentially since his death in 1953, are approaching the end of the line.

With King Abdullah eighty-nine and ailing, having lost two crown princes and anointing a third within eight months, the royal family is approaching an inflection point. It could continue to pass the crown to remaining brothers and half-brothers, the youngest of whom already is sixty-nine, but none of them appears likely to have the acumen and energy—or even the time—to usher in a new era of reform to solve the kingdom's problems. So whether by choice of the royal family sooner or by the will of Allah a bit later, the crown is going to have to pass to a new generation of princes. This entails both opportunity and risk.

The opportunity is more obvious. In theory at least, a new-generation royal who was educated, open-minded, and above all energetic could begin seriously to tackle the country's manifold problems by relaxing political and economic controls, and by providing more efficient and accountable government to relieve the frustrations of the sullen Saudi populace.

Given the stakes involved, however, the risk is that the diffuse and divided royal family will dither or, worse, splinter. The stakes are not merely which new-generation prince will wear the crown but the prospect that that prince's branch of the family will then pass the crown to its sons and grandsons in perpetuity, preventing other branches of the family from ever ruling again. For nearly sixty years, the crown has passed by family consensus from one brother to the next, occasionally skipping one deemed incapable or unsuitable for leadership but otherwise following the tradition of seniority. A king might favor his own sons with particularly plum jobs, but he understood that the crown would pass next not to his sons but to his brothers. It is a system unlike that of any other monarchy. But in a kingdom in which princes often marry multiple wives and thus produce literally dozens of progeny—now adding up to nearly seven thousand princes—it is a system that has largely worked.

But brotherly succession has not always gone smoothly. The second Saudi state collapsed in 1891 because several Al Saud brothers fought one another for preeminence. Another brother tried to pick up the pieces but was defeated by the competing Al Rashid family and fled to exile in Kuwait with his teenage son—the future founder of the modern Saudi state, Abdul Aziz. Half a century later on his deathbed, that same Abdul Aziz summoned his two eldest sons, Saud and Faisal, to his bedside to avoid a repetition of history. "Join hands across my body," he told them, "and swear that you will work together when I am gone. Swear too, that if you quarrel, you will argue in private. You must not let the world catch sight of your disagreements."

The dying king's words fell on deaf ears. The two brothers quickly began quarreling, and their feud continued for more than a decade. The elder, Saud, who followed his father on the throne, was extravagant in every way. In a kingdom that then had few resources, he spent lavishly on everything, including a garish new pink and gold palace surrounded by high walls to conceal swimming pools, palm groves, and fountains supplied from artesian wells drilled by Americans. Traffic lights regulated the flow of Cadillacs cruising within the palace walls. The palace's thousands of colored bulbs periodically lit neon inscriptions from the Koran. Lighting, cooling, and irrigating his palace and grounds was said to consume more electricity and water than did all the rest of Riyadh. As the king drove to and from this desert palace, he habitually tossed handfuls of gold and silver coins from the window of his car, watching with glee as children scrambled to gather them.

Crown Prince Faisal, by contrast, was an ascetic. Deeply religious and hardworking, he lived what for Saudi royals was a simple lifestyle, following daily religious and personal rituals down to the number of pieces into which he cut his afternoon apple. Faisal and other princes had watched as King Saud squandered the nation's resources, leaving Saudi Arabia by 1958 essentially bankrupt, notwithstanding its rising oil revenues. In that year, a delegation of royal brothers asked Faisal to head a new government of national reform and take over day-to-day governance. The Saudi people learned this only when the religious readings on Mecca radio were interrupted to announce that Crown Prince Faisal had taken over administration of the kingdom under King Saud. When Faisal went to inquire how much cash the nation had to meet its obligations, he found only 317 riyals (about $100). When he asked the National Commercial Bank, then and now the kingdom's largest, for a loan, it refused because King Saud already had defaulted on numerous large loans.

For the next six years, the brothers carried on an increasingly public tug-of-war for leadership, bringing the country to the verge of civil war. Finally in 1963 King Saud, refusing to yield power despite his misrule, surrounded his palace with his Royal Guards. The late Crown Prince Sultan, then minister of defense, put the army on alert. Prince Abdullah, then head of the National Guard and now king, called out his troops. King Saud and his immediate extended family remained holed up at his palace. A tense nation waited to see what would happen.

Crown Prince Faisal went to work as usual each day, driving past the palace where King Saud's guards, cradling loaded machine guns, followed him with their eyes. One day Faisal stopped. "Have you got enough to eat and drink?" he asked. "You've been out here for some time. I will have some coffee sent round." The mere act of speaking to the guards was a turning point; thereafter they saluted Faisal as he drove to work. The crisis abated. But still King Saud refused to yield power.

Finally the family turned to the religious *ulama* to adjudicate the quarrel. The *ulama* noted that King Saud had voluntarily given powers to his crown prince and had no justification for revoking them. The family elders asked the *ulama* to institutionalize this decision in a fatwa. Immediately after the fatwa was issued, some seventy princes representing all branches of the family endorsed it. The decisive role played by the *ulama* is a reminder to this day that those who would be king should not offend the religious leadership.

At last King Saud departed the kingdom, with all senior family members gathered at the airport in a show of unity. The new king, Faisal, stood at the end of the farewell line with his head bowed to his elder brother and kissed his hand in respect as the deposed king flew to Dhahran, Beirut, and finally Athens, where he spent most of his remaining years. King Faisal is still widely respected by Saudis as a decisive, principled, authoritarian ruler who modernized the kingdom—ending slavery and introducing education

King Abdullah, 89, during one of his multiple hospitalizations, was visited by a group of his aged brothers, including the late Crown Prince Nayef, *at far right*. Ronald Reagan once famously said of similarly aged and infirm Soviet leaders: "They keep dying on me." (SAUDI PRESS AGENCY)

for girls both only in the 1960s—and stood up to the West with the 1973 oil embargo. After his assassination in 1975 by a nephew, the crown has passed from one half-brother to another without any visible public disagreement: from Faisal to Khalid, a reluctant and short-lived king; to Fahd, who ruled more than two decades; and now to Abdullah, who assumed the throne in 2005.

With that history in mind, and aware that a generational change was approaching that almost surely would be divisive, King Abdullah early in his reign established a so-called Allegiance Council to create a formal process for selecting future monarchs. This council consists of the remaining sons of Abdul Aziz and the eldest son or grandson of the deceased sons of the founder. Thus, all male branches of the family have representation on the council, which consisted of thirty-five princes at its founding in 2007 but now has thirty-four since one brother, Fawwaz, died leaving only an ineligible adopted son. (Abdul Aziz fathered some forty-four sons by twenty-two wives.)

Theoretically, the system gives all council members an equal say in selecting a new crown prince when the existing one becomes king. Creating this one-man-one-vote Allegiance Council was King Abdullah's way of trying to curb the power of the six surviving Sudairi brothers, a clique of senior princes occupying key government jobs, including minister of defense, minister of interior, and governor of Riyadh, for most of the past fifty years. Many branches of the family feared that if Crown Prince Sultan, a Sudairi, became king, he and his brothers would conspire among themselves to pass the throne from one Sudairi to the next, excluding half-brothers from other branches. The deaths of Sultan and Nayef leave only four Sudairis, and one, Salman, now is crown prince. (The Sudairi royals are the sons of Abdul Aziz by a favored and ambitious wife named Hassa bint Ahmad Sudairi, who dined with her seven sons weekly until her death and trained them to support each other over their half-brothers in the extended family. Her eldest son was the late King Fahd.)

The Allegiance Council, first announced in 2006, took more than a year to materialize, perhaps a sign of intrafamily struggles over its composition. Abdullah finally announced its membership at a family dinner in 2007. "We thank Allah Almighty who enabled King Abdul Aziz to realize the first Arab unity paving the way for the establishment of the Kingdom of Saudi Arabia: the purest place on earth," he said. Then each of the thirty-five princes swore an oath before the king: "I pledge to Allah Almighty to remain loyal to my religion, king and country, and not to divulge any of the state's secrets, and to preserve its interests and systems, and to work for the unity of the royal family and its cooperation as well as the national unity and to perform my duty sincerely, honestly and justly."

The Allegiance Council still has not played a role despite the deaths of two crown princes. The king, himself recuperating from back surgery only a few days before Sultan's death, rose from his hospital bed to ask his brothers to pledge their loyalty to his choice for Crown Prince, Nayef, the Sudairi he had personally named second deputy prime minister in 2009, to hold the fort at home when he traveled on business as Crown Prince Sultan was abroad for medical reasons. That 2009 appointment effectively put Nayef second in line for the throne after his ailing brother, Sultan, and seemed to undermine the very system that the king himself had created to select a new crown prince. Nayef's ultimate confirmation as crown prince a few days after Sultan's death surprised no one.

The king's decision to name Nayef deputy prime minister parted the curtain on royal family divisions. Prince Talal, older than Nayef, immediately warned through Reuters that Nayef's appointment absolutely did not mean he was crown prince in waiting. "I call on the royal court to clarify what is meant by this nomination and that it does not mean that he will become crown prince," Talal told the news agency.

Notwithstanding Prince Talal's view, Nayef would have been monarch had he not died in June 2012 from diabetes and poor circulation soon after being appointed crown prince. His death pleased reformers who had feared he would snuff out even the modest reforms of King Abdullah. Nayef, who served as minister of interior from 1975 until his death, was disliked by many Saudis for his role in smothering any hint of dissent by arresting those brave enough to criticize the regime even mildly and by imprisoning and executing those who actively oppose it. When reformers in 2003 were proposing a constitutional monarchy, one activist who met with an angry Nayef recalls that the prince retorted, "I don't want to be Queen Elizabeth." Now the crown looks likely to pass to Prince Salman, seventy-six, who was appointed minister of defense in 2011 at the death of Crown Prince Sultan, who held that portfolio for half a century. Salman became crown prince in June 2012 upon the death of Nayef eight months later. Prince Salman is described as hardworking and religiously conservative but is seen as open to at least maintaining the modest reforms of King Abdullah. Prince Salman and his half-brother Abdullah are expected to be a more harmonious duo than were Abdullah and Nayef.

But given the age of both men, at some point soon the Al Saud family will have to make the generational change to a grandson of the founder. The Allegiance Council, which already has a majority of grandsons, might be assumed to favor a member of the next generation. But given the deference to age in Saudi society, especially in the royal family, the grandsons are likely to defer to their remaining uncles' judgment. Moreover, the competing interests of the multiple grandsons may well serve to block one another's ambitions. One grandson on the Allegiance Council confides that the grandsons' numerical advantage won't affect the outcome. "We will simply follow what the senior members of the family say."

Another grandson acknowledges that groups of family members are already meeting regularly these days to discuss the changes they all know are coming. He insists all will go smoothly. "The only difference is that instead of being loyal to our uncles, we will be loyal to our cousins," he says of the impending generational change. "In the next two to five years this will cease to be an issue." The family, he says, is trying to organize a whole series of moves to arrange succession not just at the top but at key ministries like defense, interior, and foreign affairs, each of which was held for decades by the same princes who now are either dead or dying. (Defense, as noted, has been filled by Prince Salman.) "It is like a rosary," he explains. "You can't move one bead without moving them all. So the family wants to move all the beads at once."

This is another way of saying that the family hasn't yet balanced issues of internal equity, so the country simply will have to wait for better or at least more energetic leaders. The leadership has essentially been on hold since 1995, when King Fahd suffered a debilitating stroke and Crown Prince Abdullah became acting king and ruled without a functioning partner or crown prince for a decade. In 2005, when Fahd died and Abdullah became king in title as well as fact, he named Sultan his crown prince, but within two years Sultan was in New York seeking treatment for cancer; he died in October 2011. So for at least fifteen years, the kingdom has been without a team who could make the sclerotic Saudi bureaucracy function. All important decisions wind up at the king's desk. Now the kingdom once again has both a king and a crown prince, yet both are infirm and cannot provide energetic, let alone visionary, leadership.

So Saudis watch and wait, having no input into the succession decisions but aware that rivalries and tensions within the family clearly could break into the open and that a royal house divided might not stand. It obviously is in the self-interest of the Al Saud family to ensure smooth transitions, but in a family of thousands of princes and several dozen different branches, consensus could prove elusive. And if the family settles for another aged son of the founder to succeed Salman, the country's sad status quo would simply continue to run its downward course. This is most likely as Prince Mugrin bin Abdul Aziz, sixty-seven, was named next in line after his brother Crown Prince Salman in 2013.

In late 2012 King Abdullah began to name some of his younger nephews to prominent leadership roles. Muham-

Four of the princes who would be king. Each is among the not-so-young younger generation of grandsons of the country's founder.

Khalid al Faisal, 72, governor of Mecca, a moderate, modern prince known for his religious rectitude, is the son of the late King Faisal. (GETTY IMAGES)

Muhammad bin Fahd, 61, former governor of the Eastern Province and son of the late King Fahd, is widely known for amassing a personal fortune. (GETTY IMAGES)

Muhammad bin Nayef, 53, Minister of Interior and son of the late Crown Prince Nayef, works closely with U.S. security agencies on counter-terrorism. (GETTY IMAGES)

Khalid bin Sultan, 63, deputy minister of defense and son of the late Crown Prince Sultan, is a billionaire horse breeder with close ties to the U.S. military. (GETTY IMAGES)

mad bin Nayef, fifty-three, was named Minister of Interior replacing his seventy-two-year-old uncle; his brother, Saud bin Nayef, fifty-seven, was named governor of the Eastern Province and Faisal bin Salman, forty-two, son of the king-dom's Crown Prince was named governor of Medina.

If the throne can be passed to a new-generation royal, there will at least be an opportunity for change. That next genera-tion includes numerous princes with the education, experi-ence, and energy to tackle the kingdom's many problems. And several appear to be actively jockeying. These include both Muhammad and Saud bin Nayef; Khalid al Faisal, son of the late King Faisal and governor of Mecca; Muhammad bin Fahd, son of the late King Fahd and until 2013 governor of the Eastern Province; Al Waleed bin Talal, Saudi Arabia's most successful businessman and son of the crotchety Prince Talal bin Abdul Aziz, the lifelong advocate of democratic reform by the royal family; Khalid bin Sultan, son of the late Crown Prince Sultan and deputy minister of defense; and their uncle, Ahmad bin Abdul Aziz, despite his being removed in 2012 as Interior Minister. At the most simplistic level, a new-generation monarch might be capable of work-ing a full day and at least press the sclerotic bureaucracy to implement, rather than deep-six, royal decrees, as so often now occurs. Such a driver of change, of course, could crash, but in the absence of an alert and active driver, the kingdom seems doomed to sink ever deeper into the mire of unproduc-tive dependency, with all the mounting frustrations that such indignity provokes.

Saudis watch the diminishing line of Al Saud brothers and the impending generational succession as if it were an old-fashioned time bomb with a lit fuse. The wick burns ever shorter, advancing a moment of explosion that could destroy life as they know it. But they are powerless to remove the bomb or snuff out the flame. All they can do is watch, wait, and worry.

CHAPTER 13

Saudi Scenarios

Much of the Middle East remains in turmoil and transition as this book goes to press. Some of the revolution has been largely peaceful, as in Egypt; some has been suppressed for the time being, as in Bahrain; some has led to civil war, as in Libya and in Syria. Meanwhile, Saudi Arabia—far and away the most important country in the region, given its enormous oil reserves and exports, its consequent impact on the global economy, and its role as strategic counterweight to revolutionary Iran—still seems stable and largely peaceful. But on its current flight path, Saudi Arabia is in serious trouble, so how may the journey end?

Unfortunately, the most likely path, given the risk-aversion of the elderly rulers, is continuation of the status quo. That option would mean continued and deepening economic and social stagnation, with the ensuing risk of social explosion. A second option would be to open up the society and economy to relieve stagnation and begin the process of revitalization. A third course could be a reversion to the rigid religiosity and repression of the 1980s. A final outcome could be chaos and collapse. The aged, infirm, and politically paralyzed Saudi leadership for now is sticking with the status quo.

Like deer in the headlights, the senior Saudi leadership is frozen in time and place. The geriatric rulers see the turmoil in the region around them and the growing disaffection of Saudi youth. They dimly understand that there is a problem, but they don't begin to understand the dimensions of the discontent, let alone how to reduce it. Thus they fall back on the tactics that have served the Al Saud in the past—keeping society divided, playing one group off against another, dispensing large sums of money to placate angry citizens, shoring up relations with the religious, and praying that their father's social compact of loyalty to the Al Saud in exchange for stability will hold.

Early in 2011 King Abdullah, recuperating in Morocco from back surgery while revolution rolled through Tunisia and Egypt, returned home to do what Saudi kings know how to do—spend money. He dispensed $130 billion (an astounding 85 percent increment to the annual budget) to almost every group in society that was unhappy or that conceivably could become so. Some 500 billion Saudi riyals were passed out among the religious, the military, students, and the unemployed, with half the total earmarked to create housing. For the first time, a minimum wage was set for Saudi workers, though of course not for foreigners, who do most of the work. The religious were given permission to open fatwa centers in all regions of the country (as if the religious didn't already produce enough fatwas) and were allowed to fire an outspoken sheikh in Mecca whom the king personally had intervened to save only a year earlier.

The new largesse doubtless has bought a bit of time, but it will do nothing to revitalize the stultified economy. Rather, it simply increases dependency on unproductive government jobs and royal handouts, further sapping Saudi enterprise. For many Saudis, these latest tips, however generous, reinforce their sense of entitlement, their resentment over unequal distribution of wealth, and their humiliation over the indignity of dependence on royal favors that they believe should be a public right. In today's Saudi Arabia, money may buy passivity, but it rarely buys gratitude—and surely not the kind of loyalty that King Abdul Aziz once commanded from his tribal followers.

Because King Abdullah offered only money and no real reform proposals, modernizers saw his action as another lost opportunity to institute changes that might reverse the country's downward course. Might the Al Saud have been expected to do more? Not really, and for several reasons.

First, with succession tensions consuming the royal family, continuity, not change, is the safest course for all princely contenders. Second, when the Al Saud family is nervous, as now, it tilts toward pacifying its religious partners, who almost never favor change—unless it is a retreat toward seventh-century purity. Historically, only when the Al Saud are confident have they risked religious ire by offering even small reforms, such as those King Abdullah advocated early in his rule, when he championed opportunity for women, or as a confident King Faisal did in the 1960s, when he introduced girls' education and television to the kingdom.

Third, the senior royals genuinely believe that the traditional practices that have brought them through numerous challenges, both external and internal, over the past half-century remain sufficient. Prince Salman bin Abdul Aziz, governor of Riyadh, interviewed in 2010 at his sprawling modern office in downtown Riyadh, took pains to explain why democracy wouldn't work in Saudi Arabia. "If Saudi Arabia adopts democracy, every tribe will be a party," he said, and the country would be chaotic. Instead, he says, the kingdom has *shura,* or consultation. "Government asks a collection of people to consult, and when there is no consensus, the leader decides."

Finally, the royal family is absolutely convinced of the indispensability of its absolute rule. To a man, the scores of princes I've met over many years—even those who criticize the government and advocate change—invariably conclude by saying, "We are the glue that holds the kingdom together. Without us, there is chaos."

If these tried and true tactics have kept the kingdom stable in the past, why shouldn't they work now and in the future? Conceivably, they will. However, there are numerous reasons they likely will not. The most important can be summed up in one equation: the gap between aged rulers and youthful subjects grows dramatically, as the information gap between the rulers and the ruled shrinks. The average age of the king and crown prince is eighty-three, yet, as already noted, 60 percent of Saudis are under twenty. Thanks to satellite television, the Internet, and social media, the young now are well aware of government ineffectiveness and wealth inequities. A new survey of Arab youth taken before and after the revolution in Egypt found that 59 percent of young Saudis rated the wealth gap as a major concern, even ahead of concerns about unemployment (57 percent). Across the kingdom, they can see princely palaces covering city blocks that are protected not by private guards but by Saudi soldiers paid by the government.

Moreover, the multiple crises of the past five decades—Gamal Abdel Nasser's enmity, the attack on the Grand Mosque, hosting unpopular U.S. troops to repulse Saddam's threat, challenges from religious conservatives, and terror attacks at home—did not coincide with generational succession and all the risks it entails for family unity. The combination of aged rulers and intrafamily jockeying for future power consumes the limited energies of the senior princes and makes any decisive policy steps far less likely, even though mounting social pressures require bold—and inevitably risky—actions.

Further complicating future Saudi stability is the declining credibility of both the Al Saud and their religious supporters. Over the past decade, as Saudis of all ages and persuasions have gained access to information, these two pillars of stability have been tarnished by images of royal decadence and religious hypocrisy. Greater awareness has eroded what might be called the "satisfied center"—those Saudis who traditionally believed what they were told by their rulers and the religious establishment. They now know better. The new pan-Arab youth survey found the sharpest drop in confidence about the direction of their country among Saudis. Still, some 62 percent (down from 98 percent a year earlier) said their country was going in the right direction. But the downward trend is clear.

Ironically, deep divisions and distrust among Saudis, long exploited by the regime to bolster its rule, now pose a reverse risk for the Al Saud. For example, as the gap between religious conservatives and modernizers widens, the Al Saud rulers find it ever more difficult to balance between competing agendas.

Finally, the Al Saud penchant for consensus and for buying off critics to minimize opposition not only has slowed decision making but also over time has packed the bureaucracy with competing interests, leaving almost every aspect of society and the economy crippled by inefficiency and corruption. Securing decisions on almost anything is extraordinarily time consuming, all the more so with a king and a crown prince who were ill for most of the past fifteen years, and who now are old and ill. Arguably, not since King Faisal, who was assassinated in 1975, has the kingdom had a confident, activist monarch interested in modernizing and developing Saudi Arabia. Faisal's short-lived successor, Khalid, didn't want to be king, and Fahd, who followed in 1982, was so spooked by the new theocracy in Iran and by the attack on the Grand Mosque that he largely abandoned reform inside the kingdom to please the religious establishment.

In his still-seminal 1968 book, *Political Order in Changing Societies,* the late Sam Huntington, a political science professor at Harvard, examined the challenges of political change with striking relevance to Saudi Arabia. Modernizing monarchies, he wrote, initially can absorb the upwardly mobile individuals in society. Eventually, however, traditional contempt for private-sector jobs in such societies, and the government's inability to absorb all the educated people that its modernization produces, inevitably lead to disaffection among middle and lower classes left behind. One way to postpone this disaffection, he wrote, is to slow modernization and reform, "coming to an accommodation with the traditional elements in society, and enlisting their support in the maintenance of a partially modern but not modernizing system." This is precisely what the Al Saud have done. But as Huntington also predicted, monarchies like the Al Saud "will lose some or all of whatever capability they have developed for policy innovation under traditional auspices before they gain any substantial new capability to cope with problems of political participation produced by their own reforms."

Huntington, writing more than forty years ago, pinpointed the dilemma the Al Saud would face were they to pursue a policy of genuine reform. They aren't, of course, and almost surely the current elderly leadership won't.

A Saudi reform scenario would not involve democracy in any Western understanding of the concept. Most Saudis, deeply Islamic, aren't seeking that. Even most of the aggressive modernizers seek only a constitutional monarchy, in which the Al Saud would still reign but within the parameters of a written constitution and by sharing some power with others.

What most Saudis I have met say they want is not democracy or even constitutional monarchy, but a government that is efficient in providing basic services and that is accountable for its decisions. They want transparency with the uses of the nation's wealth and less corruption. They want rule of law, not of royal whim. They want to know they are being treated equitably with others in society and that punishments and penalties meted out don't change at the whim of authorities or with the status of the offender.

Beyond that, many Saudi citizens want a more open society, still devoutly Islamic but free of some of the restraints imposed by religious fundamentalists and absent the daily harassment of the religious police. One such Saudi, Khalid al Nowaiser, a Jeddah lawyer, called on the king (in an open letter published in 2011 by *Arab News* and *The Wall Street Journal*) to abolish the religious police, calling the organization "totally unacceptable, not only for a country that is a member of the G-20 but for any country that exists in the 21st century." Al Nowaiser and other such Saudis seek more personal space: outlets through which to express themselves, civic organizations through which they can cooperate with like-minded citizens to bring change. In short, they seek to escape the labyrinth in which they feel confined. Finally, the young in particular want to be free to contribute to shaping society, not merely to play the role of puppets in a gloomy theatrical production and on occasion to receive favors bestowed by those in power. For most societies, these expectations would be modest; for Saudi Arabia, they are revolutionary.

Ironically, a model of this sort of open society exists in Saudi Arabia: it is Saudi ARAMCO, the national oil company. Within the gates of its walled compound near Dhahran, some thousands of Saudis, the overwhelming majority of its employees, work together efficiently and productively. They include men and women, Sunnis and Shias, managers and employees—and a small minority of foreigners. They function together in what relative to the rest of Saudi Arabia is a meritocracy: education is prized, hard work is expected, expertise is developed, and talent is recognized and rewarded. This island of ARAMCO, off limits to the religious police and largely isolated from the rest of Saudi society, offers visible proof that Saudis can be educated, enterprising, and efficient; can work together with purpose and pride; can employ the most modern technologies to operate in world markets; and can remain uniquely Saudi while also competing in the modern world. Religion on the ARAMCO compound is individual and largely invisible. A small, square glass-walled structure with no iconic minaret serves as a mosque for Muslim employees. Three school gymnasiums host Catholic, Protestant, and Mormon services, not only for Saudi ARAMCO employees but also for Christian expatriates in the surrounding area.

"We have a corporate culture that awards competence and training," says Saudi ARAMCO CEO Khalid al Falih, the third Saudi to hold the top job since the company, founded by American oil companies in 1933 and initially led by Americans, was bought by Saudi Arabia in 1980. "We are blind to ethnicity or sect. We have a highly industrious work ethic and integrity." Asked if a minority Shia could one day be CEO, Al Falih instantly says, "Yes, he could. There are Shia vice presidents now."

Sitting in the Saudi ARAMCO cafeteria with a mix of men and women, some of them veiled and others not, many young but some older, conversing across the traditional lines of gender, sect, tribe, and class, is unlike any other experience in the kingdom. These Saudis are not all Westernized; nor are they rebels against Saudi society. They have simply created a parallel society.

A woman, Nabilah al Tunisi, is in charge of the engineering on Saudi ARAMCO's new $25 billion refinery and petrochemicals plant at Ras Tanura, a tiny protrusion into the Persian Gulf. One of the company's vice presidents, Nadmi Nasir, a Shia, was selected to lead the creation and construction of the King Abdullah University for Science and Technology, a project the king entrusted to Saudi ARAMCO rather than his moribund Ministry of Higher Education.

This Saudi ARAMCO model may seem utopian, but even much more modest reform seems out of reach for the rest of Saudi society. While small reforms would satisfy many Saudis, for the Al Saud the perceived risks to their rule outweigh any potential benefits to society. Even opening the economy to more enterprise and competition would require greater openness in society and fewer rigid rules imposed by the religious. This, in turn, would mean accommodating to a more independent-minded citizenry, less dependent on royal largesse and less accepting of regime control. It is the dilemma of glasnost and perestroika. While some of the royals would welcome more economic reforms, they fear the demands for greater glasnost or transparency, that could result.

Specifically, what the regime fears are escalating demands from frustrated youth who, if given some opportunity for expression and enterprise, will want more. The government also worries about a domino effect, in which trying to satisfy the demands of one group leads to greater demands from others—from frustrated women, disenfranchised minorities, exploited foreign workers, and more. Above all, the royals are restrained by their reliance on religious conservatives, whom they dare not alienate. After all, without the imprimatur of Islam, the Al Saud risk being seen as just another Saudi tribe. Every action in Saudi society carries the risk of a reaction, and this is nowhere truer than in dealing with modernizers and religious fundamentalists.

Finally, any prospect of even modest reform would require a new-generation monarch who sees the risk-reward relationship in reverse, who believes the greater risk to the monarchy is the status quo, and who has the confidence, energy, and longevity to see a reform agenda through. Some such princes with at least some of those qualities do exist among the grandsons of the founder. But given the royal family's devotion to age and seniority, it is doubtful any of them will be given a chance to rule until it could be too late for reform.

A third scenario—and one that comes more naturally to the Al Saud than risky reform—is to clamp a lid on social demands, bow to the dictates of the religious establishment, and impose greater repression on Saudi society. There already is a precedent: King Fahd did precisely this in the 1980s, closeting women and suppressing critics. This scenario could result either from a deteriorating status quo or from an experiment with reform that unleashed more societal demands than the Al Saud could tolerate. It is easy to imagine a situation in which repression would be a tempting tack for the Al Saud, but it would entail its own set of risks. The direction of history in the Middle East these days is not increased repression. The Al Saud never have been reluctant to deploy harsh tactics—imprisonment without trials, torture, and even summary execution against selected opponents they see as serious threats. However, the regime has never had to resort to mass repression. It is not clear that the elderly brothers would have the stomach for clubbing youth protesters in the streets, much less turning out the military to shoot them. For all the criticisms of the Al Saud, they are not hated the way some other rulers in the Middle East were before they were toppled. They are resented, especially by young Saudis who neither fear nor respect them as earlier generations did. But were the family to engage in wholesale brutal repression to cling to power, today's sullen resentment would explode among many Saudis into active hatred.

Conformity is such a strong strain in Saudi society that the Al Saud may never need to resort to brutal repression. Targeted repression of protest leaders, coupled with billion-dollar bribes to wide swaths of society, may prove sufficient. Saudi youth, however, seem determined to have a say in shaping their future, so they may not be intimidated by repression or seduced by traditional bribes. Almost certainly a key determinant in how they will react in coming years will be the success or failure of revolutions in Egypt and elsewhere in the region. If, a few years hence, revolutions are seen to have yielded improvements in economic and political life, Saudis will be more likely to demand the same freedom for themselves. If the liberalization experiments have brought chaos without progress, even young, frustrated Saudis will be inclined to opt for stability. In short, failure elsewhere will mean success for the Al Saud monarchy.

A final scenario could result from any of the three already outlined—disintegrating status quo, failed reform, or repression—and that is collapse and chaos. However unlikely it seems today in a still-stable kingdom, no one can be completely confident that events will not spiral out of control in a country with no institutions to allow expression and resolution of differences. If, as seems likely, clinging to the status quo results only in further social and economic deterioration; if attempts at reform unleash excessive expectations—or prompt a harsh backlash by conservatives—and resulting repression inflames rather than suppresses opponents, then chaos could erupt.

The regime has long fed fears of chaos—*après moi la deluge*—and the religious have preached that chaos is sinful and obedience is the way of Allah. Still, it is not unimaginable that Saudi Arabia's many deep divisions could erupt into conflict. The kingdom's security forces are divided into at least three groups—Defense, National Guard, and Interior—under the control of different princes of the family. The religious are divided among themselves, ranging from the tame *ulama* who support the Al Saud to both moderates and fundamentalists unhappy with royal family rule and perhaps open to supporting new leaders. The kingdom's regional divisions are always there to be exploited. The Eastern Province (home to the oil reserves and to the perennially ill-used and unhappy Shiite minority) and the Hejaz (site of the holy cities of Mecca and Medina with their more open, international outlook) both resent the overwhelming dominance of religious conservatives from the Nejd, home of the

Al Saud, at all levels of national governance. These regional divisions—and tribal divisions within each region—are stronger than any sense of Saudi national identity. The Al Saud princes, of course, never sought to instill nationalism or patriotism but only loyalty to their family. Thus, should royal family divisions, now festering beneath the surface, erupt over succession, little could prevent society's larger fault lines from cracking. In that environment of civil strife— a Libya writ large—the extremists would see opportunity and the West, especially the United States, would face the agonizing choice of military intervention to safeguard global oil supplies.

Optimists believe that even in the worst of scenarios, even if Islamic extremists were to gain control, they would continue exporting the oil that fuels the global economy. That seems entirely too sanguine an assumption about Saudi religious fundamentalists who believe that society would be better off with a more medieval lifestyle that wouldn't require earning hundreds of billions of dollars from exporting oil to the infidel West. Islamic terrorists, of course, who seek to destroy the West, have an even clearer reason to curb oil exports. As unlikely as this scenario sounds in a country notable for the passivity and conformity of its people, just as unlikely, in a different way, is a twenty-first-century society totally ruled by a family of seven thousand princes.

CHAPTER 14

On Pins and Needles

Do you know what is better than charity and fasting and prayer? It is keeping peace and good relations between people as quarrels and bad feelings destroy mankind.

—PROPHET MUHAMMAD

Most countries predicate their foreign policy on some consensus definition of core national interests. Such national interests can be subject to internal political debate and are not always pursued consistently or successfully, but they do exist. Not so for Saudi Arabia. Only one interest guides Saudi foreign policy, and that is the survival of the House of Saud.

Just as Al Saud survival is based on a policy of balancing competing forces within the kingdom, its foreign policy consists of a constant effort to play off or buy off more powerful regional forces. And just as the Al Saud's balancing act at home is becoming increasingly precarious, so too is the regime's high-wire act in the dangerous Middle East neighborhood where the local bully—Iran—is expanding its influence and thus diminishing Saudi Arabia's. Meanwhile Saudi Arabia's tether to the United States, its protector for more than half a century, is fraying badly at both ends.

Saudi Arabia is like a rich schoolboy and teacher's pet who seeks to mask his dependence on the teacher's protection by currying favor with the schoolyard bullies. While he goes to great lengths to avoid being seen as the teacher's pet, he also frets that the teacher will be upset at the bad company he is keeping. As a result, he is not respected or trusted by anyone.

Much as many in the West might like to dismiss the Saudis as religious zealots who are reaping the results of Islamic extremism that they set in motion, the decisions of the Al Saud affect both the economic prosperity of Western societies and, of course, the lives of Western citizens who continue to be targets of radical Islamic terrorists. As a result, the West needs to understand, if not sympathize with, the high-wire act of the Al Saud amid the changing winds that are buffeting the region and the regime.

Theirs is not a neighborhood given to peaceful resolution of differences, and clearly, conducting a successful Saudi Arabian foreign policy is no easy task. The country is rich but weak. It owns massive amounts of modern military equipment but has almost no military might. It is banker to many, but money alone does not buy influence. And the Saudis are surrounded by increasingly hostile and unstable neighbors.

The Arab Spring of 2011, which some in the West viewed with optimism as a long-overdue force for freedom in the region, shocked and alarmed the Al Saud. Most shocking was the fate of Egyptian strongman Hosni Mubarak, toppled largely by angry youth. To the Al Saud, the revolution in Egypt was a double disaster. Not only did the Saudi regime lose a longtime friend and ally; even worse, the United States, Saudi Arabia's ultimate protector, conspired in forcing the Egyptian president to resign after thirty years of faithful cooperation with Washington. Not surprisingly, Saudis within and without the royal family wondered how loyal the United States one day might prove to be to them. The regime showed its pique by refusing a visit from U.S. defense secretary Robert Gates. Meanwhile, next door to Saudi Arabia, Bahrain's Sunni royal family faced widespread civil unrest from its Shiite majority, prompting the anxious Al Saud to dispatch one thousand troops to help shore up a beleaguered fellow monarchy.

Across the Arabian Gulf, Shiite Iran is spreading its regional tentacles via proxies like Hamas in Gaza and

Hezbollah in Lebanon. On the Saudis' northern border is Iraq: under Saddam Hussein it was pugnacious but at least Sunni-dominated, but now Saudis see their neighbor as an unstable Shiite-led country that is falling under the sway of Iran. On Saudi Arabia's southern border sits the semifeudal nation of Yemen, where a longtime and largely pliable dictator has been displaced by prolonged citizen protest, where Iran surreptitiously supports anti-Saudi rebels, and where Al Qaeda plots terrorist attacks against both the Saudi regime and the United States. Just beyond and across the narrow Red Sea lie the failed rogue states of East Africa, Somalia and Sudan.

Small wonder that Saudi Arabia needs a protector, and it long has had one in Uncle Sam. If security for loyalty is the regime's domestic compact with its people, Saudi-U.S. relations for more than half a century have been based on an implicit pact of oil for security. The United States gets oil at reasonable world prices and implicitly guarantees Al Saud security.

This pact began with a handshake, when President Franklin Roosevelt met King Abdul Aziz aboard the USS *Quincy* in the Suez Canal in 1945, and it has been strengthened, or at least sustained, by every American president since. There have been periodic strains, as when Saudi Arabia embargoed oil to the West to protest U.S. support for Israel in the October 1973 war with Egypt. There also have been moments of intense embrace, as when the two countries cooperated in the 1980s to arm and fund mujahedeen in evicting Soviet occupiers from Afghanistan, or when the United States dispatched half a million troops to the kingdom in 1990 to drive Saddam Hussein's troops from Kuwait and thwart his ambition to occupy Saudi oil fields.

Ironically, even as tensions were escalating during the 1973 oil embargo, Prince Fahd, then the minister of interior, summoned his security officers to show them clips of the U.S. airlift of war matériel to Israel. "This is why we need to maintain close relations with the U.S.," Prince Fahd told them. "They are the only ones capable of saving us in this manner should we ever be at risk." Indeed, in 1990, when Saddam Hussein invaded neighboring Kuwait, then king Fahd called on the United States, which responded with an even more massive airlift of men and matériel to Saudi Arabia.

The last decade has seen the rising tide of radical Iranian influence and, particularly in the last few years, an ebbing of U.S. prestige in the Middle East. That severely complicated the U.S.-Saudi oil-for-security relationship even before it hit a new low with U.S. acquiescence in the ouster of Mubarak. Further complicating the Saudi-U.S. relationship is the rise of Islamic fundamentalism across the region, largely fueled over the past thirty years by the Saudis themselves. Ever since the terrorist attacks of September 11, 2001, the Saudi regime has faced a deepening dilemma between catering to Islamic fundamentalists to protect its reputation and rule at home and risking further alienating, through this support, its U.S. protector, so often the target of Islamic terrorists. The Saudi dilemma is on display in Palestine. There Iran's shrewd diplomacy over the past decade has made Tehran, not Riyadh, the widely perceived champion of Palestinian aspirations. The more Iran establishes itself as the Palestinian defender, the harder it is for the Saudi regime to acquiesce in requests by its U.S. protector to support peace efforts requiring Palestinians to compromise with Israel.

On this issue, as on so many others, the regime's foreign policy is driven less by the rights of the Palestinians or others than by the needs of the Al Saud. The royal family believes it must present itself as the leader of Islam and defender of the faithful in order to sustain its legitimacy and rule at home. Maintaining this posture in the face of competition from the real revolutionaries in Iran and without further upsetting its U.S. sponsor might be an insurmountable challenge for any regime, and it is proving ever more difficult for the Al Saud, as politically aware young Saudis wield Islam as a weapon in criticizing their government for being disingenuously Islamic.

As so often is the case, the Saudi regime finds itself hoist on its own petard. After the 1979 triumph of Ayatollah Khomeini and the establishment of his theocracy in Iran, Sunni clerics inside Saudi Arabia began to chafe at sharing power with the Al Saud and sought a larger role in ruling the country. To thwart this power play and to appear as devout as the *ulama,* the late King Fahd shoveled money into spreading radical Wahhabi Islam around the world and granted the religious leaders at home wide sway over virtually every aspect of Saudi life. A former U.S. Treasury Department official is quoted by *Washington Post* reporter David Ottaway in a 2004 article as estimating that the late king spent "north of $75 billion" in his efforts to spread Wahhabi Islam. According to Ottaway, the king boasted on his personal Web site that he established 200 Islamic colleges, 210 Islamic centers, 1,500 mosques, and 2,000 schools for Muslim children in non-Islamic nations. The late king also launched a publishing center in Medina that by 2000 had distributed 138 million copies of the Koran worldwide. Indeed, a meeting with almost any Saudi royal concludes with the gift of a copy of the Koran.

To this day, the regime funds numerous international organizations to spread fundamentalist Islam, including the Muslim World League, the World Assembly of Muslim Youth, the International Islamic Relief Organization, and various royal charities such as the Popular Committee for Assisting the Palestinian Mujahedeen, led by Prince Salman bin Abdul Aziz, now minister of defense, who often is touted as a potential future king. Supporting *da'wah,* which literally means "making an invitation" to Islam, is a religious requirement that Saudi rulers feel they cannot abandon without losing their domestic legitimacy as protectors and propagators of Islam. Yet in the wake of 9/11, American anger at the kingdom led the U.S. government to demand controls on Saudi largesse to Islamic groups that funded terrorism. "Iran is buying Muslim loyalty throughout the Middle East for a fraction of the money we used to provide until the U.S. blocked us," says one Al Saud prince, who argues that the United States is wittingly or unwittingly helping Iran against Saudi Arabia.

Trapped between the twin needs for maintaining domestic legitimacy and sustaining U.S. protection, King Abdullah did what the Saudi government so frequently does when confronted with a challenge: it said one thing and did another. After initial denials that fifteen of the nineteen September 11 hijackers were Saudis, the government finally launched a verbal campaign against extremism inside the country and an even more visible campaign abroad to champion religious tolerance. But a decade later, the rigid religious authorities inside Saudi Arabia seem as entrenched as ever. Despite widely publicized visits by King Abdullah to the Vatican and his organization of an Interfaith Dialogue in Madrid, followed a few months later by another among heads of state at the United Nations, the kingdom's estimated 1.5 million Christians (almost all foreign workers) still are not allowed to worship publicly. Saudis insist that the Prophet Muhammad established the tradition that only Islam can be practiced within Arabia, home of Islam's two holiest sites. Nor has Saudi Arabia's Shiite Islamic minority seen any real decrease in government-sanctioned discrimination.

The Saudi-sponsored Interfaith Dialogue at the United Nations in November 2008 was typical of Saudi diplomacy—much more show than substance. UN organizers who worked with the Saudis to arrange the king's visit—the first ever by a Saudi king to the UN—say his primary goal was to present himself as the "pope" of all Islam, thereby diminishing Iran's Shiite sect and pleasing the conservative clerics in Riyadh, for whom Shiites are heretics. For this reason, the king's staff insisted that protocol for his visit parallel that of Pope John Paul II's visit to the United Nations. The chief of protocol, the Saudis insisted, must meet the king at the airport, and the UN secretary general must greet him at the base of the escalator bearing him up to the General Assembly, an honor given to no other head of state.

"The Interfaith Dialogue meeting was one of the toughest we've ever dealt with," recalls a UN official shortly after the many heads of state departed. Despite hosting an interfaith dialogue, King Abdullah declined to meet or shake hands with Israeli president Shimon Peres. So those arranging dinner for the many Arab heads of state, the Israeli president, U.S. president George W. Bush, and UN secretary general Ban Ki-moon had to ensure the Saudi and Israeli leaders never got close enough to have to shake hands. The solution: since the secretary general had sat by Peres at the October General Assembly opening dinner, this time he sat by the Saudi king, while Peres sat at another table. All this seemed at odds with the king's brief four-minute address in which he said, "Human beings are created equals and partners on this planet," and added, "We can leave our differences for God to make His judgment on the Day of Judgment."

The hapless secretary general had hoped to avoid the whole imbroglio by flying to Los Angeles for a previously scheduled visit with California's governor and some of Hollywood's top movie stars, including Angelina Jolie, but the Saudis demanded—and won—cancellation of those plans in order that he be on hand to meet the king and attend the Interfaith Dialogue.

More complex even than the seating arrangements was securing a final statement at the close of the event. The Saudis wanted a statement, but they did not want a UN resolution that would have to be negotiated among 180-plus nations. The king's staff drafted a statement and negotiated it with the United States and the Vatican, but the ever prickly French and some other European Union nations objected to the statement because it mixed religion and politics and, perhaps more relevantly, because they had no hand in writing it. One UN official said the Saudis called President Nicolas Sarkozy, who was scheduled to visit the kingdom a few weeks later, and told him not to come if the impasse over the UN statement wasn't quickly resolved. This same official says the French president called his UN ambassador and relayed a blunt message: Get the European Union on board or resign his post. (France was head of the European Union's rotating presidency at the time.)

When the conference concluded forty-eight hours later, Saudi foreign minister Prince Saud al Faisal stood alongside the grounded Ban Ki-moon, who read the statement, said to represent a "sense of the United Nations" in support of greater religious tolerance. In a final irony, the statement was not reported in the Saudi press. It was Saudi foreign policy at its most elaborately artificial.

To be fair to King Abdullah, most Saudis believe he is a deeply religious man and also a tolerant one. Some approve of his tolerance, while more conservative critics see his willingness to allow mixing of men and women at KAUST or small steps to reduce discrimination against Shiites in the Eastern Province as evidence that he is a pawn of the liberal-minded United States. But whatever Abdullah's true sentiments, the driving priority of Al Saud survival means he does not directly challenge the conservative religious orthodoxies that still dominate Saudi Arabia.

To further calm angry Americans after the events of 9/11, then crown prince Abdullah unveiled a new Arab-Israeli peace initiative in 2002, promising to recognize the Jewish state as soon as Israel withdrew from all occupied territories and permitted the establishment of a Palestinian state with East Jerusalem as its capital. Here again the Saudi initiative was more public relations than foreign relations. While it was the first offer by a Saudi regime to accept the state of Israel more than half a century after its founding, the conditions for that acceptance—withdrawal from all occupied territories with no border rectifications to enhance Israeli security—had been rejected repeatedly by Israel for decades. Thus the offer of normal relations with Israel may have sounded good in the United States and Europe, but it wasn't likely to become a reality that would upset conservative religious Saudis inside the kingdom. Sure enough, nearly a decade later, Saudi Arabia remains in the shadows of international efforts to bring Palestinians and Israelis to an accommodation.

Whether in the presidency of Bill Clinton or George W. Bush, whenever Israeli and Palestinian leaders are brought together at the White House flanked by moderate Arab leaders, the Saudis are conspicuously absent. Whatever efforts the Saudis might make to please an American president by encouraging Palestinians to make peace are whispered from far offstage. The Saudi regime would like a resolution of the Palestinian issue because it would deny Iran further opportunity to exploit Middle Eastern tensions to Riyadh's detriment, but the Al Saud are unwilling to take any risks that might backfire with religious conservatives and with political cynics inside the country who already see the royal family as handmaidens of the United States.

Given Saudi Arabia's fear of Iran and its increasingly strained alliance with the United States, the Saudi regime has been busy spinning a wider web of diplomatic relationships. Upon becoming regent in 2005, King Abdullah's first foreign trip was to China, an emerging economic powerhouse hungry for Saudi oil. China, Japan, South Korea, and India over the past decade have become the primary purchasers of Saudi oil production, with nearly 60 percent of Saudi oil exports going to Asia. Since then, Saudi-Chinese relations have deepened, including the signing in 2012 of an agreement to cooperate in the use of atomic energy for peaceful purposes.

Abdullah also reached out to Russia, welcoming Vladimir Putin to Riyadh and awarding him the kingdom's highest honor, the King Abdul Aziz Medal. More significantly, Saudi Arabia and Russia concluded a joint venture between Saudi ARAMCO and LUKOIL to develop new Saudi gas fields. During his February 2007 visit to the kingdom, Putin said that in a world of growing energy demand, Saudi Arabia and Russia are "not competitors but partners."

Clearly Saudi Arabia has shifted from singular dependence on the United States to more of a multipolar foreign policy. Saudi foreign minister Prince Saud al Faisal has succinctly summed up the shift in Saudi-U.S. relations: "It's a Muslim marriage, not a Catholic marriage." This is a clever way of saying Saudi Arabia now has multiple marriage partners, as allowed in Islam. That said, however, there is no doubt that the United States remains Saudi Arabia's first and paramount wife.

For all the outreach and obfuscation, only two powers are central to Saudi survival—Iran and the United States. Fearful Saudis see Iran as their major threat for both religious and political reasons. Many Saudis are convinced Iran's goal is to occupy Islam's two holiest sites and to declare a Shiite state in Saudi Arabia's oil-rich Eastern Province and in the neighboring Gulf sheikdoms of the United Arab Emirates and Bahrain, where Shiites are a majority. For the Al Saud, the loss either of its oil or its religious legitimacy would spell the catastrophic end of the dynasty.

Prince Turki al Faisal, one of the Al Saud's most thoughtful public servants (he served for two decades as his country's head of intelligence and more recently as ambassador to Great Britain and then to the United States) shies from this apocalypse but expresses concern at Iran's goals. "We talk to some who say Iran wants a Shiite crescent or that Iran wants to take Mecca and Medina and create a Persian empire. I don't know." But he adds, "I see no benign scenario with Iran. The question is how actively malignant it is. We have to be very careful and always on our toes in Bahrain, UAE, Lebanon, and Afghanistan."

The Saudis have every reason to be fearful. Iran now is the dominant influence in Iraq, Syria, and Lebanon, and with Hamas in Gaza. Its rising influence across the region is encouraging Shiites in the Gulf states and Saudi Arabia to become more assertive and to agitate against Sunni rulers. In some Saudi neighbors such as Yemen, Iran actively is supporting terrorist groups targeting the Al Saud. The skittish Saudis pay periodic courtesy calls in Tehran, and King Abdullah invited Iranian president Ahmadinejad to Riyadh in 2007, where he posed smiling and holding hands. But the Saudis understand it was the smile of a crocodile.

As one effort to protect the kingdom, the Saudis have nuzzled up to Islamic Pakistan, in hopes the Pakistanis will provide a nuclear umbrella. But this reliance is problematic given that Pakistan is a fragile polity held together by an army that is showing signs of cracking under the pressure of Islamic radicalism.

While the Iranians focus their hostile rhetoric almost entirely on Israel and the Great Satan of the United States, the truth is that neither has as much reason to fear Iran—at least in the short run—as does Saudi Arabia. As the world's leading military power, the United States is unlikely to be attacked militarily by Iran. Israel, as a not-so-secret nuclear power, surely would respond in full force to any Iranian attack. Saudi Arabia, however, is a much softer, weaker, and more tempting target. Saudi oil fields are a short distance across the Persian Gulf from Iran, and former CIA operative Robert Baer estimates Iran could seize those Saudi fields in less than forty-eight hours.

The kingdom's military spending has totaled nearly $500 billion over the past quarter-century, according to the Stockholm International Peace Research Institute. And in 2010 the government won approval from the United States Congress to purchase another $60 billion in modern aircraft from the United States. Still, few believe the Saudis could defend against such an attack without major U.S. intervention. While the United States doubtless could drive out the Iranian invaders with aerial bombing and boots on the ground if needed, the retreating Iranians likely would disable or destroy Saudi oil fields, crippling some or all of the country's oil production, with calamitous global economic consequences. Repairing the Saudi oil fields could take at least two years in Baer's view.

Or, Iran could, as it threatened in December 2011, try to close the Strait of Hormuz, the narrow passageway though which some 17 million barrels a day, or 20 percent of the world's traded oil, pass daily. The United States would take military action to reopen the strait with Saudi cooperation, inevitably raising a new wave of Islamic rage against America, underscoring Saudi dependence on American military might, and creating a new opportunity for fundamentalists to condemn the Al Saud as lapdogs of the United States.

Despite Prince Saud's elliptical talk of multiple wives, the truth is that Saudi Arabia is stuck in a very "catholic" marriage with the United States. While Saudi Arabia may not always be a faithful marriage partner, it dare not risk divorce, considering the consequences of going it alone in its dangerous neighborhood. At the same time, being perceived in the

Islamic world as being too friendly to America is a problem for the Al Saud—one that extremists inside and outside the kingdom exploit to undermine the legitimacy of the regime. Any situation in which the Saudis again would require U.S. military intervention could well be the kiss of death.

Prince Turki al Faisal acknowledges the mutual reluctance to cooperate too visibly. Asked if an Iranian invasion of Kuwait or another Gulf sheikdom would elicit the same Saudi request for U.S. military protection as in 1990, the prince says, "It would not be as clear-cut now as then. We would need more time for our public to be brought along." He hastens to add the obvious: "America too would have a little more hesitation to organize public opinion there for supporting Saudi Arabia." Nevertheless, he says, "It is good sense for the two countries to maintain a relationship that would allow them to cooperate in such a situation."

If marriage to the United States is an embarrassment to the Saudis, it has become increasingly embarrassing to U.S. administrations as well. The spectacle of newly elected President Obama bowing to King Abdullah at their first meeting was a reminder of several things that Americans would prefer to ignore or forget—the degree of U.S. dependence on Middle Eastern oil, the role of Saudis in the horrifying events of 9/11, Saudi Arabia's funding of extremist Islam, and a relationship with an absolute monarchy that pays little heed to civil society and human rights.

The relationship is so fraught with mutual chagrin that the U.S. ability to influence the Saudi regime in the direction of modernity and reform is virtually nonexistent. Indeed, the American government is so unpopular in Saudi Arabia these days that overt promotion of reform would only arouse greater opposition to it. King Abdullah's critics already attack his modest reforms by charging they are intended to please "liberal" reformers, a code phrase for U.S. sympathizers in Saudi Arabia. So cautious is the United States on this point that President Obama didn't even mention Saudi Arabia in a major speech enunciating U.S. Middle East policy and priorities after the Arab Spring.

Notwithstanding the tension and embarrassments on both sides, protecting the flow of Saudi oil to the world market is unquestionably a high national interest of the United States. That is no less true today than when Saudi Arabia embargoed oil to the West in 1973 and the Nixon administration alarmed Great Britain by discussing a military seizure of Saudi oil fields. Britain in 2003 declassified long-secret documents revealing that Percy Cradock, head of Britain's Joint Intelligence Committee, considered a U.S. move against the Saudi oil fields likely to be executed "without any prior consultation of allies." Indeed, James Schlesinger, Nixon's secretary of defense, had warned Britain's ambassador to Washington that the United States would not tolerate threats from "under-developed, under-populated" countries and that it was no longer obvious to him that the United States "could not use force."

Only five days into the 1973 war, Defense Secretary Schlesinger called Secretary of State Henry Kissinger to warn that the United States was going to find itself in a position in which its interests in Saudi Arabia were at risk and suggested that they review the "fundamentals of our position."

Oil has been the glue in the Saudi-U.S. relationship. Shown here in 1973 is the late King Faisal, with then secretary of state Henry Kissinger, who warned him of "incalculable consequences" should the Saudis again embargo oil to the United States. (AP PHOTO)

"Well," asked Kissinger, "what are the fundamentals of our position, as you see it?"

Schlesinger replied, "The fundamentals are that we may be faced with the choice that lies cruelly between support of Israel [and] loss of Saudi Arabia and if [our] interests in the Middle East are at risk, the choice between occupation or watching them go down the drain."

"Occupation of whom?" Kissinger asked.

"That's one of the things we'd like to talk about," responded Schlesinger.

"Who's we?"

"Me," Schlesinger acknowledged.

Secretary Kissinger, architect of the airlift to replenish Israeli military needs during the 1973 war with Egypt that sparked Saudi outrage and prompted the oil embargo, was also the one who negotiated with the late King Faisal to end the embargo. Dr. Kissinger warned the Saudi king that any future embargoes might well trigger a U.S. invasion. "I did not threaten, but it is true I did say there could be incalculable consequences from another oil embargo," Kissinger acknowledged in a 2011 interview. Prince Turki, son of the late King Faisal and Saudi ambassador to the United States more than thirty years after the embargo, demurs when asked to confirm that Kissinger made such a threat to his father, but offers an anecdote to indicate he believes it true.

"I don't know if what I am about to say is true, but it is pervasive in the Arab world," Prince Turki says. "When Henry Kissinger said that to the late King Faisal, the king is reported to have responded, 'We Saudis can go back to living in tents and eating dates and drinking camel milk. But what can you do?'" The king's clear implication: Saudi Arabia would destroy its own oil wells before allowing the United States to seize them. "I don't recall such a statement," Kissinger says.

While it may well be true that some Saudis could return to living in tents and dining on dates and camel milk, that kind of subsistence society almost certainly no longer would be ruled by the Al Saud. While the Al Saud family often displays pride and petulance, it is not suicidal.

Continuing Saudi oil flows at reasonably stable world prices is essential both to the industrial world and to the Al Saud. While a spiking oil price produces more short-term revenue for Saudi Arabia, that has not been the kingdom's strategy. For one thing, the conservative royal family does not want to risk the enmity of its U.S. protector and of the wider industrial world whose prosperity is so dependent on oil. Furthermore, the Saudi government invests its oil revenues in U.S. dollars and other foreign currencies and has no interest in seeing those currencies collapse. Finally, prolonged oil prices at extremely high levels might actually prompt industrial countries to get serious about developing alternative energy sources, which is not in Saudi Arabia's longer-term interest. So stability at reasonable prices serves all interests. "The Saudis learned that the oil weapon is a boomerang," said Schlesinger, America's first secretary of energy, in an interview nearly forty years after the Saudi embargo. "The Saudis want us using oil for as long as possible."

Schlesinger, long retired, now says he never supported seizing Saudi oil fields. He acknowledges he did think seizing the tiny UAE's oil fields might serve as a "demonstration" to the Saudi regime. But he calls the idea of seizing Saudi oil fields "kind of crazy." The country's large population, he notes, would make occupying Saudi Arabia very difficult. On the other hand, he continues, "splitting off the Eastern Province, with its large Shiite population, might be doable." The Eastern Province, of course, is where the great majority of Saudi oil is located. An uprising among Shiites, who are concentrated in the Eastern Province, where they account for about 30 percent of the population, is among the Al Saud's worst nightmares. The regime fears that trouble in the Eastern Province might be exploited by Iran or used by the United States as a pretext for intervention.

These days the United States is a relatively modest importer of Saudi oil; imports are around 1.2 million barrels a day or roughly 12 percent of total U.S. oil imports. More Saudi oil is being sold to Asia and more Canadian and Mexican oil is being sold to the United States. Direct imports are not the point, however, since global oil flows are fungible, and any significant change in Saudi production immediately would affect global prices and thus the price American consumers pay at the pump.

The ultimate irony in the U.S.-Saudi relationship based on oil for security is that in coming years Saudi Arabia's oil exports are virtually certain to decline sharply, both because of the rapid rise in Saudi domestic consumption and because Saudi production may have peaked and may already be in decline. In a country where a gallon of gasoline at roughly fifty-three cents is cheaper than bottled water and government energy subsidies are roughly $35 billion annually, Saudi energy consumption is rising at what one energy official calls an "alarming rate." If this trend continues, Saudi consumption of energy could more than double to 8.3 million barrels a day of oil (or equivalent other energy) by 2028, roughly equal to the 8.6 million barrels a day of oil the kingdom exported in 2010.

King Abdullah contemplated imposing unpopular cuts in energy subsidies to induce efficiency among Saudis but abandoned the idea in 2011 in the wake of political unrest across the Middle East. The regime didn't want to risk citizen anger. Instead, the government is investing in solar and nuclear energy, so Saudi Arabia can try to meet domestic energy demand that way and conserve oil production for export. The kingdom has announced plans to build sixteen nuclear reactors at a cost of $7 billion each by 2030.

As domestic energy demand grows—along with global demand—so does the number of oil experts who insist that Saudi oil production has peaked and, indeed, is already in decline. Saudi Arabia refuses to provide transparency on either production or reserve numbers. Indeed, shortly after it took full control of Saudi ARAMCO in 1980 from the Americans, Saudi ARAMCO abruptly announced that reserves were 150 billion barrels, far more than the 100 billion barrels the American management had said existed in 1977. By 1982 the number was put at 160 billion barrels. Then in 1988 Saudi ARAMCO raised its reserve estimate by yet another

100 billion barrels, a nearly 150 percent increase in the nine years of Saudi control! No convincing evidence ever has been provided to support the increase. And tellingly, in 1982 the kingdom and other OPEC oil producers ceased releasing production data by field, reducing the transparency on depletion of oil. Finally, Saudi Arabia has not revised its reserve estimate since 1988, even though it has pumped somewhere between 5 million and 9 million barrels a day for the intervening two decades, for a total of nearly 50 billion barrels.

All this led Matthew Simmons, chairman of Simmons & Company International in Houston and the author of *Twilight in the Desert: The Coming Saudi Oil Shock,* to challenge Saudi reserve estimates and the country's ability to continue to serve as the world's "swing producer," raising production in times of high demand and then taking oil off the market when demand declines to keep prices stable. In short, Saudi leverage on the world market has become more limited.

In this meticulously researched book on Saudi oil fields and their production past, present, and future, Simmons, now deceased, examined data in published scientific papers on the four biggest Saudi oil fields, which account for 90 percent of Saudi oil production. He makes a convincing case that they are in decline, even though Saudi ARAMCO refuses to publish production numbers by field or allow any independent audit of production or reserve estimates. The giant Ghawar field, the country's largest, which alone accounts for fully 50 percent of Saudi oil production—and 8 percent of total world production—is 60 percent depleted, he argues. In production since 1951, Ghawar has yielded in excess of 55 billion barrels of oil. Still, Saudi Arabia hasn't reduced its total reserve estimate. "The death of this great king leaves no field of vaguely comparable stature in the line of succession," Simmons writes.

That oil is a finite resource obviously is true. That most of the world is oblivious to such momentous events until they recognize them in the rearview mirror also is true. In 1970, the year U.S. oil production peaked at 9.63 million barrels of oil a day, hardly anyone was worried that the world's largest oil producer was about to see rapid decline in its production. But since 1970 U.S. oil output has fallen, to 5.5 million barrels a day in 2010, even as U.S. oil consumption has risen to roughly 20 million barrels a day, or some 25 percent of worldwide consumption. The United States, which in the 1950s accounted for 50 percent of global energy production, now provides only about 7 percent. Clearly major shifts in oil production over brief periods are possible.

"We are not good at recognizing distant threats even if their probability is 100 percent," says former energy secretary Schlesinger. "Society ignoring this peak oil is like the people of Pompeii ignoring the rumblings below Vesuvius." In a foreword to a new report predicting that world oil production will peak in 2015, Schlesinger notes that the decline rate from presently producing fields is roughly 4 million barrels each year. To replace that production and find additional oil to meet growing world demand over the next quarter-century would require the discovery of the equivalent of five new Saudi Arabias. No one expects that level of new oil discoveries. Since the 1970s the world has discovered only one new barrel of oil for every three it has pumped from the ground, as Schlesinger notes in his foreword to *The Impending World Energy Mess*. (Of course, the world contains other actual and potential sources of energy but none are yet able to replace oil.)

Has Saudi oil production peaked and entered inexorable decline? Obviously only the Saudi leadership knows for sure. Beyond examining arcane data by experts, however, nonexperts observe some telltale signs. For starters, King Abdullah, while Saudi regent, warned his countrymen in 1998 that "the oil boom is over and will not return . . . All of us must get used to a different lifestyle." Since becoming king in 2005, he has pressed his country to diversify its economy to create wealth, not simply extract it from the ground. Perhaps this is just an elderly king seeking to motivate a lazy populace, but one obvious implication is that the king knows oil is running out sooner rather than later.

Even more to the point, in the summer of 2010 King Abdullah told Saudi students that he had ordered a halt to oil exploration to save the kingdom's remaining hydrocarbon wealth for future generations. Speaking in Washington, D.C., to some of the thirty thousand Saudi students studying in the United States on King Abdullah Scholarships, the monarch recounted that he had once asked his cabinet ministers to repeat a prayer after him, "May Allah prolong its life." The ministers, the king recounted, asked him, "What is 'it'?"

" 'It' is the oil wealth," the king answered. "I told them that I have ordered a halt to all oil explorations so part of this wealth is left for our sons and successors, God willing," Abdullah said.

The monarch went on to tell the students, "You are ambassadors of your homeland. Thank God, your homeland is proceeding resolutely to a prosperous future. God willing. And what is unknown is even better." No official clarification of exactly what the king meant by a halt in exploration or of what is "unknown" has yet been issued, leaving all to wonder if it means Saudi Arabia no longer will serve as "swing producer"—raising production in times of high demand—or if it means Saudi Arabia *cannot* much longer raise oil production because its big fields are nearing depletion and new discoveries aren't keeping pace.

Saudi ARAMCO CEO Khalid al Falih is similarly opaque about Saudi oil production. When I asked him in the spring of 2009 whether Saudi Arabia can continue to play the price-stabilizing role of swing producer, he insisted the kingdom still can increase production to balance supply in times of great demand but added, "The question is should we do so? Our long-term depletion strategy is to allow our economy to evolve away from oil so we need to calibrate our production to use our oil slowly so our economy can transform to a non-oil economy. We don't want to produce so much oil that people in Saudi have no incentive to diversify the economy."

The sentiments are eminently sensible, but do they derive from choice or necessity? And if the latter, if Saudi Arabia's total reserves are rapidly being depleted and if production already is in decline, the consequences for the world economy as well as for the Al Saud are alarming. In terms of U.S.-Saudi relations, however, a gradual decline in oil production would almost certainly not mean an end to U.S. protection of the Al Saud.

Even if Saudi oil output is in decline, the pact between the United States and Saudi Arabia likely will remain important for other reasons. It would shift from a relationship built largely on oil for security to one increasingly based on security for security—U.S. security for the Al Saud's. It is hard to imagine a scenario in which the United States could be agnostic about who rules Saudi Arabia. In theory, the United States might be happier with a more pluralistic Saudi polity, but that is the least likely future scenario. The reality is that any regime that might follow the Al Saud—revolving military coups, radical fundamentalist rule, chaos in which terrorism flourishes—would be far more inimical to U.S. interests. For that reason, the United States seems certain to continue to protect the Al Saud, in the belief that the Saudi royal family, however flawed, is more likely to avoid overt hostility to U.S. interests and to try to control terrorism than any regime that might follow it. The House of Saud is busy spreading just that message.

CHAPTER 15

Endgame

Most Saudi experts—diplomats, businessmen, and scholars—while not oblivious to the country's multiple challenges, still conclude that the kingdom, resting as it does on a foundation of Al Saud rule, conservative religious orthodoxy, and bountiful oil revenue, remains fundamentally stable. In this view, coming U.S. presidents will be dealing with Al Saud monarchs long into the future.

Optimists about the current and future stability of Saudi Arabia invariably cite prior pessimistic predictions that did not materialize. If the Al Saud regime has survived numerous crises over the past five decades, there is little reason to think it cannot continue to do so. To the optimists, past is prologue. But history is not always a reliable guide, and the status quo will not be the future. Few "experts" foresaw the fall of the shah of Iran or of Mubarak in Egypt, and fewer still predicted the sudden collapse of the Soviet Union. One fears that the optimists, who see "strawberry fields forever," may be whistling past the graveyard.

No single problem in Saudi Arabia—and as we have seen it has many—is likely to be fatal to the regime. Rather, it is the confluence of so many challenges coupled with the rigidity of the regime, the sullenness of the society, the escalating demands of youth, and most important, the instability inherent in generational succession that could well prove fatal to Al Saud rule. It is not that Saudis are worse off than other Arabs—they lead more comfortable lives than most. It is not that King Abdullah has been a worse monarch than his predecessors—on the contrary, he is more sincere and benevolent than most. It is not that Saudi Arabia is making no progress. But the confluence of challenges is far greater than at any time in the past. More important, the Saudi people are less patient and more demanding than they were in the past. And the ever-expanding and increasingly divided Al Saud family, once upon a time both feared and respected, these days is neither.

There is a growing lawlessness in Saudi Arabia that is at odds with its reputation for rigid adherence to Sharia law. King Abdullah has promised more freedom to women, more space for open political and religious discourse, and reforms of education and of the economy. But hardly any of these reforms have been institutionalized and codified in law, and even where new rules and regulations have been announced, they are often not enforced. So authorities and citizens are not accountable to each other. Day to day the princes and the prominent do as they like, while most of the kingdom's passive people dare not confront society's unwritten rules or unenforced regulations. Instead, most have the temerity for only myriad minor infractions they think will go unnoticed or unpunished, from flagrant traffic violations to bribing officials for access to government services; from mistreating domestic servants to erecting ostensibly illegal satellite dishes; from lying to authorities to lying to each other. But the list grows longer, as more and more Saudis do whatever they feel they can get away with. These all are signs of a disintegrating society, and the deterioration is only accelerating.

Alexis de Tocqueville, in *The Ancien Regime,* described a kingdom of France "made up from different, disunited orders and from a people whose citizens have only a small number of ties in common. As a result, no one concerns himself with anything but his own private interests." Louis XVI was the only French king in that nation's long history to make an effort to unite his people in anything other than "an equal state of dependency." But after so many years of divide-and-conquer rule, the French discovered, de Tocqueville wrote, that "it had been much simpler to divide them than it was thereafter to reunite them." He could have been describing today's Kingdom of Saudi Arabia.

A monarchy is at greatest risk, de Tocqueville wrote, when it acknowledges the need to reform and begins to offer small changes. "Only a great genius can save a ruler who is setting out to relieve his subjects' suffering after a long period of oppression. The evils, patiently endured as inevitable, seem unbearable as soon as the idea of escaping them is conceived." Louis XVI's regime on the eve of its downfall "still looked unshakeable even to those who were about to topple it." Louis XVI's reward for small reforms, of course, was the guillotine.

As we have seen throughout this book, Saudi society is cracking in multiple ways. Religion, the glue that long has bound the kingdom, is a source of division, with contending forces wielding the Koran to challenge each other and the regime. An overwhelmingly youthful society with access to outside information and influences is challenging authority of all sorts. The oil-based Saudi economy remains one-dimensional and unable to create jobs to absorb the youth bulge. Saudi women, notwithstanding some small new freedoms in recent years, remain largely subjugated, frustrated, and sidelined from contributing to the stagnant economy. Oil production may well have peaked.

From abroad, Iran poses a far greater threat to Saudi Arabia than has any foreign power in recent decades. A confident President Ahmadinejad has said Iran feels no threat from Saudi Arabia's latest purchase of $60 billion in sophisticated U.S. arms, but he wryly observed at a New York press conference in 2010 that those arms "might fall into the wrong hands" if the House of Saud lost power. It was a clever way of saying the arms might one day wind up threatening the United States, as did those the Americans sold to the shah in the years before his sudden ouster.

Most significant is the generational leadership change that will be forced on the Al Saud somewhere in the next decade unless the family finds the courage to preempt Father Time and make it sooner. Either way, the change is sure to be more difficult than the one nearly six decades ago, when the strong-willed founder died. Even with shared fealty to their father, Abdul Aziz's eldest sons, King Saud and Crown Prince

Faisal, squabbled for nearly a decade before Faisal emerged triumphant. Today none of the elderly surviving sons of Abdul Aziz has the clout to establish a clear generational transition that would pass the monarchy down through one branch of the family. This has set up an intense rivalry among the remaining sons and many grandsons of the founder. Power sharing is not a feature of absolute monarchies. The prospect of Al Saud family feuds frightens ordinary Saudis, who are impotent to influence the outcome. "When elephants fight, we gnats get crushed" is the way Saudis so often express their fear.

So what might the Al Saud do to resolve some of the kingdom's challenges and prolong its rule? Doubtless, if regime changes in Tunisia and Egypt are seen a few years hence to have yielded no improvements, the Al Saud will benefit. Saudis almost surely will again be grateful at least for stability, even at the price of dependency and indignity. But if the Al Saud, rather than banking on failure elsewhere, prefer to take the initiative to improve their standing with Saudis, they could consider a number of steps.

For starters, the royal family should codify into law and enforce the modest reforms that King Abdullah has enunciated over the past half-dozen years, so that they do not fade away under a new monarch. Moreover, the Al Saud should find a way, presumably well short of Western democracy, to provide elements of political pluralism that would engage the best and brightest of Saudi society, not just more and more princes, in governance.

Such reforms could include a parliament at least partially elected by Saudi society and a prime minister and council of ministers chosen for competence rather than genes. The Al Saud should take economic reform far more seriously and sharply accelerate it, not just plan it on paper with teams of consultants and then bury it in bureaucracies, if the country's youth bulge is to be employed. They should curb the influence of the conservative clergy in education and elsewhere in society, to enable the female half of society to become part of a productive workforce—the Saudi ARAMCO model writ large. And today, not tomorrow, the Al Saud should be announcing a formal line of royal succession to what will be something less than an absolute monarchy, in order to demonstrate that national unity and stability are more important than the fates and fortunes of princely factions.

Reforms of this magnitude would amount to the dismantling of traditional Saudi Arabia, so it is almost impossible to imagine the royal family undertaking them. In my five years of meeting dozens of princes, only one, Prince Talal bin Abdul Aziz, has ever proposed a path that would lead to the Al Saud eventually sharing power with the people. The prince was exiled to Lebanon in 1962 after he and several of his half-brothers—the so-called Free Princes—proposed democratic reform and a constitution for Saudi Arabia while their two eldest brothers, the king and crown prince, squabbled over power. Prince Talal, now eighty and long since returned home, has softened his contrarian style but has not shed his ideas.

"We have to go step by step," the elderly but still forceful prince explains in his modest Riyadh office, adorned with black-and-white photos of more than three dozen of his half-brothers. "The Majlis and the king should create a plan for five to ten years of reform, and people would be happy to wait." But the country, he insists, must start by giving its Potemkin political bodies some real power. For instance, he advocates giving local municipal councils, elected for the first time in 2005, the right to tax citizens to fund programs they favor. He wants members of the Majlis Ash Shura, or parliament, to be elected by citizens, not appointed by the monarch, and empowered to play a role in selecting and removing government ministers and in naming a prime minister to help the king run the government. These proposals are being ignored now as they were in the 1960s. "I made up my mind I would give my honest advice to the king, but I will do what he says," Prince Talal concludes with a small shrug of resignation.

What, if anything, might the United States do to encourage enlightened evolution inside the kingdom? The sad truth is the United States doesn't have much influence and seems unwilling to try to use even what little it has. Once upon a time Washington did. It was 1962; John F. Kennedy was president; Egypt's Nasser was the Middle Eastern bully; Yemen, then as now, was in turmoil. Saudi prince Faisal came to Washington seeking a U.S. commitment to defend Saudi Arabia's territorial integrity if threatened by Nasser and his Yemeni allies. Kennedy, no fan of the Saudis, offered the commitment but conditioned it on a package of Saudi reforms that included some limits on Al Saud absolute rule and the abolition of age-old slavery in the kingdom. Absolute rule, of course, continues to this day, and reforms remain more talk than substance, but slavery, at least, is gone since 1962. It was a small victory for U.S. pressure.

In all the decades since, Washington has been wedded to the Saudi status quo. Successive U.S. administrations found any significant change in that status quo to be so threatening as to be almost unthinkable. But the greater danger now lies precisely in clinging to the status quo, as rapid changes swirl both inside and outside the kingdom.

It is undoubtedly true that the United States cannot itself reform Saudi Arabia. Any effort at doing so through public pressure is bound to backfire, dooming the reforms with an infidel kiss of death and further weakening the monarchy. Only an Al Saud can save the Al Saud. And therein lies Washington's one slim opportunity.

American self-interest dictates that it convince the royal family that its self-interest—indeed, its preservation—requires the aging band of brothers to forsake tradition and ambition, to forswear brief turns on the throne. Rather, they now need to coalesce and crown the son of one of them who has the energy, the boldness, and the longevity to proclaim and then actually to implement a panoply of social, economic, and political reforms that hold government accountable for serving people.

Such younger princes do exist. The United States, as the Al Saud's ultimate protector, does have some influence. The United States also has multiple channels of communication to multiple senior princes. But for U.S. diplomacy—not known for subtlety, secrecy, or prescience—it would be a new challenge. The United States has a rich history of sticking with losers too long. It has some experience with helping to depose dictators, such as Iran's shah or Egypt's Mubarak, but too late to shape what follows. In the case of Saudi Arabia, the change the United States would be seeking would be relatively modest; after all, it would be all in the family, merely asking old princes to make way for a younger, more energetic one of their choice while there still is time to save the Al Saud. Given the mutual U.S.-Saudi dependency and their common self-interest, this should not be an impossible diplomatic mission.

So America conceivably could influence the kingdom, but in no way is the United States the role model for Saudi Arabia. Increasingly educated Saudis want to modernize, but they most surely do not want to Westernize, and they resent the American view that modernization means Westernization. Saudis don't pine for democracy, but they do seek a more open civil society where they are free to congregate and express views and where society's rules are clear and enforced equitably on all. They want iPads and access to the Internet, but the conservative among them—and most Saudis still are conservative—do not want all the other alien infidel influences emanating from America and the West. Saudis are unique and seek to remain so.

So the Royal Saudi 747, richly appointed but mechanically flawed, flies on, its cockpit crowded with geriatric Al Saud pilots. Buffeted by mounting gales, the plane is losing altitude and gradually running out of fuel. On board, first class is crowded with princely passengers, while crammed behind in economy sit frustrated Saudi citizens. Among them are Islamic fundamentalists who want to turn the plane around, and also Islamic terrorists who aim to kill the pilots and hijack the plane to a destination unknown. Somewhere on board there also may be a competent new flight team that could land the plane safely, but the prospect of a capable pilot getting a chance at the controls seems slim. And so the 747 flies on into the headwinds, perhaps to be hijacked, or ultimately to crash.

ACKNOWLEDGMENTS

Many people, especially Saudis of widely diverse backgrounds and perspectives, have assisted me on this book. Some I can thank by name; others, given the constraints of Saudi society, ask to remain anonymous. To all these hundreds of Saudis who welcomed me, informed me, introduced me to others, and in some cases took risks to do so, I owe a deep debt of gratitude. Whatever the flaws of Saudi society, the Saudi people, once connected to me through a trusted friend, invariably were as generous with their time and thoughts as they are in sharing their tea and dates with a stranger.

Above all, I want to thank Abdullah Al Shammari, who over a four-year period during which I reported this book, frequently served as my translator, but more importantly introduced me to scores of Saudis, who then introduced me to hundreds more from Tabuk in the north to Jizan in the south, from Jeddah on the Red Sea to Dammam on the Persian Gulf. Abdullah helped me to discover the rich and remarkable diversity of Saudi society beneath its veneer of white robes and black *abayas*. Abdullah is not a journalist, but in a freer and more open society, he would be a great reporter, researcher, and analyst.

Among the many Saudis I visited, special thanks go to the wife and mother identified in the book as Lulu, who invited me to live in her modest home with her family in order to share all aspects of her deeply religious and conservative family life. While Lulu did not succeed in her effort to convert me to Islam, she did profoundly impress me with the genuine religious devotion she lives out daily. Among the many other families I repeatedly visited I owe a special thanks to Abdul Malik Al Ashshaikh and his professor wife, Noura, both direct descendants of Muhammad ibn Abd al Wahhab, and their six accomplished daughters. With their respect for religion and tradition, but also their openness to modernity and change, they represent to me the very best in Saudi society. Prince Abdul Aziz bin Sattam, a scholar who also happens to be one of many royals I met, provided knowledgeable insights into Islamic religion and Sharia law.

Saudi ambassador to the United States, Adel al Jubeir, encouraged me to pursue this project and made it possible by granting a five-year multiple-entry visa. He never tried to influence my reporting; the analysis and conclusions of this book are mine. Graham Allison, director of the Belfer Center at Harvard's John F. Kennedy School of Government, also encouraged this project while I was a senior fellow at the center in 2007.

Robert Asahina, a gifted editor, reviewed early drafts and helped me greatly with organization of the manuscript. Vicky Wilson, my editor at Knopf, and her associate, Carmen Johnson, were tolerant of a first-time author and provided expert guidance and support through the whole process from book contract to publication. Janet Biehl was a skilled and rigorous copy editor. I am also grateful to Mort Janklow, my agent, for his support throughout. Finally, thanks to my husband, Peter Kann, a fine reporter and writer, for his constant encouragement and help. He patiently read every page of every draft, and his suggestions for improvement were invaluable. Also thanks to our children, Hillary, Petra, Jason, and Jade, who were tolerant of my frequent travel to and focus on Saudi Arabia. Then again, at least some of them may have found that preferable to my focusing on messy rooms and inattentive studies.

CHAPTER I · *Fragile*

3 **Because Saudi Arabia:** CIA, "Saudi Arabia, People," *World Factbook,* https://www.cia.gov/library/publications/the-world-factbook/geos/sa.html.

4 **So fanatical was this preacher:** Natana J. Delong-Bas, *Wahhabi Islam: From Revival and Reform to Global Jihad* (New York: Oxford University Press, 2004), p. 33.

5 **These young people:** A minister and a deputy minister of two separate ministries, interviews by author, March 2009.

5 **and at least 60 percent cannot afford a home:** "Saudis wishing to own homes left with limited options," *Arab News,* April 19, 2011, arabnews.com/saudiarabia/article366591.ece?service=print.

5 **They know that nearly 40 percent:** John Sfakianakis, "Employment Quandary: Youth Struggle to Find Work Raises Urgency for Reform," Banque Saudi Fransi, February 16, 2011, p. 3.

5 **They know that 90 percent:** Adel Fakieh, Saudi minister of labor, interview by author, February 5, 2011.

5 **Yet it is no secret:** Ibid.

6 **The first flood, in 2009:** "302 Face Flood Probe," *Arab News,* April 21, 2011, arabnews.com/saudiarabia/article368405.ece?service=print.

8 **"They keep dying on me":** Jim Kuhn, *Ronald Reagan in Private: A Memoir of My Years in the White House* (New York: Penguin, 2004), p. 165.

9 **"We are hypocrites":** Anonymous imam, interview by author, Riyadh, February 3, 2011.

10 **With seventy thousand mosques:** Abdullah Alheedan, assistant deputy minister for Islamic Affairs, interview by author, Riyadh, October 26, 2009.

11 **"If we do not share responsibility":** Prince Saud bin Abdul Mohsin al Saud, interview by author, Jeddah, January 28, 2011.

CHAPTER 2 · *Al Saud Survival Skills*

13 **How has an absolute monarchy:** Prince Abdul Aziz bin Sattam al Saud, interview by author, April 10, 2010.

13 **A strapping man:** Alexei Vassiliev, *The History of Saudi Arabia* (New York: New York University Press, 2000), p. 203.

16 **The imam had taught:** Christine Moss Helms, *The Cohesion of Saudi Arabia* (Baltimore: The Johns Hopkins University Press, 1981), p. 92.

17 **But unlike Washington:** Simon Henderson, "After King Abdullah: Succession in Saudi Arabia," Washington Institute for Near East Policy (August 2009), Policy Focus no. 96, p. 8.

17 **But he is estimated:** David Howarth, *The Desert King* (London: Quartet Books, 1980), pp. 117–18.

19 **"Draw the sword":** Ameen Rihani, *Maker of Modern Arabia* (New York: Houghton Mifflin, 1928), p. 75.

19 **"Are there not a number":** Helms, *Cohesion*, p. 114.

19 **The lessons learned:** H. C. Armstrong, *Lord of Arabia Ibn Saud: The Intimate Study of a King* (London: Kegan Paul, 2005), p. 97.

20 **Thus began the first jihadist:** Yaroslav Trofimov, *The Siege of Mecca* (New York: Doubleday, 2007), p. 4.

20 **But the siege claimed:** Ibid., p. 225.

23 **In 2009, to reinforce his call:** King Abdullah's endowment for KAUST is undisclosed, but KAUST is said to be "among the world's best endowed" by its public relations officer, who, like the kingdom's U.S. ambassador, Adel al Jubeir, doesn't discourage the "second only to Harvard" description given by numerous Saudis.

24 **"Neither I nor my ancestors":** Armstrong, *Lord of Arabia*, p. 151.

24 **In 1938 Standard Oil:** Rachel Bronson, *Thicker Than Oil: America's Uneasy Partnership with Saudi Arabia* (New York: Oxford University Press, 2006), p. 17.

24 **"Do you know":** Ibid., p. 19.

25 **At least 80 percent:** CIA, "Saudi Arabia: Economy," *World Factbook*, at www.cia.gov/library/publications/the-world-factbook/geos/sa.html.

25 **Fully 40 percent of the budget that is:** Robert Lacey, *Inside the Kingdom: Kings, Clerics, Modernists, Terrorists, and the Struggle for Saudi Arabia* (New York: Viking Penguin, 2009), p. 252.

27 **A popular hadith:** Imam Ahmad, 4/126, muttagun.com /scienceofhadith.html.

28 **"Obey me for so long":** Barnaby Rogerson, *The Heirs of Muhammad* (Woodstock, N.Y.: Overlook Press, 2007), p. 129.

28 **Within fifty years:** Ibid., p. 342.

28 **The conquerors invited:** Tamim Ansary, *Destiny Disrupted* (New York: Public Affairs, 2009), p. 85.

30 **The security directorate:** Dr. Abdulrahman al Hadlag, general director of Ideological Security Directorate, Ministry of Interior, interview by author, Riyadh, October 10, 2009.

30 **The Al Saud have taken a lesson:** Prince Abdul Aziz bin Sattam, interview by author, Riyadh, April 29, 2010, www .ummah.com/forum/showthread.php?257654-Mu-awiyah-s -Hair, accessed May 14, 2011.

CHAPTER 3 · *Islam: Dominant and Divided*

33 **"That is her home":** Lulu, interview by author, Riyadh, May 5, 2010.

34 **"Men are in charge":** Koran 4:34.

35 **Her eldest daughter:** Lulu's daughter, interview by author, Riyadh, January 18, 2011.

36 **"The angel asks you":** Anonymous family, interview by author, Riyadh, January 27, 2010.

36 *"Allahu akbar":* Frederick Mathewson Denny, *An Introduction to Islam* (New York: Macmillan, 1994), p. 120.

41 **Public anger forced:** Sarah Abdullah, "Court Grants 12-year-old Bride Divorce," *Arab News,* April 29, 2010, p. 2.

42 **"The Prophet consulted":** Sheikh Abdullah Mutlag, interview by author, Riyadh, October 26, 2009.

42 **Muslims believe that each human:** Sahih Muslim, book 1, hadith no. 2033, hadithcollection.com/about-hadith-books /129-Sahih%20Book%2001.%20faith/8551-sahih-muslim, accessed May 11, 2011.

43 **"For nearly 1,400 years":** Seyyed Hossein Nasr, *Ideas and Realities of Islam* (Chicago: ABC International Group, 2000), p. 74.

44 **The Prophet is quoted:** Denny, *Introduction,* p. 113.

44 **When Muslims pray:** Ibid., 122.

44 **"In the name of God":** Koran 1:1–7.

45 **The grand mufti, the kingdom's senior:** M. D. Humaidan,

"Al-Asheikh Tells Hai'a Official to Stay Out of Shariah Issues," *Arab News,* April 24, 2010, p. 2.

46 **Within hours of the firing:** "*Hai'a* Denies Statement Accuracy," *Saudi Gazette,* April 27, 2010, p. 1.

46 **In another unprecedented:** Sheikh al Ghamdi, interview by Al Arabbiyah TV, April 30, 2010.

48 **"There is only one change":** Sheikh Salman al Awdah, interview by author, Riyadh, February 18, 2008.

48 **"Saudi society is slow":** Sheikh Salman al Awdah, interview by author, Riyadh, May 1, 2010.

50 **Using a few non-Arabic words:** Y. Admon, "Anti Soccer Fatwas Led Saudi Soccer Players to Join the Jihad in Iraq," Middle East Media Research Institute, Inquiry & Analysis Series, Report no. 245 (October 2005), pp. 1–4, www.memri.org/report/en/print1494.htm, accessed May 11, 2011.

50 **"First, practicing masturbation":** "Fasting person committing masturbation," Fatwa No. 10551, www.alifta.com, Fatwas of the Permanent Committee, browse by page number, group 1, pt. 10, p. 259.

50 **The *ulama* insist:** Chapter on nullifications of Wudu', "Whether touching or shaking hands with a non-Mahram woman . . . ," www.alifta.com, Fatwas of the Permanent Committee, browse by page number, group 1, pt. 5, p. 268.

50 **Similarly it is acceptable:** Salam, "Raising the hand when greeting someone far, " www.alifta.com, Fatwas of the Permanent Committee, browse by page number, group 1, pt. 24, p. 124.

51 **"Things that used to be *haram*":** Young Imam University students and graduates, interview by author, Riyadh, October 9, 2009.

52 **During the first two centuries:** Tilman Nagel, *The History of Islamic Theology* (Princeton, N.J.: Marcus Wiener, 2000), p. 239.

52 **The Prophet further said:** "Gold-coated tableware and sanitary ware," www.alifta.com, Fatwas of the Permanent Committee, browse by page number, group 1, pt. 22, p. 158.

53 **Those who live by Allah's:** Koran 37:42–48.

53 **"We have made it":** Koran 37:63–68.

54 **Only martyrs are spared:** Dr. Shadiah Hamza Sheikh, "Eternal Life: Rewards and Punishments," p. 2, www.wefound.org/texts/Islam_files/EternalLife.htm, accessed May 11, 2011.

56 **Ironically, this breakdown:** Hamid Mowlana and Laurie J. Wilson, *The Passing of Modernity: Communication and the*

Transformation of Society (New York: Addison-Wesley, 1990), p. 9.

CHAPTER 4 · *The Social Labyrinth*

60 **Saudi Arabia boasts 9.8 million:** International Telecommunications Union, www.internetworldstats.com/me/sa.htm, accessed May 11, 2011.

60 **And with 5.1 million Saudis:** Spot On Public Relations, http:// www.spotonpr.com/egypt-facebook-demographics, accessed September 10, 2011.

60 **Tellingly, Saudi users are:** *Middle East and North Africa Facebook Demographics* (Spot On Public Relations, May 2010); also "Saudi Arabia Facebook Statistics," Socialbakers .com, www.socialbakers.com/facebook-statistics/saudi-arabia, accessed March 12, 2012.

62 **More ominously:** Muhammad al Sulami, "Kingdom Amends Media Laws," *Arab News,* April 29, 2011, arabnews.com/saudi arabia/article377672.ece?service=print, accessed April 30, 2011.

62 **"Honor is what makes":** David Pryce-Jones, *The Closed Circle: An Interpretation of the Arabs* (Chicago: Ivan R. Dee, 2002), p. 35.

63 **"Between the poles":** Ibid., p. 41.

63 **Rana, the mother:** University-educated daughter of a professor, interview by author, Riyadh, October 11, 2009, and January 16, 2011.

66 **Thus, tribal raiding:** Marcel Kurpershoek, *Arabia of the Bedouins* (London: Saqi Books, 1992), p. 65.

66 **There he heads:** Abdul Rahman bin Humaid, interview by author, Yanbu, February 2, 2010.

CHAPTER 5 · *Females and Fault Lines*

75 **"The resistance to change":** Madawi al Hassoun, interview by author, Jeddah, April 6, 2009.

75 **"We don't want to be":** Nashwa Taher, Jeddah Chamber of Commerce board member, interview by author, Jeddah, April 4, 2009.

75 **"We feel sorry":** Amal Suliman, King Saud University, interview by author, Riyadh, October 18, 2009.

76 **"Oh Allah, I ask":** Sa'eed ibn ali ibn Wahf al Qahtaani, *Fortification of the Muslim Through Remembrance and Supplication from the Quran and the Sunnah,* trans. Ishmael Ibraheem (Riyadh: Ministry of Islamic Affairs, 1998), no. 74, p. 209.

76 **In sum, the religious:** Mai Yamani, *Changed Identities: The Challenge of the New Generation in Saudi Arabia* (London: Royal Institute of International Affairs, 2000), p. 97.

77 **"A woman is made":** Salwa Abdel Hameed al Khateeb, interview by author, Riyadh, February 18, 2008.

79 **As women become:** Dr. Muhammad A. al Ohali, deputy minister of educational affairs, Ministry of Higher Education, interview by author, Riyadh, October 6, 2009.

79 **They want divorces:** Khalad al Jabri, "Half of Wedding Hall's Marriages End in Divorce," *Saudi Gazette,* February 20, 2010.

80 **Women make up less than 12 percent:** Dr. John Sfakianakis, "Employment Quandary: Youth Struggle to Find Work Raises Urgency for Reform," Banque Saudi Fransi, February 16, 2011, p. 6.

80 **Despite efforts by King Abdullah:** Noura Alturki and Rebekah Braswell, *Businesswomen in Saudi Arabia: Characteristics, Challenges and Aspirations in a Regional Context* (Jeddah: Chamber of Commerce, July 2010), p. 10.

80 **A new survey:** Ibid., p. 11.

84 **A month later:** Geraldine Brooks, *Nine Parts of Desire: The Hidden World of Islamic Women* (New York: Doubleday, 1995), p. 197.

85 **Before their demonstration:** Ibid., p. 198.

85 **"Allowing women to drive":** Fatwas of Ibn Bin Baz, "Ruling on Female Driving of Cars," browse by page, pt. 3, p. 351, www.alifta.com.

86 **"The king wants":** A close relative of King Abdullah, interview by author, Jeddah, January 26, 2011.

86 **"Son of mine uncle":** Martin Lings, *Muhammad: His Life Based on the Earliest Sources* (Rochester, Vt.: Inner Traditions, 2006), p. 35.

87 **She is estimated by:** Karen Armstrong, *Muhammad: A Biography of the Prophet* (San Francisco: Harper, 1992), p. 80.

87 **"You are striving":** Ibid., pp. 84–85.

87 **Kadijah became the first:** Leila Ahmed, *Women and Gender in Islam* (New Haven, Conn.: Yale University Press, 1992), p. 47.

87 **Once Kadijah died:** Safiur Rahman Mubarakpuri, *When the Moon Split: A Biography of the Prophet Muhammad,* trans.

Tabassum Siraj, Michael Richardson, and Badr Azimabadi
(Riyadh: Darussalam, 1998), p. 413.

87 **Aisha was only six:** Armstrong, *Muhammad,* p. 145, Brooks,
Nine Parts, p. 79.

87 **One story recounts how Aisha:** Bukhari Hadith, vol. 5, bk.
58, no. 168.

87 **This marriage violated:** Brooks, *Nine Parts,* p. 83; Armstrong,
Muhammad p. 196.

88 **The Prophet laughed:** Barnaby Rogerson, *The Heirs of
Muhammad* (Woodstock, N.Y.: Overlook Press, 2007), p. 111.

88 **Instead, he beckoned to:** Lings, *Muhammad,* p. 282.

88 **Women in his day:** Ahmed, *Women and Gender,* p. 72.

88 **Nusaybah, a woman of Medina:** Lings, *Muhammad,* p. 191.

89 **Unfortunately for women:** Ahmed, *Women and Gender.* p. 90.

89 **"Establishment Islam's version":** Ibid., p. 239.

90 **"Our religious leaders say":** Suhaila Zein Al Abdein Hammad, interview by author, Riyadh, February 14, 2008.

90 **That exclusion held:** M. D. Humaidan, "Women May Not
Vote in April 23 Municipal Polls," *Arab News,* March 24,
2011, p. 2; Reuters, March 28, 2011, www.reuters.com/assets
/print?aid=USTRE72R65E20110328, accessed May 12, 2011.

90 **"I am the first woman":** Norah al Faiz, interview by author,
Riyadh, April 14, 2009.

91 **In 2010 he conferred:** *Arab News,* January 12, 2010, p. 1.

93 **Or as the princess:** Princess Adelah, interview by author,
Riyadh, January 13, 2010.

93 **"If a woman can stand up":** Maha Muneef, interview by
author, Riyadh, January 10, 2010.

93 **"We have the opportunity":** Princess Adelah, interview by
author, Riyadh, January 28, 2009.

94 **"People had less means":** Ibid.

95 **All this helps account:** *Arab News,* May 10, 2009.

95 **"Sometimes I feel overwhelmed":** Reema, interview by
author, Jeddah, October 5, 2009.

97 **"Women rode":** Alya al Huwaiti, interview by author, Riyadh,
January 29, 2009.

98 **"I am like my sister":** Sara al Huwaiti, interview by author,
Riyadh, January 29, 2009.

98 **"We have had some progress":** Alia Banaja, interview by
author, Jeddah, April, 8, 2009.

99 **"I'm not advertising":** Manal Fakeeh, interview by author,
Jeddah, April 5, 2009.

99 **The tale of one woman from:** Rania Salamah, "Saga of the

Forcefully Divorced Couple," *Arab News,* September 21, 2006, archive.arabnews.com/?page=13&section=0&article+86 892&d=29&m=9&y=2006, accessed July 1, 2010.

100 **Within months:** Walaa Hawari, "Judiciary Council Overturns Forced-Divorce Decision," *Arab News,* January 31, 2010.

100 **Fatima's tale, however horrifying:** Walaa Hawari, "Forced-Divorce Victims; Fatima, Mansour Finally Together," *Arab News,* February 19, 2010, arabnews.com/saudiarabia/article 19435.ece, accessed July 1, 2010.

100 **"Girls wait to be selected":** Fawzia al Bakr, interview by the author, Riyadh, April 25, 2010.

CHAPTER 6 · *The Young and the Restless*

102 **Strolling alone:** Kris Kristofferson, "Sunday Morning Coming Down," 1970, www.songfacts.com/detail.php?id=3904, accessed May 13, 2011.

103 **Yet religious fundamentalists:** Abdullah al Shammary, Ministry of Information, e-mail to author, March 2, 2001; Majed al Maimouni and Nawaf Afit, "Religious Group Disrupts Riyadh Book Fair," *Saudi Gazette,* May 3, 2011, www .saudigazette.com.sa/index.cfm?method=home.regcon& contentID=2011030395019, accessed May 13, 2011.

103 **"Youth want freedom":** Saker al Mokayyad, Prince Naif Arab University for Security Sciences, interview by author, Riyadh, January 27, 2009.

105 **In a recent survey, some 31 percent:** ASDA'A Burson-Marsteller, *Arab Youth Survey,* March 2011, p. 24, www.Arab youthsurvey.com.

106 **A second youth video:** "Businessman Donating 200,000 Sq. Meters Land to Solve Housing Woes," *Arab News,* November 14, 2011, arabnews.com/saudiarabia/article533299.ece?service =print.

107 **When the conversation didn't go:** Adnan Shabrawi and Obaidallah al Ghamdi, "Ministry Slams 'Inaccurate' Media Reports over School Girl's Sentence," *Saudi Gazette,* January 28, 2010, p. 4.

107 **But some of the 225 youths:** "Youths Ransack Al Khobar Shops," *Arab News,* September 26, 2009; "Rioters Caused Huge Losses, Al Khobar Businesses Claim," *Arab News,* September 27, 2009, http://archive.arabnews.com/services/print/print .asp?artid=126786&d=260&m=9&y=2009&pix=kingdom .jpgandcategory=kingdom, accessed September 27, 2009.

107 **A dozen of the teens:** Siraj Wahab and Molouk Y. Ba-Isa, "Dozen Teens Flogged for Role in Rampage," *Arab News,* September 30, 2009, p. 2.

107 **Traffic accidents are:** Faisal Aboobacker Ponnani, "Saher Seminar Held for EP Expats," *Saudi Gazette,* January 18, 2011, www.saudigazette.com.sa/index.cfm?method=home.regcon &contentID=2011011891564, accessed May 13, 2001.

108 **The younger answers:** Anonymous teenager, interview by author, Jeddah, February 14, 2008.

109 **"Our concentration was on":** Mustafa, interview by author, Riyadh, October 29, 2009.

109 **Indeed, according to public security:** Muhammad al Negir, Public Security, Ministry of Interior, interview by author, Riyadh, April 1, 2009.

110 **Some 90 percent of stolen cars:** Ibid.

111 **"I don't accept":** Anonymous young man, interview by author, Riyadh, October 9, 2009.

113 **The artist "perceives a culture":** Eyad Meghazel, "Installation," *Young Saudi Artists* exhibition, Athr Gallery, Jeddah, January 12–31, 2001.

114 **"It is like pressing":** Prince Saad bin Muhammad, interview by author, Jeddah, January 29, 2011.

114 **"The government has become":** Mai Yamani, *Changed Identities: The Challenge of the New Generation in Saudi Arabia* (Washington, D.C.: Brookings Institute Press, 2000), p. 148.

115 **In mosques, they hear:** "Sheikh Al-Qaradawi: Kaust Will Lead to 'Renaissance of the Ummah,'" *Saudi Gazette,* October 24, 2009, 64.65.60.109/index.cfm?method=home.regcon &content ID=2009102452459, accessed May 13, 2011.

115 **How can a film festival:** Omaima al Fardan, "Jeddah Film Festival Canceled," *Arab News,* July 19, 2009, http://archive .arabnews.com/?page=1&section=0&article=124684&d =19&m=7&y2009&hl-Jeddah_Film_Festival_canceled, accessed May 15, 2011.

115 **Why did the kingdom:** Salman al Malki, interview by author and written responses to author's questions, Riyadh, January 23, 2011.

116 **"Facebook opens the doors":** Anonymous young man, interview by author, Riyadh, January 9, 2009.

116 **"I saw things change":** Anonymous source, interview by author, Jeddah, January 23, 2011.

116 **"The young are at a crossroads":** Anonymous source, interview by author, Jeddah, April 8, 2009.

116 **"Religion here is just":** Ahmad Shugairi, interview by author, Jeddah, January 21, 2009.

118 **"We cover everything":** Prince Turki bin Khalid, interview by author, Riyadh, October 12, 2009.

119 **"The young generation is demanding":** Abdulaziz al Khayyal, senior vice president for industrial relations Saudi ARAMCO, interview by author, Dhahran, March 21, 2009.

120 **In recent years, the company:** Samir Tubayyeb, executive director for employee relations and training, Saudi ARAMCO, interview by author, Dhahran, March 21, 2009.

121 **"As Gandhi said":** Young women at Saudi ARAMCO, interview by author, Dhahran, March 21, 2009.

122 **Because he has no way:** Salim al Fafi, interview by author, Faifa, April 9, 2009.

CHAPTER 7 · *Princes*

123 **"Please excuse me":** Prince Abdullah bin Musa'id, interview by author, Riyadh, October 11, 2009.

123 **"In the United States 'we tried'":** Prince Abdullah bin Musa'id, interview by author, Riyadh, April 15, 2009.

124 **"Soccer is our only":** Ibid.

125 **Third-generation princes:** Robert Baer, "The Fall of the House of Saud," *Atlantic,* May 2003, p. 6, www.theatlantic.com /magazine/print/2003/05/the-fall-of-the-house-of-saud/4215, accessed May 14, 2011.

126 **When the monarch reached:** Robert Lacey, *The Kingdom: Arabia and the House of Saud* (New York: Harcourt Brace Jovanovich, 1981), pp. 425–26.

127 **"Here Saudis prefer":** Prince Abdullah bin Musa'id, interview by author, Riyadh, April 15, 2009.

129 **Prince Abdul Aziz earned:** Prince Abdul Aziz bin Sattam, interview by author, Riyadh, March 26, 2009.

130 **"Over the next thirty to fifty years":** Prince Abdul Aziz bin Sattam, interview by author, Riyadh, January 29, 2011.

131 **The kingdom is undertaking a $2 billion:** Abdullah bin Muhammad al Yahya, president of the Court of Appeal, general secretary, Supreme Judicial Council, interview by author, Riyadh, October 27, 2009.

131 **But Prince Abdul Aziz argues:** Prince Abdul Aziz bin Sattam, interview by author, March 24, 2009.

132 **"I am only fifteen days":** Prince Abdul Aziz bin Sattam, interview by author, October 6, 2009.

133 **When Prince Sultan was born:** Prince Sultan bin Salman, interview by author, Riyadh, January 14, 2010.

134 **"We cannot believe anyone":** Robert Lacey, *Inside the Kingdom: Kings, Clerics, Modernists, Terrorists, and the Struggle for Saudi Arabia* (New York: Viking Penguin, 2009), p. 88.

134 **Given the speed:** Prince Sultan bin Salman, interview by author, Riyadh, January 14, 2010.

134 **"He didn't ask":** Ibid.

135 **"On the first day":** Prince Sultan bin Salman, keynote speech, Global Space Technology Forum, Abu Dhabi, UAE, December 7–9, 2009, p. 4.

135 **"There is no doubt":** Prince Sultan bin Salman, interview by author, Riyadh, January 14, 2010.

136 **"Do you want to know":** Princess Hala bint Sultan bin Salman, interview by author, Riyadh, January 14, 2010.

136 **"We can't continue":** Prince Sultan bin Salman, interview by author, Riyadh, January 14, 2010.

136 **Turki served as director:** "Prince Turki al Faisal," Saudi Embassy, www.saudiembassy.net/about/turkibio.aspx, accessed May 14, 2011.

136 **The prince now:** Prince Turki al Faisal, King Faisal Foundation, www.kff.com/ENo1/KFCRIS/KFCRISIndex.html, accessed May 14, 2011.

137 **The prince reportedly is:** Barbara Ferguson, "Prince Turki al Faisal Resigns as Saudi Ambassador to U.S.," *Arab News,* December 13, 2006, archive.arabnews.com/services/print/print.asp?artid=89943&d=13&m=12&y=2006, accessed May 14, 2011.

137 **"We miss you too":** Prince Turki al Faisal, interview by author, Riyadh, May 4, 2008.

138 **In that post:** Lawrence Wright, *The Looming Tower* (New York: Alfred A. Knopf, 2006), p. 104.

138 **"In the fifties to the nineties":** Prince Turki al Faisal, interview by author, Riyadh, January 27, 2008.

CHAPTER 8 · *Failing Grades*

140 **No less an exemplar:** Koran 62:2.

140 **At that time, only 2 percent:** Helen Chapin Metz, ed., *Saudi Arabia: A Country Study* (Washington, D.C.: GPO for the

Library of Congress, 1992), Education, p. 1, countrystudies.us /saudi-arabia/, accessed March 7, 2010.

140 **In comparison with students:** "Mathematics Achievement of Fourth and Eighth Graders in 2007," *Trends in International Mathematics and Science Study,* table 1, nces.ed.gov/timss /table07_1asp, accessed May 16, 2011.

141 **Native Saudi male teachers:** Consultant to the Ministry of Education, interview by author, Riyadh, January 13, 2009.

141 **This helps explain:** Dr. Mohammad A. al Ohali, deputy minister of educational affairs, Ministry of Higher Education, interview by author, October 6, 2009.

141 **In a country where more than 60 percent:** Michaela Prokop, "The War of Ideas: Education in Saudi Arabia," in Paul Aarts and Gerd Nonneman, eds., *Saudi Arabia in the Balance* (New York: New York University Press, 2005), p. 77.

141 **More alarmingly:** Dr. John Sfakianakis, "Employment Quandary: Youth Struggle to Find Work Raises Urgency for Reform," Banque Saudi Fransi, February 16, 2011, p. 3.

141 **At 137 billion Saudi riyals:** "Saudi Arabia Promises to Support Economic Recovery in 2010," Middle East North Africa Financial Network, *Arab News,* December 24, 2009, p. 2, www.menafn.com/qn_print.asp?StoryID=1093291161&sub1 =true, accessed March 4, 2010.

142 **At the elementary school:** Metz, *Saudi Arabia,* p. 2.

142 **Indeed, Saudi educational policy:** Ibid.

142 **As a result of this educational:** Abdulwahed al Humaid, deputy for planning and development, Ministry of Labor, interview by author, Riyadh, February 8, 2007.

143 **Saudi schools weren't always:** Tewfiq al Saif, interview by author, Dammam, February 20, 2007.

144 **The religious leaders departed:** Abdul Mohsen al Akkas, former minister of social affairs, interview by author, Al Khobar, March 22, 2011.

144 **When Nasser, a nationalist:** Abdullah Uthaimin, historian, King Faisal Foundation, interview by author, Riyadh, February 16, 2008.

145 **"Invading a country":** Ghazi al Gosaibi, minister of labor, interview by author, Riyadh, January 29, 2008.

145 **"I always referred to Abdullah":** Ibid.

146 **Teachers were sent:** Faisal bin Muammar, deputy minister of education, interview by author, Riyadh, April 13, 2009.

147 **"If you are serving":** Visit to School 48 in Riyadh by author, April 26, 2010.

148 **The new textbooks:** Naif H. al Romi, deputy minister of educational planning and development, Ministry of Education, interview by author, Riyadh, April 19, 2010.

148 **By contrast, in the tiny:** Ibid.

149 **While Saudis came to the United States:** Ambassador Adel al Jubeir, e-mail to the author, February 26, 2012.

149 **Determined to reverse that:** P. K. Abdul Ghafour, "Over 106,000 Saudis Get King Abdullah Scholarships," *Arab News,* March 13, 2011, arabnews.com/saudiarabia/article316284 .ece?service=print, accessed May 15, 2011.

149 **To try to jump-start:** Shafquat Ali, "KAUST: King's Gift to the World," *Arab News,* September 24, 2009, www.arabnews .com/services/print/print.asp?artid=126714&d=24&m=9&y =2009&hl=KAUST:kingsgifttotheworld, accessed September 24, 2009.

149 **On campus, most students:** Visit to KAUST by author, October 18, 2009.

150 **"Throughout history, power":** KAUST press release, available at kaust.edu.sa.

150 **By one estimate, fully 70 percent:** Majlis Ash Shura member who asks to be anonymous, interview by author, Riyadh, January 30, 2008.

150 **"There is no critical thinking":** King Saud University professor who asks to be anonymous, interview by author, Riyadh, February 16, 2008.

151 **"Students aren't curious":** King Saud University professor who asks to be anonymous, interview by author, Riyadh, October 11, 2009.

151 **The regime is seeking to make up:** "Saudi Arabia Promises to Support Economic Recovery in 2010," Middle East North Africa Financial Network, *Arab News,* December 24, 2009, p. 2, www.menafn.com/qn_print.asp?StoryID=1093291161& sub1=true, accessed March 4, 2010.

151 **"On a visit to Hail":** Former official of city of Hail who asks to remain anonymous, interview by author, Riyadh, January 11, 2009.

152 **The girls who tried to flee:** "Saudi Arabia: Religious Police Role in School Fire Criticized," Human Rights Watch, March 14, 2002, www.hrw.org/en/news/2002/03/14/saudi-arabia -religious-police-role-school-fire-criticized, accessed May 15, 2011.

153 **There are some outposts:** Visit to Ahliyya School in Dammam by author, March 22, 2009.

154 **"The time has come":** Maha Fozan, interview by author, Riyadh, October 13, 2009.

154 **"A woman is allowed to speak":** Muhammad Abdul Kareem al Eisa, minister of justice, March 2, 2010, written response to a question asked in an interview by author, Riyadh, January 19, 2010.

156 **The kingdom's 5.5 million:** Salah al Amr, vice governor for development, Technical and Vocational Training Center, interview by author, January 25, 2009.

156 **even though between 2002 and 2006:** Dr. Muhammad A. al Ohali, deputy minister of educational affairs, Ministry of Higher Education, interview by author, Riyadh, October 6, 2009.

156 **"Families put kids":** Ibid.

156 **Prince Faisal bin Abdullah, minister:** Prince Faisal bin Abdullah, interview by author, Riyadh, April 15, 2009.

156 **Easier said than done:** Stephane Lacroix, telephone interview by author, March 6, 2009.

CHAPTER 9 · *Plans, Paralysis, and Poverty*

157 **Two out of every three people:** Abdulwahed al Humaid, deputy minister for planning and development, Ministry of Labor, interview by author, Riyadh, January 26, 2010.

157 **And in Saudi Arabia's anemic:** Adel Fakieh, minister of labor, interview by author, Riyadh, February 5, 2011.

158 **In 2011, thanks primarily:** "Economy: Saudi Arabia," *The World Factbook,* CIA, 2012, www.cia.gov/library/publications /the-world-factbook/geos/sa.html, accessed March 9, 2012.

158 **As a result, on a per capita income:** "Country Comparison: GDP Per Capita (PPP)," *The World Factbook,* CIA, 2012, www .cia.gov/library/publications/the-world-factbook/rankorder /2004rank.html, accessed March 9, 2012.

159 **"By 2030, foreign assets":** Brad Bourland, "Saudi Arabia's Coming Oil and Fiscal Challenge," Jadwa Investment (July 2011), p. 1.

159 **Not only is unemployment:** John Sfakianakis, "Employment Quandary: Youth Struggle to Find Work Raises Urgency for Reform," Banque Saudi Fransi, February 16, 2011, p. 3.

159 **but 40 percent of all Saudi citizens:** Senior officials at two separate ministries, interview by author, Riyadh, 2010.

160 **The king's decision to institute:** Muhammad Ibrahim, "SR500bn Social Spending Package Outlined," *Arab News,*

March 18, 2011, arabnews.com/saudiarabia/article321419.ece?
service=print, accessed March 26, 2011.

160 **With this latest largesse:** John Sfakianakis, "Holding Back:
State Spending Focus Restrains Private Sector, Diversification," Banque Saudi Fransi, May 17, 2011, p. 2.

160 **Indeed, adjusted for inflation:** Ibid., p. 7.

160 **So while the private sector:** Sfakianakis, "Employment Quandary," p. 3.

161 **The previous plan called:** Ibid., p. 5.

162 **Now, as in the days:** Dr. Muhammad al Zolfa, member of
Majlis Ash-Shura, interview by author, January 24, 2009.

162 **One may well wonder:** OPEC Net Oil Export Revenues,
OPEC Revenues Fact Sheet, Energy Information Administration, www.eia.doe.gov/emeu/cabs/OPEC_Revenues/Fact
sheet.html, accessed July 7, 2009.

162 **down to \$215.3 billion in 2010:** John Sfakianakis, "Quota
Counting: New Saudi Employment Rules to Shake Up Private Sector," Banque Saudi Fransi, June 14, 2011, p. 9.

163 **"At least 85 to 90 percent":** Dr. Khalid al Falih, CEO
Saudi ARAMCO, interview by author, Dhahran, March 21,
2009.

163 **A 2011 survey of three hundred projects:** "Only Three Percent
of Projects Finish on Time: Study," *Arab News,* May 19, 2011,
arabnews.com/saudiarabia/article415376.ece?service=print,
accessed May 20, 2011.

164 *Arab News,* **the kingdom's major:** Ghazanfar Ali Khan,
"King Lays Foundation Stone for Women's University," *Arab
News,* October 30, 2008.

164 **but it actually had cost 20 billion:** Ghazanfar Ali Khan,
"World's Largest University for Women Opened," *Arab News,*
May 16, 2011.

164 **One sad snapshot:** "Patents by Country, State, and Year—All
Patent Types," U.S. Patent and Trademark Office (December
2010), p. 3, www.uspto.gov/web/offices/ac/ido/oeip/taf/cst_all
.htm, accessed May 17, 2011.

164 **"We want to move from":** Dr. Khalid al Sulaiman, deputy
minister of industry, Ministry of Commerce and Industry,
interview by author, March 30, 2009.

165 **In addition to the new Industrial:** Dr. Turki Saud Mohammed al Saud, vice president for research institutes, King Abdulaziz City for Science and Technology, interview by author,
Riyadh, March 28, 2009.

165 **A Higher Education Plan:** Dr. Muhammad A. al Ohali, dep-

uty minister of educational affairs, Ministry of Higher Education, interview by author, Riyadh, October 6, 2009.

166 **Yet in 2009 the government:** Sfakianakis, "Employment Quandary," p. 3.

166 **For instance, a business procures:** Abdulrahman Zamil, interview by author, Riyadh, January 18, 2011.

166 **Of course, occasionally:** Mishaal al Tamimi, "In Visa Scams, Crooks Become Victims," *Arab News,* March 31, 2011, arabnews.com/saudiarabia/article336633.ece?service=print, accessed May 16, 2011.

166 **This illegal conduct:** Saleh al Rasheed, "This Business Will Finally Ruin Us," *Arab News,* April 28, 2011, arabnews .com/opinion/columns/article375117.ece?service=print, accessed April 28, 2011.

167 **If the private-sector workforce:** John Sfakianakis, "Holding Ground: Saudi H2 Economic Outlook Sound in Face of External Stress," Banque Saudi Fransi, June 14, 2010, p. 8.

167 **A survey by the Riyadh Chamber:** Steffen Hertog, *Princes, Brokers, and Bureaucrats: Oil and the State in Saudi Arabia* (Ithaca, N.Y.: Cornell University Press, 2010), p. 251.

167 **Some 60 percent of university:** Sfakianakis, "Employment Quandary," p. 6.

167 **More recently, the government has:** Prince Faisal bin Abdullah, minister of education, interview by author, October 25, 2009.

168 **"I pity my children":** Badea Abu al Naja, "Unable to Pay Rent, Makkah Family Live in Tent," *Arab News,* May 11, 2008, p. 3.

169 **The latest five-year development:** Salah al Amr, vice governor for development, Technical and Vocational Training Corporation, interview by author, Riyadh, January 25, 2009.

169 **Everything is state of the art:** Visit to High Institute for Plastic Education by author, Riyadh, January 28, 2009.

170 **One sign of how badly:** Monera al Aloula, assistant deputy governor of training, Girls Technical College, interview by author, Riyadh, February 7, 2007.

171 **Remittances from expat workers surged:** Sfakianakis, "Holding Ground," p. 8.

171 **Yet more than three:** Ayman Kanaan, vice president for the Industrial Steel Products Group, Zamil Steel, interview by author, Al Khobar, January 24, 2010.

171 **To meet government goals:** Ibid.

172 **"When you build":** Abdulrahman al Zamil, interview by author, Riyadh, February 17, 2008.

172 **"My brother wanted":** Abdulrahman al Zamil, interview by author, October 10, 2009.

172 **"I would put him":** Ali al Qahtani, manager of Haram Store, interview by author, Riyadh, January 14, 2010.

173 **"It is not permitted":** Rima al Mukhtar, "Saudis Shocked by Fatwa Banning Women Cashiers," *Arab News,* November 1, 2010, arabnews.com/saudiarabia/article177726.ece?service= print, accessed May 16, 2011.

174 **The state has "fundamentally":** Hertog, *Princes, Brokers,* p. 259.

176 **While the government claims:** Official at a prominent financial institution, interview by author, Riyadh, April 15, 2009.

176 **But the estimated waiting:** John Sfakianakis, "Under Construction: Saudi Steps Up Efforts to Meet Home, Loan Demand," Banque Saudi Fransi, March 20, 2011, p. 3.

176 **Lower-income Saudis:** Ibid., p. 5.

176 **As revolutionary winds swept:** Muhammad Ibrahim, "SR500bn Social Spending Package Outlined," *Arab News,* March 18, 2011, arabnews.com/saudiarabia/article321419.ece ?service=print, accessed March 26, 2011.

CHAPTER 10 · *Outcasts*

179 **Surprising as it may seem:** Study, not public, quoted to author by senior officials in two different ministries.

179 **As the Saudi population:** "Saudi Arabia, Statistics, Demographic Indicators," UNICEF, www.unicef.org/infobycountry /saudiarabia_statistics.html#78.

181 **"I need this job":** Umm Turki, interview by author, Riyadh, January 19, 2010.

182 **"Who among people deserves":** Sahih al Bukhari, *Book of Good Manners,* vol. 8.

182 **"I pray to God":** Divorcee, interview by author, Riyadh, January 19, 2010.

183 **"My life with my husband":** Widow, interview by author, Riyadh, January 19, 2010.

184 **"I don't want people":** Umm Muhammad, interview by author, Jeddah, October 19, 2009.

185 **The chamber of commerce also:** Basmah Omair, interview by author, April 6, 2009.

186 **"There are a lot":** Abdullah, interview by author, Riyadh, October 26, 2009. Abdullah declined to give his family name.

187 **"O you who have believed":** Koran 2:264.

187 **"If you disclose your":** Koran 2:271.

188 **My guide for the visit:** Mekhlef bin Daham al Shammary, interview by author, April 23, 2010.

189 **"Life was better":** Author visit to imam of Al Athla, a village near Jizan, April 11, 2009.

190 **"He is not a perfect Muslim who":** Sahih Bukhari, www.ahya .org/amm/modules.php?name=Sections&op=printpage& artid=151.

CHAPTER 11 · *. . . and Outlaws*

193 **The prince, still holding:** Dr. Abdulrahman al Hadlag, general director of Ideological Security Directorate, Ministry of Interior, interview by author, October 10, 2009.

194 **Khalid fit the profile:** Ibid.

194 **"I missed my family":** Khalid Sulayman al Hubayshi, interview by author, Jeddah, October 18, 2009.

197 **"I was not religious":** Khalid al Bawadi, interview by author, Riyadh, January 16, 2010.

198 **"I smoked":** Muhammad Fozan, interview by author, Riyadh, October 13, 2009.

200 **"So long as they":** Prince Muhammad bin Nayef, deputy minister of interior, interview by author, Riyadh, February 6, 2007.

200 **"If you just cut":** Jamal Khashoggi, interview by author, January 21, 2010.

200 **As a result, the government now is paying:** Dr. Abdulrahman al Hadlag, interview by author, Riyadh, October 20, 2009.

202 **The men, who live:** Visit to Prince Muhammad bin Nayef Care Center by author, Riyadh, October 12, 2009.

202 **"Art in Saudi Arabia":** Awad al Yami, interview by author, Riyadh, October 12, 2009.

203 **"When radicalism goes underground":** Thomas Hegghammer, interview by author, Princeton, N.J., June 23, 2010.

204 **"No one recruited me":** Hegghammer, *Jihad in Saudi Arabia: Violence and Pan-Islamism Since 1979* (New York: Cambridge University Press, 2010), p. 139.

204 **"near enemy":** Gilles Kepel and Jean-Pierre Milelli, *Al Qaeda in Its Own Words,* trans. Pascale Ghazaleh (Cambridge, Mass.: Belknap Press of Harvard University Press, 2008), p. 158.

205 **"Liberating the Muslim":** Ibid., p. 205.

205 **"Take not for friends":** Koran 4:138–39.

205 **"God prohibited":** Kepel and Milelli, *Al Qaeda*, p. 212.

205 **"We saw the noblest":** Ibid., p. 207.

205 **"Democracy is a new religion":** Ibid., p. 184.

206 **"Terrorism is criminal":** *Saudi Gazette,* March 3, 2010, www
.saudigazette.com.sa/index.cfm?method=home.regcon&
contentID=2010022063962, accessed March 12, 2012.

207 **More terrorist cells:** Hegghammer, *Jihad,* p. 216.

207 **"The only way of repelling":** Kepel and Milelli, *Al Qaeda,*
p. 49.

208 **Three of the first:** Bernard Lewis, *The Arabs in History*
(Oxford: Oxford University Press, 2002), pp. 59–64.

CHAPTER 12 · *Succession*

210 **The second Saudi state:** Alexei Vassiliev, *The History of Saudi
Arabia* (New York: New York University Press, 2000), p. 187.

210 **"Join hands across":** Robert Lacey, *The Kingdom: Arabia and
the House of Saud* (New York: Harcourt Brace Jovanovich,
1981), p. 318.

210 **In a kingdom that then:** David Howarth, *The Desert King*
(London: Quartet Books, 1980), p. 198.

210 **As the king drove:** Lacey, *Kingdom,* pp. 300–302.

211 **When Faisal went:** Ibid., p. 323.

211 **"Have you got enough":** Ibid., p. 351.

212 **Immediately after the fatwa:** Ibid., pp. 353–56.

212 **The new king, Faisal:** Ibid., p. 356.

213 **With that history in mind:** "King Abdullah Names Members
of the Allegiance Commission," Royal Embassy of Saudi Arabia, December 10, 2007, www.saudiembassy.net/latest_news
/news12100801.aspx, accessed May 17, 2011.

213 **Abdul Aziz fathered some:** Simon Henderson, "After King
Abdullah: Succession in Saudi Arabia," Washington Institute
for Near East Policy (August 2009), Policy Focus no. 96, p. 3.

213 **Her eldest son:** For more on the Sudairis, see ibid., p. 6, and
Joseph A. Kechichian, *Succession in Saudi Arabia* (New York:
Palgrave, 2001), pp. 6–8.

214 **"I pledge to Allah Almighty":** "King Abdullah Addresses
Princes," Leadership News, Ministry of Foreign Affairs, December 10, 2007, http://mofa.gov.sa/sites/mofaen/Servicesand

Information/news/statements/Pages/NewsArticleID72858
.aspx, accessed March 29, 2008.

214 **That 2009 appointment, made without:** Henderson, "After
King Abdullah," p. 8.

214 **"I call on the royal court":** "Prince Talal Bin Abdul Aziz
Questions Saudi Succession Plan," Reuters News Agency,
March 29, 2009, http://gulfnews.com/news/gulf/saudi-arabia
/prince-talal-bin-abdul-aziz-questions-saudi-succession
-plan-1.60019, accessed May 21, 2011.

CHAPTER 13 · *Saudi Scenarios*

220 **He dispensed $130 billion:** Muhammad Ibrahim, "SR500bn
Social Spending Package Outlined," *Arab News,* March 18, 2011,
arabnews.com/saudiarabia/article321419.ece?service=print,
accessed March 26, 2011.

221 **"If Saudi Arabia adopts democracy":** Prince Salman bin
Abdul Aziz, governor of Riyadh Province, interview by author,
Riyadh, April 28, 2010.

222 **A new survey of Arab youth:** "3rd Annual ASDA'A
Burson-Marsteller Arab Youth Survey," March 2011, p. 15, www
.asdaa.com.

222 **The new pan-Arab youth survey:** Ibid., p. 18.

223 **One way to postpone:** Samuel Huntington, *Political Order in
Changing Societies* (New Haven, Conn.: Yale University Press,
1968), p. 187.

223 **Al Saud "will lose some":** Ibid., p. 191.

224 **One such Saudi:** Khalid al Nowaiser, "An Open Letter to
King Abdullah," *Wall Street Journal,* March 18, 2011.

225 **"We are blind":** Khalid al Falih, interview by author, Dhahran, March 21, 2009.

CHAPTER 14 · *Pins and Needles*

232 **"This is why we":** Rachael Bronson, *Thicker Than Oil: America's Uneasy Partnership with Saudi Arabia* (New York: Oxford
University Press, 2006), p. 118.

234 **"north of $75 billion":** David Ottaway, *The King's Messenger*
(New York: Walker, 2008), p. 185.

234 **Indeed, a meeting:** Ibid., p. 186.

236 **"Human beings are created":** "Principle of Justice Is Key," *Arab News,* November 13, 2008, http://archive.Arabnews .com/?page=4&section=0&article=116308&d=13&m=11&y =2008, accessed September 7, 2010.

238 **China, Japan, South Korea:** U.S. Energy Information Administration, Country Analysis Briefs, "Saudi Arabia Oil Exports and Shipping," http://204.14.135.140/countries/cab.cfm?f.ps =SA., accessed March 14, 2011.

238 **Abdullah also reached out:** "Saudi King Holds Talks with Russian President, Says Relations 'Stronger,'" *BBC Worldwide Monitoring,* February 12, 2007.

238 **"not competitors but":** "Russia's Strategic and Economic Alignment with the Arab States," *Globalia Magazine,* September 26, 2008.

238 **"It's a Muslim marriage":** Ottaway, *King's Messenger,* p. 226.

239 **"We talk to some":** Prince Turki al Faisal, interview by author, Riyadh, March 31, 2009.

240 **Saudi Arabia, however, is:** Robert Baer, *The Devil We Know* (New York: Three Rivers Press, 2008), p. 138.

240 **The kingdom's military spending:** milexdata.sipri.org/result .php4, accessed September 14, 2010.

240 **Repairing the Saudi oil fields:** Baer, *Devil We Know,* p. 138.

241 **"It would not be as clear-cut":** Prince Turki, interview by author, Riyadh, March 31, 2009.

242 **Indeed, James Schlesinger:** Bronson, *Thicker Than Oil,* p. 107.

243 **"Well," asked Kissinger:** Kissinger Telephone Transcripts, at foia.state.gov/documents/kissinger/0000C284.pdf.

243 **"I did not threaten":** Henry Kissinger, interview by author, New York, July 13, 2011.

243 **"I don't know if what":** Prince Turki, interview by author, Riyadh, March 31, 2009.

243 **"I don't recall such":** Kissinger, interview by author, New York, July 13, 2011.

244 **"The Saudis learned that":** Dr. James Schlesinger, interview by author, Washington, D.C., September 28, 2010.

245 **If this trend continues:** "Saudi Arabia Looks to Solar, Nuclear Power to Reduce Its Oil Use by Half," Bloomberg, April 3, 2011, www.bloomberg.com/news/2011-04-03/solar -nuclear-energy-to-reduce-Saudi-oil-demand-official-says .html, accessed July 19, 2011.

245 **The kingdom has announced plans:** Brad Bourland, "Saudi

Arabia's Coming Oil and Fiscal Challenge," Jadwa Investment, July 2011, p. 19.

245 **Then in 1988 Saudi ARAMCO:** Matthew R. Simmons, *Twilight in the Desert: The Coming Saudi Oil Shock and the World Economy* (Hoboken, N.J.: John Wiley & Sons, 2005), p. 273.

246 **In production since 1951:** Ibid., p. 152.

246 **"The death of this great":** Ibid., p. 179.

247 **But since 1970:** U.S. Energy Information Administration, Petroleum and Other Liquids, Annual U.S. Field Production of Crude Oil, http://www.eia.gov/dnav/pet/hist/LeafHandler.ashx?n=PET&sMCRFPUS2&f=A, accessed May 19, 2011.

247 **"We are not good":** James Schlesinger, "Energy Security," keynote at Association for Study of Peak Oil, Cork, Ireland, September 2007.

247 **"Since the 1970s the world":** Robert Hirsch, Roger Bezdek, and Robert Wendling, *The Impending World Energy Mess* (Eugene, Ore.: Mud City Press, 2010).

248 **" 'It' is the oil wealth":** "New Oil Fields Saved for Future Generations: King," *Saudi Gazette,* September 7, 2010.

248 **"The question is should we":** Khalid al Falih, interview by author, Dhahran, March 21, 2009.

CHAPTER 15 · *Endgame*

251 **"made up from different":** Alexis de Tocqueville, *The Ancien Regime and the Revolution* (London: Penguin Group, 2008), p. 112.

251 **"it had been much simpler":** Ibid., p. 111.

252 **"Only a great genius":** Ibid., p. 175.

252 **"still looked unshakeable":** Ibid., p. 200.

252 **A confident President Ahmadinejad:** Neil MacFarquhar, "Iran's Leader Warns U.S. as He Rebuts Criticism," *New York Times,* September 22, 2010, www.nytimes.com/2010/09/22/world/middleeast/22iran.html, accessed September 25, 2010.

254 **"We have to go step":** Prince Talal bin Abdul Aziz, interview by author, Riyadh, May 11, 2008.

255 **"Kennedy, no fan of":** Lacey, *The Kingdom: Arabia and the House of Saud,* p. 345.

BIBLIOGRAPHY

Ahmed, Leila. *Women and Gender in Islam: Historical Roots of a Modern Debate.* New Haven, Conn.: Yale University Press, 1992.

Al-Bukhari. *Sahih.* Translated by Dr. Muhammad Muhsin Khan. Riyadh: Darussalam, 1997.

Al-Qahtaani, Sa'eed Ibn Ali Ibn Wahf. *Fortification of the Muslim Through Remembrance and Supplication from the Quran and the Sunnah.* Riyadh: Ministry of Islamic Affairs, 1998.

Al-Rasheed, Madawi. *Contesting the Saudi State: Islamic Voices from a New Generation.* Cambridge, U.K.: Cambridge University Press, 2007.

Ansary, Tamim. *Destiny Disrupted: A History of the World Through Islamic Eyes.* New York: Public Affairs, 2009.

Armstrong, H. C. *Lord of Arabia Ibn Saud: The Intimate Study of a King.* London: Kegan Paul, 2005.

Armstrong, Karen. *Muhammad: A Biography of the Prophet.* New York: HarperCollins, 1993.

Asad, Talal. *Genealogies of Religion: Discipline and Reasons of Power in Christianity and Islam.* Baltimore: Johns Hopkins University Press, 1993.

Baer, Robert. *The Devil We Know.* New York: Three Rivers Press, 2008.

Bennison, Amira. *The Great Caliphs: The Golden Age of the 'Abbasid Empire.* New Haven, Conn.: Yale University Press, 2009.

Bronson, Rachael. *Thicker than Oil: America's Uneasy Partnership with Saudi Arabia.* New York: Oxford University Press, 2006.

Brooks, Geraldine. *Nine Parts of Desire: The Hidden World of Islamic Women.* New York: Doubleday, 1995.

Cook, Michael. *Commanding Right and Forbidding Wrong in Islamic Thought.* Cambridge, U.K.: Cambridge University Press, 2006.

Cooper, Andrew. *The Oil Kings: How the U.S., Iran, and Saudi Arabia Changed the Balance of Power in the Middle East.* New York: Simon & Schuster, 2011.

Cordesman, Anthony. *Saudi Arabia: National Security in a Troubled Region.* Santa Barbara, Calif.: ABC CLIO, 2009.

Delong-Bas, Natana J. *Wahhabi Islam: From Revival and Reform to Global Jihad.* New York: Oxford University Press, 2004.

Denny, Frederick. *An Introduction to Islam.* New York: Macmillan, 1994.

De Tocqueville, Alexis. *The Ancien Regime and the Revolution.* London: Penguin Group, 2008.

Feldman, Noah. *The Fall and Rise of the Islamic State.* Princeton, N.J.: Princeton University Press, 2008.

Hegghammer, Thomas. *Jihad in Saudi Arabia: Violence and Pan-Islamism Since 1979.* New York: Cambridge University Press, 2009.

Helms, Christine. *The Cohesion of Saudi Arabia.* Baltimore: Johns Hopkins University Press, 1981.

Hertog, Steffen. *Princes, Brokers, and Bureaucrats: Oil and the State in Saudi Arabia.* Ithaca, N.Y.: Cornell University Press, 2010.

Hirsch, Robert, Roger Bezdek, and Robert Wendling. *The Impending World Energy Mess.* Eugene, Ore.: Mud City Press, 2010.

Holdren, David, and Richard Johns. *The House of Saud.* London: Sidgwick & Jackson, 1981.

Howarth, David. *The Desert King.* London: Quartet Books, 1980.

Huntington, Samuel. *Political Order in Changing Societies.* New Haven, Conn.: Yale University Press, 1968.

Kechichian, Joseph. *Succession in Saudi Arabia.* New York: Palgrave, 2001.

Kepel, Gilles. *The War for Muslim Minds: Islam and the West.* Translated by Pascale Ghazaleh. Cambridge, Mass.: Belknap Press of Harvard University Press, 2004.

Kepel, Gilles, and Jean-Pierre Milelli. *Al Qaeda in Its Own Words.* Translated by Pascale Ghazaleh. Cambridge, Mass.: Belknap Press of Harvard University Press, 2008.

Kuhn, Jim. *Ronald Reagan in Private: A Memoir of My Years in the White House.* New York: Penguin Books, 2004.

Kurpershoek, Marcel. *Arabia of the Bedouins.* London: Saqi Books, 1992.

Lacey, Robert. *The Kingdom: Arabia and the House of Sa'ud.* New York: Harcourt Brace Jovanovich, 1981.

———. *Inside the Kingdom: Clerics, Modernists, Terrorists, and the Struggle for Saudi Arabia.* New York: Viking Penguin, 2009.

Lewis, Bernard. *The Arabs in History.* New York: Oxford University Press, 2002.

Lings, Martin. *Muhammad: His Life Based on the Earliest Sources.* Rochester, Vt.: Inner Traditions, 2006.

Lyons, Jonathan. *The House of Wisdom: How the Arabs Transformed Western Civilization.* London: Bloomsbury, 2009.

Mabarakpuri, Safiur Rahman. *When the Moon Split: A Biography of the Prophet Muhammad.* Edited and translated by Tabassum Siraj, Michael Richardson, and Badr Azimabadi. Riyadh: Darussalam, 1998.

Mernissi, Fatima. *Beyond the Veil: Male-Female Dynamics in Modern Muslim Society.* Bloomington: Indiana University Press, 1987.

Meulen, D. van der. *The Wells of Ibn Sa'ud.* New York: Frederick A. Praeger, 1957.

Mowlana, Hamid, and Laurie Wilson. *The Passing of Modernity: Communication and the Transformation of Society.* New York: Longman, Addison-Wesley, 1990.

Nagel, Tilman. *The History of Islamic Theology from Muhammad to the Present.* Princeton, N.J.: Marcus Wiener, 2009.

Nasr, Seyyed Hossein. *Ideas and Realities of Islam.* Chicago: ABC International Group, 2000.

Philby, Harry. *Sa'udi Arabia.* New York: Frederick A. Praeger, 1955.

Prokop, Michaela. "The War of Ideas: Education in Saudi Arabia." In Paul Aarts and Gerd Nonneman, eds., *Saudi Arabia in the Balance.* New York: New York University Press, 2005.

Pryce-Jones, David. *The Closed Circle: An Interpretation of the Arabs.* Chicago: Ivan R. Dee, 2002.

Quandt, William. *Saudi Arabia in the 1980s: Foreign Policy, Security, and Oil.* Washington: Brookings Institution, 1981.

Rihani, Ameen. *Maker of Modern Arabia.* New York: Houghton Mifflin, 1928.

Rogerson, Barnaby. *The Heirs of Muhammad: Islam's First Century and the Origins of the Sunni-Shia Split.* Woodstock, N.Y.: Overlook Press, 2007.

Simmons, Matthew. *Twilight in the Desert: The Coming Saudi Oil Shock and the World Economy.* Hoboken, N.J.: John Wiley & Sons, 2005.

Strahan, David. *The Last Oil Shock: A Survival Guide to the Imminent Extinction of Petroleum Man.* London: John Murray, 2007.

Thesiger, Wilfred. *Arabian Sands.* London: Penguin Books, 2007.

Trofimov, Yaroslav. *The Siege of Mecca.* New York: Doubleday, 2007.

Vassiliev, Alexei. *The History of Saudi Arabia.* New York: New York University Press, 2000.

Wright, Lawrence. *The Looming Tower: Al Qaeda and the Road to 9/11.* New York: Knopf, 2006.

Yamani, Mai. *Changed Identities: The Challenge of the New Generation of Saudi Arabia.* London: Royal Institute of International Affairs, 2000.

ACADEMIC JOURNALS AND ARTICLES

Admon, Y. "Anti Soccer Fatwas Led Saudi Soccer Players to Join the Jihad in Iraq." The Middle East Media Research Institute, Inquiry & Analysis Series Report no. 245 (October 2005). Online at www.memri.org/report/en/print1494.htm, May 11, 2011.

Al Turki, Noura, and Rebekah Braswell. "Businesswomen in Saudi Arabia: Characteristics, Challenges and Aspirations in a Regional Context." Jeddah: Chamber of Commerce, July 2010.

Bourland, Brad, and Paul Gamble. "Saudi Arabia's Coming Oil and Fiscal Challenge." Jadwa Investment (July 2011).

Henderson, Simon. "After King Abdullah: Succession in Saudi Arabia." Washington Institute for Near East Policy, Policy Focus no. 96. (August 2009).

Metz, Helen, ed. *Saudi Arabia: A Country Study.* Washington, D.C.: GPO for the Library of Congress, 1992. Online at http://countrystudies.us/saudi-arabia.

Sfakianakis, John. "Employment Quandary: Youth Struggle to Find Work Raises Urgency for Reform." Banque Saudi Fransi (February 16, 2011).

———. "Under Construction: Saudi Steps Up Efforts to Meet Home, Loan Demand." Banque Saudi Fransi (March 20, 2011).

———. "Holding Back: State Spending Focus Restrains Private Sector Diversification." Banque Saudi Fransi (May 17, 2011).

———. "Holding Ground: Saudi H2 Economic Outlook Sound in Face of External Stress." Banque Saudi Fransi (June 14, 2010).

———. "Quota Counting: New Saudi Employment Rules to Shake Up Private Sector." Banque Saudi Fransi (June 14, 2011).

AUTHOR INTERVIEWS

Princess Adelah bint Abdullah bin Abdul Aziz
Prince Abdulaziz bin Salman bin Abdulaziz
Prince Abdul Aziz bin Sattam bin Abdul Aziz
Prince Abdulaziz bin Talal bin Abdul Aziz
Prince Abdullah bin Musa'id bin Abdul Aziz
Prince Abdul Rahman bin Musa'id bin Abdul Aziz

Prince Bandar bin Saud bin Muhammad al Saud
Prince Bandar bin Sultan bin Abdul Aziz
Prince Faisal bin Abdullah
Prince Faisal bin Mishal bin Saud al Saud
Prince Khalid bin Sultan bin Abdul Aziz
Prince Mohammad bin Nayef bin Abdul Aziz
Prince Mugrin bin Abdul Aziz
Prince Muhammad bin Nasir bin Abdulaziz
Prince Saad bin Muhammad bin Abdulaziz al Saud
Prince Salman bin Abdul Aziz
Prince Saud Abdul Mohsin bin Abdul Aziz
Prince Sultan bin Fahd Abdulaziz
Prince Sultan bin Salman bin Abdul Aziz
Prince Talal bin Abdul Aziz
Prince Turki al Faisal bin Abdul Aziz
Prince Turki bin Khalid
Prince Turki bin Muhammad bin al Kabeer
Prince Turki bin Sultan bin Abdulaziz
Prince Turki bin Talal bin Abdul Aziz
Dr. Salah al Aayed
Abdulaziz al Abdulkader
Mohammed Aboudawood
Elliott Abrams
Dr. Hussein Muhammad Ageely
Muhammad al Ahmari
Jenan al Ahmed
Bandar al Aiban
Abdul Mohsin al Akkas
Fawaz al Almy
Monera al Aloula
Salah al Amr
Thuraya Arrayed
Abdullah bin Muhammad al Ashaikh
Noura al Ashaikh
Munira Ashgar
Sheikh Salman al Awdah
Awada al Badi
Omar Bahlaiwa
Fawzia al Bakr
Muhammad al Balawi
Alia Banaja
Abdul Rahman al Barrack
Khalid al Bawadi

Hussein al Bayat
Mohammed al Blahei
Christopher Boucek
Brad Bourland
Noura Bouzo
Osama Bunyan
George H. W. Bush
Christopher Clayton
Anthony Cordesman
Abdullah Dabbagh
Amr al Dabbagh
Soad al Dabbagh
Sheikh Salah al Dawish
Nawal Abdullah al Egagi
Muhammad Abdul Kareem al Essa
Salim al Fafi
Abdulaziz Fahad
Abdul Wahab al Faiz
Norah al Faiz
Manal Fakeeh
Adel Fakieh
Khalid al Falih
Najla al Faraj
Samar Fatany
Maha Fitaihi
Maha Fozan
Muhammad Fozan
Charles Freeman
Abdulaziz al Gasim
Sheikh Ahmad Gelan
Michael Gfoeller
Khaled Mohammed al Ghefaili
Ghazi al Gosaibi
Abdulrahman al Hadlag
Steve Hadley
Suhaila Zein Al Alabdein Hammad
Mansour al Harbi
Madawi al Hassoun
Dr. Sulaiman al Hattlan
Dr. Selwa al Hazzaa
Abdullah al Heedan
Thomas Hegghammer

Steffen Hertog
Sheikh Salah bin Abdullah bin Homaid
Khalid Sulayman al Hubayshi
Abdulwahed al Humaid
Abdul Rahman bin Humaid
Alya al Huwaiti
Sarah al Huwaiti
Somayya Jabarti
Saad al Jabri
Adel al Jubeir
Sadeem al Kadi
Ayman Kanaan
Gilles Kepel
Abdullah al Khalaf
Haila Abdullah al Khalaf
Haifa Khalid
Khalil al Khalil
Amr Khashoggi
Jamal Khashoggi
Salwa Abdel Hameed al Khateeb
Saleh al Khathlan
Abdulaziz al Khayyal
Qsai Khider
Omar Kholi
Nabil al Khowaiter
Henry Kissinger
Abdullah Ibrahim el Kuwaiz
Stephane Lacoix
Khaled al Maeena
Sadig Malki
Salman al Malki
Khalid al Matrafi
Saker al Mokayyad
Majid Abdullah al Moneef
Mazin Motabagani
Faisal bin al Muammar
Dr. Maha al Muneef
Sheikh Abdullah al Mutlag
Nadme Nasr
Aisha Natto
Mohammad al Negir
James Oberwetter

Muhammad al Ohali
Lubna Olayan
Basmah Omair
Yousef al Othaimeen
Ali al Qahtani
Muhammad Quanibet
Fahd al Rasheed
Haifa Rasheed
Turki Faisal al Rasheed
Naif al Romi
David Rundell
Ahmad Sabri
Abdulrahman al Saeed
Abdulaziz Sager
Tawfiq al Saif
Mujtaba Tawfiq al Saif
Moddi Saleh al Salem
Turki Saud Muhammad al Saud
James Schlesinger
Brent Scowcroft
Abdulaziz al Sebail
Fahd al Semmari
Maha al Senan
Hamza Serafi
John Sfakianakis
Abdulaziz al Shamah
Mansour al Ammar al Shammary
Mekhlef bin Daham al Shammary
Jafar al Shayeb
Authug Sultan al Shehail
Hussein Shobacshi
Ahmad Shugairi
Turki Suderi
Suliaman al Sulaim
Muna Abu Sulayman
Khalid al Sulaiman
Amal Suliman
Nashwa Taher
Fahad al Tayash
Samir Tubayyeb
Khalid al Turki
Noura al Turki

Saleh al Turki
Sally al Turki
Suliaman al Turki
Ali Twairqi
Abdullah Uthaimin
David Welch
Abdullah bin Muhammad al Yahya
Dr. Suad al Yamani
Awad Yami
Hassan Yassin
Abdulrahman al Zamil
Muhammad al Zolfa
Lulu (name withheld)
Rana (name withheld)
Reema (name withheld)
And hundreds of other Saudis who asked for complete anonymity

INDEX

Page numbers in *italics* refer to illustrations.
Members of the House of Saud are listed under first names.